Black Labor
in America

Contributions in Afro -American and African Studies

87- 273

Black Labor in America

MILTON CANTOR

Editor

Introduction by
Herbert G. Gutman

*Contributions in Afro-American and
African Studies
No. 2*

NEGRO UNIVERSITIES PRESS

WESTPORT, CONNECTICUT

First printing 1970
Second printing 1977
Third printing 1979

Greenwood Press, Inc., 51 Riverside Avenue, Westport, Connecticut 06880

Library of Congress catalog card number 74-111265
ISBN 0-8371-4667-4

Printed in the United States of America

Contents

Preface

The articles which follow first appeared in the Summer 1969 issue of *Labor History* (vol. 10, no. 3). For the most part, they have not been greatly altered. Some authors, to be sure, requested limited revisions; and these requests were granted in the belief that their articles were thereby improved in style and/or in substance. Witness, for example, Paul Worthman's, which, we think, gains in clarity and incisiveness. The articles of James Olson and Kenneth W. Porter have also benefitted from modest changes. Finally, the title of Raymond Wolters's contribution has been altered and, we believe, is now more consonant with the subject it treats. Throughout, the editor has sought to eliminate unfortunate solecisms and inadvertent distortions of meaning—made by him in the course of editing—toward the end of producing a volume which, we trust, represents the best traditions in American scholarship.

MILTON CANTOR

Amherst, Massachusetts
February 1970

Introduction

When the Board of Editors of *Labor History* agreed a few years ago to ask younger as well as established scholars to contribute to a special issue devoted to the Negro and the American labor movement, it did so for good reason. The editors meant neither to rehash relatively well-explored aspects of this subject nor to publish informative but rather general articles. Instead, they sought out men and women engaged in original and important research concerning the black worker's history, hoping that such a collection of essays would serve as a model for further serious study of this nearly altogether neglected historical subject. The articles gathered came from persons with quite diverse interests. Some cannot be narrowly defined as specialists in labor history. Kenneth W. Porter has long been known for an admirable study of John Jacob Astor, and Harry N. Scheiber's reputation rests solidly on an outstanding study of transportation and enterprise in antebellum Ohio. Nor are the younger authors traditional labor historians. William Tuttle, for example, is a specialist in early twentieth-century black history, and Thomas Wagstaff's main concern is the South during Presidential Reconstruction. Paul Worthman's larger study of the Birmingham working class reaches outside the narrow boundaries of traditional labor history and seeks to recreate the life-style of black and white workers in a city that symbolized the essence of the New South; nevertheless it has escaped the attention of specialists on the American labor movement. The other authors are just as diverse in their interests. But all bring to their subjects a fresh set of questions, a dissatisfaction with the standard treatment or nontreatment of the black worker, and a willingness to engage primary materials all too often neglected by historians of the American worker, black or white.

Individual readers will assess differently the value of this volume and its particular essays, but one of its strengths derives as much from the fresh materials examined as from what the authors tell us. Wagstaff's evidence about how those politicians who dominated the immediate postbellum southern political scene felt toward the freedman as worker draws heavily from the manuscript letters of these white politicians. Porter has exhausted the literature on cattlemen to create an unusually authentic portrait of the Negro cowboy as worker. Worthman has uncovered a mine of new information about black and white workers and their unions in Birmingham, Alabama, from that city's labor and regular press. Tuttle's extraordinary use of the "Alschuler

Hearings" sheds unusual light on the background of the 1919 Chicago race riots in ways that make clear how little is yet known about the urban black worker before 1920. Similarly, the Scheibers draw upon unused materials in the Papers of Woodrow Wilson and in National Archives collections to probe wartime efforts by the Wilson Administration to "mobilize" black Americans after that administration's policies had "proved detrimental to black men's interests in nearly every respect." My point is quite simple. Traditional labor sources count for much in some of these articles, but their great strength lies partly in the many ways in which they utilize sources often neglected by historians concerned with workers or with blacks. So much in the not-so-distant past has been made of the "fact" that it is difficult if not impossible to write about black workers because of the paucity of primary materials that these essays deserve attention only because they belie that myth once and for all.

But more is involved. The history of the black worker can be written, and it must be written afresh. That is another reason to welcome these essays. They are a good start. We are all familiar with the standard works on this subject: Charles Wesley's *Negro Labor in the United States 1850–1925;* Lorenzo Greene and Carter G. Woodson's *The Negro Wage Earner;* Abram Harris and Sterling Spero's *The Black Worker: The Negro and the Labor Movement;* Horace Cayton and George Mitchell's *Black Workers and the New Unions;* Herbert Northrup's *Organized Labor and the Negro;* and Robert C. Weaver's *Negro Labor: A National Problem.* All of these remain valuable and essential works but share a common vintage that tells much. Their respective dates of publication are 1927, 1930, 1931, 1939, 1944, and 1946. Except for Ray Marshall's *Negro and Organized Labor* (1965), a collection of essays edited by Julius Jacobson entitled *The Negro and the American Labor Movement* (1968), and some useful but scattered journal articles, the study of the black worker and his history has been dormant for exactly a quarter of a century. That fact alone tells a great deal. And this volume hopefully marks a fresh start but just a beginning in the reexamination of the black worker's history. These essays hint at what is to be found in the sources, and they whet the appetites of those of us concerned with black history as well as labor history.

Its strengths are apparent, but this volume has its weaknesses, too. They deserve brief note because an awareness of them may spark readers to remedy them. Despite some effort, the editors could not solicit high quality articles on such diverse but important subjects as the free black workers of antebellum southern cities, their northern and western counterparts, and southern black rural workers between 1865 and 1910. So the volume focuses entirely on the black workers since emancipation, and even that emphasis is selective. In addition, the total collection devotes too little attention to the "local scene" so as to balance the regional and national emphasis quite properly stressed by Wagstaff and Porter, and by the Scheibers, Wolters, and Olson. Only Worthman and Tuttle delve deeply into the local context, but in doing so they make it clear, once more, that the history of black working people, largely unorganized, can be studied best in such a setting. E. P. Thompson urged British labor historians to shift gears at times and give attention to "the goings-on 'in the provinces.'" Too frequently, he worried, they view labor history there as little more than "shadowy incidents or unaccountable upheavals on the periphery of the national scene." Such advice counts as much (perhaps more) for the study of American black workers as for the study of British workers. What we now know about black workers in Birmingham and Chicago must be measured carefully against the experience of black and white workers in quite diverse local settings. Only in that fashion will the essential larger mosaic—the social history of the black worker—emerge. And that is a task for a generation of scholars.

These essays call attention to yet another word of advice from a contemporary British labor historian. "In order to understand how people respond to industrial change, it is necessary to examine fully what kind of people they were at the beginning of the process, to take account of continuities and traditions as well as new ways of thinking and feeling." So writes Asa Briggs. The behavior of black (and white) workers can be fully understood only by a careful delineation of the external and internal context that helped shape such behavior. Quite recently, for example, William Toll has cogently criticized those who examine the historic lower-class black experience as if only three "variables" affected it: "white attitudes, economic institutions and Negro middle-class organizations." Put another way, the culture of lower-class black workers has not yet received the attention it deserves from those historians who write their social or labor history. We need to know much more, for example, about the culture of rural and urban Southern blacks between 1865 and 1900 before we can understand fully what attracted black workers to Birmingham labor organizations. Similarly, the movement of black lower-class culture from the South to the North between 1890 and 1940 deserves sensitive reexamination by social historians so as to make the behavior of migrating black workers and their families in Chicago and other places more comprehensible. Tuttle and Worthman, among others, show that it is entirely misleading to argue just that "continual Negro migration acted . . . as a disruptive force."

In another connection, sociologist Norman Birnbaum has written recently: "The United States, insofar as major aspects of its past are concerned, remains an unknown country. . . . We are at the beginning of a voyage of self-discovery that may yet revise some of our notions of our social provenance." This collection of essays helps us to chart that course, and its authors deserve credit for their effort and for not having engaged in the tendentious task of creating counter-myths or in the game of numbers which some consider a satisfactory substitute for a serious history of American lower classes.

HERBERT G. GUTMAN

University of Rochester
Rochester, New York, 1970

Black Labor
in America

1

Call Your Old Master—"Master": Southern Political Leaders and Negro Labor During Presidential Reconstruction

THOMAS WAGSTAFF

In August 1865, William Marvin, Andrew Johnson's newly appointed Provisional Governor of Florida, attempted to define the status of Florida's recently emancipated slaves. Addressing a primarily Negro audience with a speech aimed at the entire black population of the state, he told them that their new freedom had come to them as an unintended by-product of the Civil War, which had been a "white man's war" from start to finish, fought entirely over the material and political interests of white men. Marvin warned the Negroes not to delude themselves into thinking that their interests had been the central issue in that cataclysmic struggle. They should thank "no one but God" for their freedom and consider very carefully what that freedom meant: "You must not think [that] because you are as free as white people you are their equal, because you are not." Equality might be achieved one day in the distant future, Marvin said, but first, "You will have to do a great many things you cannot do, before you begin to be as great as they. You will have to be able to write a book, build a railroad, a steam engine, a steamboat and a thousand other things you know nothing of."

Marvin exhorted the Freedmen to work hard and develop their abilities. Only thus could they hope for economic and social advancement. He called on them to renounce any dreams of free land and equipment. Neither their former masters nor the government owed them any special consideration or assistance; none, in any case, would be forthcoming. If it were, he declared, it would "prove a curse" to them, killing the in-

THOMAS WAGSTAFF *is an Assistant Professor of History at Chico State College.*

centive to work that alone held hopes for their future: "Before the war, each of you was worth in dollars and cents to your owners, eight hundred or a thousand or fifteen hundred dollars, worth more than fifty acres, or eighty acres of land and a mule thrown in. Well the President in giving you your freedom, has taken so many dollars and cents from your old masters, and he thinks as I do, they have lost enough, and you by it have had enough given to you."

Therefore, Marvin concluded, the Negro should prove his worth to society in the only way open to him, by returning to his old plantation and faithfully performing his accustomed tasks. "Make the best contracts you can," he advised them. Show the white employers of the South "that you are willing to work better" as free men. "Be faithful, be honest, be interested in the affairs of the plantation; see that the mules are fed, that the hogs get good attention....If you wish to be esteemed as ladies and gentlemen, you must conduct yourselves accordingly —call your old Master, 'Master,' and your old Mistress, 'Mistress.' "[1]

Marvin's speech exemplified the ambiguous attitudes toward black labor held by the new group of southern political leaders who came briefly to power under Andrew Johnson's Reconstruction plan.[2] Generally they welcomed the death of slavery and believed that the establishment of a new labor system, based on the principles of *laissez-faire* capitalism and the Protestant Ethic, would bring greater prosperity and more rapid economic development to the South. But they also had strong, contradictory perceptions of class and caste that kept them from applying those principles consistently in the labor codes they adopted in 1865-1866.

The logic of their position, as succinctly stated by Henry J. Raymond, editor of *The New York Times* and Johnson's chief spokesman in the House of Representatives, called for the southerners to learn the "art of managing Negroes as *paid laborers* and without the aid of the lash."[3] Had the southern states rigorously applied that logic in 1865, they would have placed no controls over their black labor force beyond those supplied by the economic force of the free market. Had they done so, they might well have disarmed Johnson's opponents and made his Reconstruction policy a success. Instead they passed the harshly dis-

[1] Vicksburg (Miss.) *Weekly Herald*, October 21, 1865.
[2] Relationships between Johnson and those leaders are described in Thomas Wagstaff, "The Arm in Arm Convention," *Civil War History*, XIV (1968), 101-119.
[3] *The New York Times*, May 12, 1865.

criminatory and repressive black codes, discredited Johnson, and paved the way for the institution of Congressional Reconstruction.[4]

Why they did so is one of the central problems of the Reconstruction period. The black codes were not simply devices for the disguised perpetuation of slavery. No influential body of southern opinion believed that slavery could be restored. Nor can the codes be explained solely by reference to the southern landowners' undoubted desire to continue to exploit black labor. Southern leaders knew that they could grant the Freedman economic freedom in a competitive society without thereby granting him economic or social equality; that, lacking a massive and extended program of economic and educational assistance, the great mass of southern Negroes, crippled in mind and spirit by two centuries of slavery, devoid of property, prestige, learning, experience and organization, were doomed to remain indefinitely in a submerged position. No legislation was necessary to keep him there. Andrew Johnson stated the formula in simple terms: The Freedmen "without land of their own . . . will continue to work for those who have it." Southerners had long argued that the employer of free labor could exploit his labor force more effectively than the slave owner. Johnson referred to that staple point of the pro-slavery argument when he said: "Slavery exists. It is black in the South and white in the North, and it will continue to exist."[5]

Neither can the repressive attitudes reflected in the codes be explained by references to race prejudice alone. Southern leaders unquestionably believed, as did the great majority of white Americans, in the biological and cultural inferiority of the Negro. They may have derived from slavery even stronger racial attitudes than those held by white Americans generally, though the evidence for this is far from clear. Recent scholarship strongly suggests that in this respect North and South differed little.[6] In any case, racial prejudice did not have to be ratified by law to be effective. One perceptive southerner stated that

---

[4] Theodore Brantner Wilson, *The Black Codes of the South* (University of Alabama Press, 1965), 138-152.

[5] George Fort Milton, *The Age of Hate: Andrew Johnson and the Radicals* (New York, 1930), 90-91; Robert W. Winston, *Andrew Johnson: Plebian and Patriot* (New York, 1928), 143, 147, 229; *The New York Times*, June 26, 1865; William E. B. Du Bois, "Reconstruction and its Benefits," *American Historical Review*, XLV (1910), 781-799.

[6] Leon F. Litwack, *North of Slavery: The Negro in the Free States* (Chicago, 1961), *passim;* C. Vann Woodward, "White Racism and Black 'Emancipation,'" *The New York Review of Books*, XII (February 27, 1969), 5-11, summarizes several relevant recent works.

point clearly in 1865: "If the negroes are inferior, why should white men need any special legislation to enable them to maintain their superiority?"[7]

Slavery, however, did impart to the southern elite a set of class attitudes that were unique to themselves. Such attitudes did not, in theory, exist elsewhere in the United States. But the southern slave owner belonged to a self-conscious propertied class that had always thought in terms of sharp and clear class divisions—had always believed the gap between themselves and their laboring class to be permanent and unbridgeable.[8] It was the attitudes of these slave owners that were represented in the state governments established during Johnsonian Reconstruction and were embodied in the black codes.

With a sharpened class awareness went a heightened fear of class hostility and an instinctive dread of class conflict. Despite the extreme rarity of organized attempts at rebellion by American Negro slaves, obsessive terror of such uprisings had pervaded the *ante-bellum* South.[9] These fears remained after slavery perished. Although the southern leaders who controlled the South in 1865 professed their willingness to abandon slavery and accept a free labor system, at the same time their exaggerated fear of class conflict led them to dread the effects of relaxing the traditional controls on their black labor force.

The dilemma is poignantly revealed in the private correspondence of Alexander H. Stephens. As an old-style republican "of the Jefferson school," Stephens claimed to have "no personal antipathies against race or color" and to hope that "all the sons & daughters of Adam's family" could enjoy every right "set forth in the Declaration of Independence." He believed that the successful establishment of racial equality in the South would be "the sublimest exhibition . . . of the workings of American institutions of self government . . . not only the dawn but the rising sun . . . the *renaissance* of the political world." Stephens pledged "to give the experiment of the civil equality of the black race . . . the fairest possible trial." Yet, he admitted, however earnestly he might wish that white and black could exist on a plane of "perfect political equality," he instinctively feared that it could never be done: "Sooner or later

---

[7] Ulysses H. Ritch to Benjamin S. Hedrick, July 4, 1865, Benjamin S. Hedrick Mss., Duke University Library, Durham, North Carolina.
[8] Eugene D. Genovese, *The Political Economy of Slavery* (New York, 1965), 31-34.
[9] Stanley Elkins, *Slavery: A Problem in American Institutional and Intellectual Life* (Chicago, 1959), 136-137; Clement Eaton, *The Growth of Southern Civilization* (New York, 1961), 72-97.

broils, mobs, massacres, collisions and wars of races will ensue."[10]

An unsigned editorial in *De Bow's Review* in 1865 put this same attitude in theoretical terms, in the context of a discussion of the implications of northern anti-slavery radicalism. "Radicalism is rationalism," stated the author. The chief characteristics of the Radicals lay in their lack of any religious, political, moral, or social faith and their reliance "on the suggestions of their own reason." Before the war northern radicalism had been checked by the "excessive Conservatism of the South," which had held that "human nature never materially changing, the religion, the laws and the political institutions adapted to it in the past will be equally well adapted to it in the future." The South, the author continued, had fought a defensive war, "under the banner of faith, wholly rejecting reason" when it conflicted with that faith. Northern radicalism had been victorious:

> It fully achieved its professed object. It emancipated all the negroes. Yet so far from being satisfied, it threatens and prepares for war again. . . . When will all this war against human inequality end? Why only by the attempt to equalize properties, which beget the only real inequalities of condition—the men of property being, in all save the name, the owners and masters of those without property.[11]

Benjamin F. Perry, Johnson's Provisional Governor in South Carolina expressed the same fear in 1866, arguing that northern radicals harbored a "fiendish purpose" to unleash class war in the southern states: "First, the negro is to be invested with all political power, and then the antagonism of interest between capital and labor is to work out the result," Benjamin F. Moore, of North Carolina, feared that the grant of suffrage to the Negroes would "speedily engender, among the whites, hosts of vile and reckless demigogues [sic] whose flatteries, promises, and agitation would keep the public mind constantly inflamed with agrarian projects. . . ."[12]

Indicative of the attitudes of the South's new leaders are the statements about race and labor made by the former Tennnessee slave owner who occupied the White House in 1865. Andrew Johnson hailed the

---

[10] Alexander H. Stephens to Dr. E. M. Chapin, March 29, 1867; see also Stephens to "Dear Sir," April 9, 1867 and Stephens Mss. "Speech to the Georgia Assembly," February 22, 1866, Alexander H. Stephens Mss., Emory University Library, Atlanta, Georgia; C. Mildred Thompson, *Reconstruction in Georgia* (New York, 1915), 160.

[11] "Terribly in Earnest," *De Bow's Review*, August 18, 1866.

[12] Benjamin F. Perry to Horace Greeley, April 15, 1866, Perry Mss., University of North Carolina Library, Chapel Hill, North Carolina; Wilmington (N.C.) *Herald*, September 1, 1865.

emancipation of the slaves with enthusiasm. Slavery, he told a group of southern visitors shortly after the war, had been the "worst evil of the South" because it had "practically shut out all the influences which have so mightily elevated all other parts of the country." It had wasted resources, deadened incentive, and allowed a parasitic class of slave-holders to monopolize political and economic power. Its removal, he predicted, would vastly stimulate the material progress of the South. But Johnson also pointed out that he neither expected nor desired the abolition of slavery to endanger the economic, political, and social superiority of the white race. The two races of the South, said Johnson in 1865:

> have hitherto lived together under the relation of master and slave—capital owning labor. Now suddenly that relation is changed. . . . In this new relation . . . there will be a new adjustment . . . and if left to *the laws that regulate capital and labor* it is confidently believed that they will satisfactorily work out the problem.

In a free market situation, he assured the South, the Freedmen would "remain dependent upon the planters, will rely upon them for their livelihoods and will be particularly subject to their influence." Johnson believed that the transition to a free labor system would drastically improve the economic situation of the southern states; "the incoming of free industry [and] . . . the removal of slave labor is a pledge," he stated, "that those regions . . . will vie with any in the Union in . . . inventive genius, wealth and industry." But Johnson also believed that the change in economic relationships would not change race and class relationships: abolition had "freed more whites than blacks." Johnson made his views on this subject very clear to the southerners he appointed to office during Reconstruction. Harvey M. Watterson, touring the South as Johnson's emissary during the summer of 1865, recommended a prospective appointee to the President on the grounds that, "like yourself, too, he is for a white man's government, and in favor of free white citizen's controlling this country."[13]

Thus Johnson's objections to Congressional interference with Reconstruction were couched not so much in terms of the threat that inter-

---

[13] Winston, *op. cit.,* 229; *The New York Times,* April 16, June 12, 1865; Harvey M. Watterson to Andrew Johnson, June 20, 1865, Andrew Johnson Mss., (microfilm), University of Wisconsin Historical Society, Madison, Wisconsin; William A. Williams, *The Contours of American History* (New York, 1960), 318. (Italics added.)

vention posed to the traditional racial order in the South, but rather in terms of the way it endangered the class structure of a *laissez-faire* economy. In April 1866 Congress passed the first Civil Rights Bill, designed to extend federally supervised equal protection of the laws to the Freedman. Johnson vetoed that act, insisting that: "it intervenes between capital and labor and attempts to settle questions of political economy through the agency of numerous officials whose interest it will be to foment discord."[14]

Johnson's closest allies in the Republican Party held very similar views. Before the Civil War, William H. Seward had defined the "irrepressible conflict" between slavery and freedom in terms of the superior economic efficiency of free labor. He called slavery a relic of the ancient system of "monarchical power." It had been established in the Americas by the backward Spanish and Portuguese and was founded on the reactionary principle that all labor was "necessarily unintellectual, groveling and base." Its inevitable fruits, he continued, could be found "in the poverty, imbecility and anarchy which prevailed in Latin America where slave labor had long been the rule." By debasing labor, "which alone can produce wealth and resources," slavery wasted "energies which might otherwise be employed in national development and aggrandizement." The northern free labor system, established by energetic and progressive peoples "of German extraction," had on the other hand unleashed the mighty forces of industrialism and effected the "great melioration of human society which modern times exhibit." To free labor, Seward stated, "we justly ascribe . . . the strength, wealth, greatness, intelligence and freedom which the whole American people now enjoy." As late as the second year of the war, Seward argued that, if the South could be brought to accept the principle of free labor, the details of emancipation could be worked out "peacefully and gradually by the agency of the states which were chiefly concerned with it." It could then be accomplished "without destroying or even deeply disturbing the constitution" of southern society and without risking the "sharp trial of servile war."[15]

Henry J. Raymond's *New York Times* defended Johnson's Recon-

---

[14] James D. Richardson, ed., *A Compilation of the Messages and Papers of the Presidents, 1789-1897*, 10 vols. (Washington, 1896-1899), IX, 3610.
[15] George E. Baker. ed., *The Works of William Henry Seward* (Boston, 1884), IV, 289-302; William H. Seward, *The Elements of Empire in America* (New York, 1844), pamphlet, Wisconsin Historical Society, 26; Frederick Bancroft, *The Life of William H. Seward* (New York, 1900), II, 42.

struction policy throughout 1865-1866, asserting that its implementation and the ratification of the Thirteenth Amendment would liberate progressive political and economic forces in the South and establish a firm national economic union based on rational *laissez-faire* principles. Raymond promised that within twenty-five years this would bring "a production and general distribution of wealth never experienced in the history of the world." With slavery gone, the South would rid itself "of that old spirit of sectionalism which was the growth of slavery" and develop "a new life which shall be thoroughly identified with the national life and have a complete community of spirit with the North and the West."

The plantations, Raymond predicted, would begin to break up. The South would develop a new class of skilled workers and craftsmen. They would settle in and stimulate the growth of southern towns, and these towns would become markets for the products of the small farmers of the South. He pointed out that abolition did not diminish the aggregate wealth of the South. The Negroes remained, their labor power unimpaired and, potentially, greatly enhanced. Emancipation had simply transferred title to that power from the master to the Freedman. Consequently, "labor will become diversified, villages will become towns, towns will become cities and civilization will advance."[16]

The southern governments established by Johnson, according to Raymond, had repudiated the reactionary social and economic attitudes of the *ante-bellum* era. Southern political rhetoric, previously characterized by a "volume of drivel about slavery," now had an "air of life and business, of reparation and progress, of thorough appreciation of all the interests whose development is vital to the greatness of a modern state." The South's new leaders, concerned with the "industrial, commercial, financial, and educational interests" of their states, would make their section an active and valuable participant in the nation's march toward unexampled material greatness.[17]

But Raymond also discerned serious threats to that glowing economic future in two related disturbing influences—the unreasoning zeal of the old anti-slavery fanatics, and the burgeoning working-class radicalism in the industrial states. He argued that the Radical Republicans were

[16] *The New York Times,* October 24, 29, December 14, 1865; Carl F. Krummel, "Henry J. Raymond and the New York Times in the Secession Crisis," *New York History,* XXXII (October, 1951), 385.
[17] *The New York Times,* December 18, 22, 1865.

attacking the racial policies of the reconstructed South from the stand-point of ideas which belonged "rather to the past than the present," and threatening to disrupt the South's new concert of economic interests. When, in December 1865, Thaddeus Stevens proposed the confiscation of the great Southern estates and their distribution to the Freedmen, Raymond charged him with disheartening very many earnest and loyal southerners who were then in New York seeking northern capital for the economic rehabilitation of the South: "Quite a number of these persons have abandoned their business prospects and gone home discouraged. . . . They cannot work with heart or hope while such a sword is hanging over their heads. . . ."

Any Congressional interference with Reconstruction, even if it did not entail confiscation, would seriously retard the development of a new and harmonious system of labor relations in the South. "It is malignant and criminal" to stir up antagonism between labor and capital in the South. The Freedmen, Raymond warned, "will be made thievish if perpetually told that their late masters lived by plundering them; will be made indolent if daily told their wages are too little; will become insolent if taught to be so."[18]

At the same time, and in much the same terms, Raymond condemned the kind of labor agitation that in the North spread the dangerous "notion that capital is everlastingly and necessarily at war with labor, that employers are the natural enemies of the employed, and that it is the duty of one to organize for perpetual resistance to the other." Industrial strife fostered by such arguments threatened the economic health of the nation. The strikes that affected manufacturing and mining areas in the aftermath of the war could not be justified on rational economic grounds. "Wages are like the ocean," Raymond wrote, "thus far and no farther can they go." Let us, he pleaded, "keep wages at a certain level and preserve our moral character." Workingmen's associations should limit themselves to intelligent and moderate discussion of real grievances and eliminate "growlers" who were "ever snarling at the measures of others [and] . . . breaking up confidence in a society."[19]

Andrew Johnson and his most prominent northern advisers defined the South's post-emancipation labor problem more in terms of economics than of race. Their view of the problem and their attitude toward black

---

[18] *Ibid.*, September 15, July 11, 1865.
[19] *Ibid.*, July 26, 1865.

labor had more in common with the attitudes of nineteenth century economic conservatives toward labor in general than it had to the *ante-bellum* pro-slavery argument. The prevalence of similar attitudes among southern political leaders in 1865-1866 strongly suggests that northern and southern conservatives differed little in their attitudes toward race and class.

In 1865 Hinton Rowan Helper joyfully annnouced that slavery was "now as defunct . . . as the filthiest carrion crow that ever tasted death after surfeiting on the carcass of a skunk." Two years of free labor, Helper predicted, would put the South on "avenues of permanent peace and prosperity." When he had expressed such views a decade earlier, Helper's writings had been proscribed and he had been forced to flee the South.[20] But in 1865 his anti-slavery arguments echoed from platforms and newspapers throughout the South.

The provisional governors appointed by Johnson addressed themselves to the problem of emancipation shortly after assuming their offices. William Woods Holden of North Carolina based his statement directly on Helper's *Impending Crisis:*

> New York and North Carolina were, in 1808, on the same footing as regards population and in other respects. The difference in their wealth, prosperity and population today is due to the retarding influences of African slavery. We are now relieved of this incubus on the interests of the State.[21]

In his inaugural address as Provisional Governor of South Carolina, Benjamin Perry told his state that "the whole civilized world opposed us on this question, and as a *slave power,* would have looked on us with a jealous eye." Perry promised that the end of slavery would prove to "be a blessing."[22] Georgia's Provisional Governor James Johnson informed the people of his state that the irrevocable abolition of slavery would "remove from among us the cause of bitterness and sectional strife which has wasted our property and deluged our land in blood." Now, Johnson predicted, "all our surplus capital, instead of being laid out in negroes, will be expended in permanent improvements, increasing the comforts of our homes, manuring our lands, planting orchards,

---

[20] Hinton R. Helper to Benjamin S. Hedrick, October 18, 1865, Hedrick Mss., Chapel Hill; Hugh C. Bailey, *Hinton Rowan Helper: Abolitionist Racist* (University, Alabama 1965), 59, 123-124.

[21] *New York Herald,* May 19, 1865.

[22] Benjamin F. Perry, *Reminiscences of Public Men With Speeches and Addresses* (Philadelphia, 1883), 229-239.

building fences and in manufactures of all kinds."[23]

In Alabama, Provisional Governor Lewis E. Parsons called slavery a destructive economic institution, forced on the South by the world's demand for cheap cotton. His section had been the unwitting victim of a "commercial revolution" in both Old and New England which "in the mysterious providence of God . . . contributed beyond all other causes combined to rivet . . . the fetters of the slave." Parsons urged Alabamans to give free Negro labor a full and fair trial and to allow future social and economic relationships between the races to be governed by the workings of natural law:

> It may be . . . , as is alleged sometimes that his freedom will end in his extermination. . . . If his race is doomed to perish from the land in an equal contest with the white race, . . . let not the sin be at our doors. Let not the children of Ham rise up against us in Judgement, and say, "Ye did it."[24]

Provisional Governor Andrew J. Hamilton told his fellow Texans:

> You will live to thank God that slavery does not exist. I thank God for it now. It made you arrogant to all the world and it was rightly taken away. We can now all talk about our institutions without danger of being hung.[25]

Johnson's Provisional Governors were of course committed by their official positions to support the President's policy. These attitudes were not, however, the exclusive property of presidential spokesman. They were general throughout the South and recognized even by Johnson's opponents. When the Radical Republican Salmon P. Chase toured the South in 1865, he found everywhere "progressives" who sensed that the old order in the South had passed forever from the stage of history—"who see that slavery is stone dead & are not sorry." They, said Chase, "are the men of vision and energy [who] in the end . . . will control" the South.[26]

James I. Alcorn, shortly to be elected Governor of Mississippi on an anti-Johnson plaform, called slavery "a cancer upon the body of the nation." Henry A. Foote, former Governor of Mississippi, wrote that the southern people would never regret the loss of slavery: "They will,

[23] Huntsville (Ala.) *Advocate,* July 26, 1865; "Message to Georgia State Legislature," December 5, 1865, Executive Minute Book of Governor James Johnson, Georgia State Archives, Atlanta, Georgia.
[24] Montgomery (Ala.) *Daily Advertiser,* December 23, 1865.
[25] *The New York Times,* August 13, 1865; Andrew J. Hamilton to Andrew Johnson, August 30, 1965, Johnson Mss.
[26] Salmon P. Chase to Andrew Johnson, May 12, 1865, Johnson Mss.

indeed, be far better off . . . *without slavery* than *with it*. . . . The whole
southern people will be far more prosperous hereafter. . . . Labor in the
South will be more diversified. . . . Manufacturing and mineral industry
. . . will now be seen to flourish." "I am tired of South Carolina as she
was," said James L. Orr, while campaigning for Governor in 1865. "I
court for her the material prosperity of New England. I would have
her acres teem with life and vigor and intelligence."[27]

Even John Brown's hangman, former Virginia Governor Henry A.
Wise, perhaps recalling Brown's final admonition that "the crimes of
this guilty land will never be purged away but with blood," joined in.
In 1865, Wise called slavery "a black idol from which we could never
have been separated by any other means than those of fire, blood, sword
and sacrifice." He now realized that slavery had been a great national
weakness, "if not wickedness," intolerable to any people "who would
themselves be strong and free." Abolition was a "blessing beyond
measure" and would free the South "to build new thousands of cottages,
hamlets, towns and cities where heretofore stood lone mansions of
masters whose broad acres were scourged by slaves." Labor would become efficient "by a price laid upon it" and that price would be paid,
not only by the Negroes, but by their pleasure-loving and improvident
late masters. "No more fair hands," Wise proclaimed, "no more lazy
morning hours! No more cigars and juleps! No more card parties and
club idleness!"[28]

Senator Benjamin H. Hill of Georgia called on his fellow citizens to
hail the death of slavery. "We have given up the dusky Helen," he declared. "Pity we kept the harlot so long." It had been "a curse," the
worst ever "inflicted upon any people." It had caused the South's de-
ficiencies in "scientific, physical and educational progress and especially
in material and commercial development," impeded her "growth in
population, wealth and physical power," and encumbered her with an
unskilled and sullen labor force that could not prudently be educated.
Nothing, Hill averred, should now stop the South from claiming its
rightful place among the great industrial areas of the world. The South
had vast mineral deposits, inexhaustible supplies of coal and water

---

[27] Congressional Globe, 42nd Congress, 2nd Session, 3424; Henry S. Foote, *War of the
   Rebellion* (New York, 1866), 422; Huntsville (Ala.) *Advocate*, October 19, 1865.
[28] W. E. Burghardt Du Bois, *John Brown* (New York, 1962), 365; *The New York Times,*
   September 11, 1865; Burton H. Wise, *The Life of Henry A. Wise of Virginia* (New
   York, 1899), 396, 391.

power and a population capable of exploiting them all to the fullest extent. "The earth contains no white race superior to the southern people," Hill stated, and that race would "do all in its power to educate, elevate, protect and advance the Negro." He would, should "his capacities prove sufficient," be transformed into an "intelligent laborer." Another Georgian, former Governor Joseph E. Brown, urged his fellow Georgians to accept emancipation calmly. William L. Yerger, Senator-elect from Mississippi in 1865, termed slavery "of all the industrial systems . . . the most costly."[29]

These sentiments were not confined to political leaders anxious to make capital in Washington. All over the South newspapers, public meetings, citizens resolutions, and private correspondence echoed the same theme. "Let us not be cast down because slavery is dead," an Alabama journal pleaded shortly after the end of the war, pointing out that Alabama's water power and other resources could make her the rival of Massachusetts in cotton manufacturing. A Mississippi editor wrote that the war had removed "the causes which have hitherto retarded the Gulf States in manufacturing their own principle [sic] staple." Now "the manufactures of New England may soon encounter formidable rivals in the South."[30] A Virgina editorial charged that, before the war, less than a third of the state's arable land had been cultivated and that "merely scratched over under the imperfect and slovenly system of slave labor."[31]

The South must never again fall victim to the "old cotton mania," warned the Vicksburg *Weekly Herald*. The backwardness of the southern economy had been completely revealed during the war and that experience should be "sufficient to convince the southern people of the impolity of stinting and starving themselves in order that the world may have cheap cotton." Had the South fully developed her industrial and mineral capabilities before the war, she could never have been defeated. Under the slave system the southern planter had been no more than "a stewart and overseer" for the "Lords of the Loom in New and Old England," burdened by "the inheritance of . . . African slaves." Now "that he has been set free from this obligation," the editor con-

---

[29] Benjamin H. Hill, Jr., *Senator Benjamin Harvey Hill, His Life and Speeches* (Atlanta, 1893), 39-40, 44-45; *Daily* (Atlanta, Ga.) *Intelligencer,* July 4, 1865; Joseph E. Brown to Andrew Johnson, July 25, 1865, Brown Mss., University of Georgia Library, Athens, Georgia; New York *Daily News,* August 7, 1865.

[30] Vicksburg (Miss.) *Weekly Herald,* February 3, 1866.

[31] Richmond *Whig* quoted in Huntsville (Ala.) *Advocate,* November 16, 1865.

cluded, "it will surely argue little for his intelligence if he voluntarily returns to the old servitude."[32]

In Charleston, a mass meeting of "Mechanics and Workingmen," while resolving that they had "no shred of sympathy for or desire to elevate the blacks," nonetheless maintained that abolition had "accomplished one great good—it has elevated the workingman and made labor respectable." Only societies that maintained "privileged classes" considered honest labor degrading, the "mechanics" noted. The Old South had been such a society, but now slavery was dead and "this artificial state of society vanished with it." Before the war, no individual white workingman could hope to compete "with a master workman and his ten, twenty or more slaves" and would often himself be "compelled to become a journeyman to the slave capitalists." Competition also came from the "slave of the rich man who, himself not a mechanic or a laborer was often a contractor." The *ante-bellum* slave codes had protected merchants, doctors, lawyers and parsons from the destructive competition of slave labor, while leaving the white laborer at its mercy. Abolition, the resolution concluded, had terminated that situation.

> All these disadvantages and restrictions are now removed, and the white workingman no longer has to contend against capital and labor combined. . . . His advancement to honor respectability and wealth will be certain and sure. We are satisfied that the abolition of slavery . . . will eventually prove a great blessing to our beloved country. . . .[33]

While many southern leaders believed that the South could profitably dispense with slavery, few were willing to dispense with the labor power of the Negro. Those who urged acceptance of a free labor system also argued that under such a system the South would still retain its ability to exploit black labor. Criticizing the Negro colonization schemes popular among northern conservatives, the *Charleston Daily Courier* asked: "Is not the black man still a valuable component of the state? Is not his brawny arm necessary to develop our resources and would not the sudden withdrawal of the entire negro population be an actual calamity?"[34]

The theory that the blacks, deprived of the superintending care of their masters, might become extinct in the United States, caused similar

---

[32] Vicksburg (Miss.) *Weekly Herald*, January 20, 1866; see also North Carolina *Standard*, August 8, 1865; and Edmund Wilson, *Patriotic Gore* (New York, 1962), 351, 322, 408.

[33] Huntsville (Ala.) *Advocate*, November 9, 1865.

[34] Charleston (S. C.) *Daily Courier*, August 14, 1866.

dismay. *"His labor* is the *condition of existence to all our operations &
interests,"* a South Carolinian declared. The "negro falls, if fall he
must, draped with every interest, hope & prospect of the land." Suggestions that Negroes be encouraged to emigrate to the North raised similar objections. The South is the *"native element"* of the Negro, protested an Alabaman, "the soil and climate to which they are indis-
putably adapted." Their departure "would *impoverish the country."*
Black labor is "our labor, and it is the cheapest we can get." Besides,
the same writer pointed out, emancipation had really changed nothing
in the South. The Negro "bears the *same relation to us now, de facto,
as heretofore.* We controlled his labor in the *past* (at our own expense)
and *will* control it in the future (at his)."[35]

In a *laissez-faire* society, the southerners who advocated that course
for the South assumed, the Negro would still be assigned a subservient
role———and kept in that role not with the legal chains of the slave code,
but with the invisible bonds of natural economic and social laws. A
Mississippi delta planter made this point starkly, if unconsciously, clear
while describing his plan to make his 250 former slaves "wholly *self
sustaining."* The Negro, he said, must be taught that he had to work
hard and conscientiously: "If he does not, he cannnot eat *my* bread and
meat or wear *my* clothes . . . a proper allowance should be made for
house rent, garden space, wood, milk and butter and feeding his poultry
from *my* corn crib . . . in the amount of money wages to be paid to him."
The planter went on to suggest that the system of local government best
suited to the new situation of the South might be simply to declare each
plantation a town and make each planter "a judge of police . . . , with
power to sentence and inflict—or the neighborhood physician might be
best as feigned sickness will be one of the greatest causes of com-
plaint."

The point is clear. Given ownership of his own labor, the Freedman
might also come to own a chicken; but his employer would own the
grain to feed it, the land the Freedman worked, the bed he slept in, and
the shoes he wore. The employer would also control the coinage (wages
would be in scrip), determine the state of his employee's health, and
wield the authority of the law.[36]

---

[35] *The New York Times,* September 14, 1865; Huntsville (Ala.) *Advocate,* August 14,
1865. (Italics in original.)
[36] J. Pearce to William L. Sharkey, July 15, 1865, Sharkey Mss., Mississippi State Archives,
Jackson, Mississippi. (Italics added.)

Such a conception of the future relationships between the freed slaves and their former masters certainly did contain racist assumptions. But those assumptions were peripheral to the main issue. Fundamentally, the attitudes of leading white southerners were the attitudes of a property-owning class and their basic assumption was that their ownership of property gave them natural authority over their labor force and the natural right to exercise the power of government. "The only danger of . . . social equality between the white and black races," Senator Benjamin H. Hill argued, "exists in the lower strata of society."[37] This was a class, not a race attitude.

Secure in their assumptions, leading white southerners discerned no threat to their racial superiority during Reconstruction. "Brought into competition with the superior intellect, tact and muscle of free white labor," said a Mississippi editor, the Negro would, if he survived at all, remain "the servant of servants." An Alabama editor saw no contradiction in stating that "we will . . . extend to the freedman all his legitimate rights [and] . . . secure him in their full and complete enjoyment . . . at the same time . . . ours is a white man's government . . . Alabama must be guided and controlled by the superior intelligence of the white man. . . ."[38]

On the basis of these attitudes many southerners argued for the granting of full legal equality to the Freedmen immediately after Reconstruction. Governor Jonathan Worth told Johnson that the "educated people" of North Carolina solidly opposed the passage of the black codes. Governor Perry said that the refusal to extend the suffrage to qualified Freedmen had been the great error of presidential Reconstruction. Provisional Governor William L. Sharkey admitted that the passage of Mississippi's black code had been unconstitutional and foolish. Governor Parsons told a Congressional Committee that Alabama's black code had been a "great blunder."[39] A Mississippi newspaper hoped, after the passage of the "unfortunate" codes, that the legisla-

---

[37] *Ku Klux Conspiracy,* The Testimony taken by the Joint Select Committee to inquire into the condition of affairs in the Late Insurrectionary States (Washington, 1872), VII, 757; see also Perrin Barber to Benjamin S. Hedrick, January 8, 1865, Hedrick Mss. and A. B. Cooper to Lewis E. Parsons, September 26, 1865, Official Correspondence of Governor Lewis E. Parsons, Alabama State Archives, Montgomery, Alabama.

[38] Natchez (Miss.) *Democrat,* January 6, 1866; Huntsville (Ala.) *Advocate,* December 21, 1865.

[39] J. G. de Roulhac Hamilton, ed., *The Correspondence of Jonathan Worth* (Raleigh, N. C., 1909) II, 214; Perry, *op. cit.,* 275; *Report of the Joint Committee on Reconstruction,* 39th Congress, 1st Session (Washington, 1866), III, 132; *Ku Klux Conspiracy,* I, 77-101.

ture would be wise and patriotic enough to voluntarily rescind them. Less charitably, another editor stated that the codes had been devised by a "shallow headed majority more anxious to make capital at home than to propitiate the powers at Washington . . . as complete a set of political Goths as were ever turned loose to work destruction upon a state."[40]

Those southerners who advocated legal equality for the Negro, however, also carefully explained that it had nothing to do with social equality. The Natchez *Daily Courier* praised Governor Sharkey for proclaiming that the testimony of Negroes would be heard in the state courts on an equal basis with white testimony: There was "no more equality guaranteed to the negro by receiving his testimony . . . than the keeper of a brothel is made the equal of a Bishop because the law permits the testimony of each to be taken." Joseph E. Brown advised Georgia to advance the suffrage to the blacks, insisting that "these people were raised among us and naturally sympathize with us . . . we shall seldom have cause to complain of their refusal to respect our wishes, or consult our interests at the ballot box."[41]

What southern leaders did fear was that northern radicals, whose motives they misunderstood and mistrusted, would stir up their black laborers against them. A Mississippi journal warned against the establishment of state-supported schools for the Freedmen, pointing to the schools that had already been established by the Freedman's Bureau, and that had attracted many northerners with abolitionist views. "If any radical was ever black enough in his views to suppose the people of Mississippi would endow 'Negro schools' for their ilk to teach the rising ibo-shin hatred of his former master, but best friend; then such chaps had better take to marching on with John Brown's soul. . . . The sooner the free negro is taught that he is to support himself and his family precisely as the white man does, the better it will be for him and his descendants."[42]

Considerations of this kind led Provisional Governor Parsons to declare the Freedmen competent witnesses in all Alabama state courts. Otherwise, his legal advisers informed him, cases involving Negroes would simply be handled by the Freedmen's Bureau courts. "The single naked question," John W. Stone told him, was whether the state would

---

[40] Jackson (Miss.) *Clarion*, January 7, 1865; James Garner, *Reconstruction in Mississippi* (New York, 1901), 116.
[41] Natchez (Miss.) *Daily Courier*, October 5, 1866; Atlanta *Daily Era*, February 23, 1867.
[42] Vicksburg (Miss.) *Weekly Herald*, October 28, 1865.

rather have Negro testimony brought before "courts of our own creation and before the tribunals who understood the character of the
parties." A group of Montgomery lawyers concurred, supporting Parsons' proclamation *"so as* to get these cases under state control."[43] Several South Carolina jurists offered Governor Orr the same advice.[44] Chief
Justice Campbell of the Mississippi Supreme Court insisted that "The
idea that it is dangerous to admit negro testimony . . . will be dis-
sipated in the mind of every sensible man who reflects calmly on the
fact . . . that a jury of white men with all their knowledge of negro
character, jealousy of caste . . . and a white judge with court house
crowded with white spectators, with white men as attorneys on both
sides, will not be likely to be deceived and duped. . . ."[45]

Wade Hampton and James L. Alcorn urged the South to make
greater concessions to the Negro in order to keep him more securely
under the control of the traditional southern ruling class. "We must
make the negro our friend," Alcorn counseled, "and we can do this if
we wish." For the South "to let the negro approach the witness stand
and the ballot box" did not threaten the status of the southern elite:
"We don't recognize the equality of the low and base of our own color
who enjoy those perogatives." The real threat to the established order
in the South, Alcorn argued, were northern agitators who would drive
a wedge between white employer and black employee: "If we make
him our enemy under the promptings of the Yankee . . . then our path
is through a way red with blood and damp with tears."[46]

Many southern property owners shared that fear. Towards the end
of 1865 a wild rumor that white and black radicals were plotting to
seize the plantations during the Christmas holidays spread throughout
the South. A Mississippi newspaper reported:

> It is very evident that there exists among negroes in various parts of the
> state, an expectation that something will be done about Christmas time. . . .
> In some places they openly announce the fact that the lands will be divided
> amongst them. In others they assert . . . that if they are not divided peace-
> ably they will fight for them.

---

[43] John W. Stone to Lewis E. Parsons, August 11, 1865, "Montgomery Lawyers" to Parsons,
August 11, 1865, E. L. Dorgen to Parsons, August 29, 1865, Parsons Correspondence,
Montgomery, Alabama.

[44] L. W. Logan to James L. Orr, April 11, 1866, Orr Mss., South Carolina State Archives,
Columbia, South Carolina.

[45] *The New York Times,* October 11, 1865.

[46] James L. Alcorn to Amelia Alcorn, August 26, 1865, Alcorn Mss., University of North
Carolina Library, Chapel Hill, North Carolina.

"They are all Christmas negroes in this section," said another Missis-sippi journal. Howell Cobb wrote to General Richard Taylor that it would be impossible to say how the new system of free labor would work out in Georgia "until Christmas passes" and the Negroes were convinced "that they are not to divide the lands with their former owners."[47]

The provisional governors were deluged with letters announcing the discovery of vaguely defined revolutionary plots among the Freedmen. A correspondent of Governor Perry blamed "the incendiary teachings of the colored troops and white abolitionists" who had convinced the Freedmen that the "whole property of the country, lands included, is theirs and soon to be divided among them." And Perry agreed that there was "a great deal more danger of 'Cuffee' than Thad Stevens tak-ing over lands." Alabama Negroes, Governor Parsons was informed, were collecting arms in preparation for "a division of lands and other property about Christmas." An irate Mississippi planter wrote to Gov-ernor Sharkey demanding that he arm the whites against the coming insurrection: "The negroes here have an idea that by the first of January next the lands are to be divided out amongst them." When informed of the falsity of that hope, they threatened to "kill the whites from the cradle up and take the lands." Negro ministers were charged with planting the seeds of revolution in their sermons, preaching that "the whites are the descendants of Cain; . . . the Negroes are the original race, the perfection of mankind." In December, Governor Marvin re-ported from Florida that "Christmas will soon be here and everyone of a timid mind . . . believes that the 'niggers are going to clean us out.' A great many think there will be attempts at insurrection."[48]

Shortly before the holiday season began, Governor James L. Orr of South Carolina informed General Daniel E. Sickles of "an apprehension felt in many sections of the state that there will be some insurrectionary

[47] Vicksburg (Miss.) *Weekly Herald,* November 4, December 23, 1965; Meridian (Miss.) *Daily Clarion,* August 8, 1865; Cobb to Richard Taylor, December 8, 1865, Howell Cobb Mss., University of Georgia Library, Athens, Georgia (quoted by permission of Mr. Howell Irwin, Jr.).

[48] Sanford W. Barber to Benjamin F. Perry, July 10, 1865, Perry Mss., Alabama State Archives, Montgomery; Perry to F. Marion Nye, May 25, 1867, Perry Mss., University or North Carolina Library; W. A. McClure to Lewis E. Parsons, December 2, 1865, Parsons Mss; H. H. Montgomery to William L. Sharkey, August 18, 1865, Sharkey Mss; Meridian (Miss.) *Daily Clarion,* August 15, 1865; *The New York Times,* December 25, 1866; see also John L. Manning to Perry, November 27, 1865, Perry Mss., Alabama, and Thomas W. Holloway to James L. Orr, December 18, 1866, Orr Mss., Columbia, South Carolina.

movement . . . during the Christmas holiday." Orr stated that he did not take the fabled revolt seriously, but did believe the Freedmen to be in a restive mood because "they expect a division of the land." Therefore he suggested that Sickles deploy federal troops about the towns of the state where, during the roisterous holiday celebrations, Negroes and whites would be crowded together under conditions that might lead to serious riots.

Orr also warned Sickles that grave danger of a future revolt of the blacks did exist, if labor relations were not quickly stabilized. Unless the Freedman's Bureau ceased interfering in labor disputes and encouraging the Negroes in their utopian fantasies, they would not contract with the landlords or work regularly. During the winter months food would be scarce:

> Then our troubles will commence in earnest. They will not starve so long as any provisions remain in the country—to supply themselves they must resort to robbing, plundering and assassination. I do not think I overdraw the picture.

Sickles responded that he had simply seen no evidence of revolutionary intent among the Freedmen, "nor any indication of any purpose or combination to seize the property of others." He insisted that all federal officials had the strictest orders to convince the Freedmen that they could expect to receive "no land" and would have to work for the "property owners." Labor difficulties arose from the unwillingness or inability of the planters to pay "regular wages in cash," Sickles concluded, not from radical agitation; and the real threat to order arose from the efforts of the state authorities to arm and train white militia units which "arouse among the colored people a sense of insecurity in their freedom."[49] General Wager Swayne made a similar response to charges against the Freedman's Bureau by Alabama's Governor Parsons. Swayne told Parsons that the reported depredations of the Freedmen were greatly exaggerated and begged him to remember that the Negroes' "Bill of Wrongs" against the white community was "at least as full and better supported." Social "turbulence," Swayne admitted, would surely attend "the cession to these people of their rights." But social change was just and necessary and its worst effects would be "lessened by every inflexible friend." He exhorted Parsons to remember

---

[49] James L. Orr to General Daniel E. Sickles, December 13, 1865, Sickles to Orr, December 17, 1865, Orr Mss., Columbia.

that "those who are early and uncompromising" in insisting on the extension of full and equal rights to the Freedmen would "be held for ages in exalted & affectionate remembrance."[50]

Parsons, along with most of the southern leaders of Johnsonian Reconstruction, did believe that the old order in the South would have to change. But they wanted that change to come without "turbulence" and without endangering established class relationships. They represented a propertied class and had a greater interest in protecting its position than they had in the accolades of history.

William Henry Trescott, a wealthy planter and former diplomat, represented South Carolina in Washington during 1865-1866, when southern representatives were excluded from Congress. Trescott concerned himself particularly with the effort to secure the return of the valuable Sea Island plantations that had been seized early in the war and were then still held by federal authorities. Throughout the negotiations, he argued that occupation of those lands by the Freedmen made other property owners insecure, encouraged other Negroes to hope that they would be given land and, therefore, hindered the resumption of normal labor relationships throughout the South.[51]

Trescott later derived from those views a general theory of the problems of Reconstruction and presented them to Senator Henry Wilson in a letter warning the Massachusetts radical of the dangers of the Congressional Reconstruction plan. He told Wilson that southern Negroes were convinced that federal policy would "in some way . . . secure them the possession of the land" and could not be dissuaded, "especially when the argument is made by the present land owner." Should the Congressional plan be enacted, rootless white agitators, "whose only hope of power and profit is the perpetuation of this hostility," would generate continual turmoil by advocating "legislation against all the established interest of the state." Thus, Trescott continued, "the natural influence of capital on labour, of employer on employed, that influence which in the development of civilization has always existed and must always exist in every society where public and private pros-

[50] General Wager Swayne to Lewis E. Parsons, July 31, 1865, Parsons Mss. Montgomery.
[51] James L. Orr to William H. Trescott, February 27, 1865, Trescott to Orr, January 25, February 4, 6, March 4, 6, 10, April 15, 1866, Orr Mss., Columbia; Trescott to Benjamin F. Perry, October 9, 1865, Perry Mss., Montgomery; Willie Lee Rose, *Rehearsal for Reconstruction: The Port Royal Experiment* (Indianapolis, 1964), brilliantly describes the situation in the Sea Islands and its implications for Reconstruction. See particularly, 188, 346-377.

perity go hand in hand, has been utterly destroyed." Trescott did refer
to the problem of race, but made clear his feeling that race and color
were superficial differences compared to the primary divisions:

> You know—every man in this country, white and black, knows that this
> is, *in no invidious or offensive sense, but as a fact,* the white man's gov-
> ernment. You and they know the spirit of independence which settled it,
> the courage which won its liberty and has maintained its existence, the
> brain which devised its constitution, the enterprise which extended its
> territory, the capital which freights its ships, ploughs its fields, digs its
> mines and builds its railroads—the arts and science, the effort and the
> achiev(e)ment which make sum of its civilization, belong to the white
> man. This civilization you cannot intend, you cannot desire to destroy. . . .
> If you wish these Southern States restored, you very naturally wish them
> to be restored with *changed opinions and altered feelings,* but just as cer-
> tainly you do not wish to receive them back with their State Governments
> utterly disorganized and their means of Social and industrial prosperity
> completely destroyed.[52]

Trescott was right. In the final analysis, northern radicals had no
greater desire to disturb the traditional relationships between capital
and labor than southern conservatives. In the end they granted the
southern blacks legal and political rights, but denied them the massive
concerted economic and educational assistance that could have made
those rights meaningful. As one of the most stalwart of those radicals,
Albion W. Tourgee, later admitted:

> They granted to the ignorant, unskilled and dependent race—a race who
> could not have lived a week without the support or charity of the dominant
> one—equality of political right! Not content with this, they went farther,
> and, by erecting the rebellious territories into self-regulating and sovereign
> states, they abandoned these parties like cocks in a pit, to fight out the
> question of predominance without the possibility of national interference.
> They said to the colored man, in the language of one of the pseudo-
> philosophers of that day, "Root, hog, or die."[53]

Andrew Johnson tersely summed up the future of the Negro as
Freedman and laborer when he said that the Negro should be given
only "the right to rise by his own energies" and hastened to add that
he did not thereby "mean to argue that the Negro race is equal to the
Anglo-Saxon"; the certain outcome would be the relegation of the
blacks to "the inferior condition of society."[54]

[52] Galliard Hunt, ed., "Letter of William Henry Trescott on Reconstruction in South
  Carolina, 1867," *American Historical Review,* XV (1910), 574-582 (Italics added.)
[53] Albion W. Tourgee, *A Fool's Errand* (New York, 1966), 137.
[54] W. E. Burghardt Du Bois, *Black Reconstruction* (New York, 1935), 244.

In the fall of 1865, Johnson addressed a regiment of Negro troops. He warned them not to expect "to fall back on the government for support and live in idleness and debauchery." As the President advised the black Civil War veterans that liberty "consisted in the right to work and enjoy the profits of one's labor," a Negro Sergeant was heard to murmur softly: "Thank God it means that much."[55]

[55] Vicksburg (Miss.) *Weekly Herald*, October 21, 1865; see also *The Philadelphia Press*, May 20, 1865 and New York *Herald*, May 13, 1865.

2

Negro Labor in the Western Cattle Industry, 1866-1900

KENNETH W. PORTER

INTRODUCTION

The range-cattle industry in its various aspects, and in its importance to the United States and particularly to the Great Plains for the post-Civil War generation, has been the subject of numerous studies. This industry was rendered possible by such factors as vast expanses of grazing land, projected railroad lines across the Missouri and onto the Great Plains, the rise of heavy industry and the consequent demand for beef of less-than-high quality by the meat-hungry industrial population. But like the steel, mining, packing, and other industries, it also needed a labor force—workers with special abilities and qualities—for although the cowhand or cowboy possibly was no more than a "hired man on horseback,"[1] he was a hired man with skills in riding, roping, and branding which could not be easily acquired. Most of his working hours were spent in such routine tasks as riding the range and turning back drifting steers; rounding up, branding, and castrating calves; selecting beeves for the market; and, even on the "long drive," jogging along and daily "eating dirt" on the flanks or in the rear of a few

Research for this paper and for the larger project of which it is a part was facilitated by grants from the American Philosophical Society and the Graduate School of the University of Oregon. This article is extracted from seven chapters of a nearly-completed book-length manuscript tentatively entitled *Black Riders: The Negro on the Frontier of the Cattle Country*, which is a functional and interpretative study. Therefore, it would hardly be an exaggeration to state that complete documentation of every statement might occupy almost as much space as the text. Consequently, I have frequently restricted my references to the more important and particularly controversial statements. The most nearly complete published account of the Negro in the cattle country is Philip Durham and Everett L. Jones, *The Negro Cowboys* (N. Y., 1965), which is to a large extent regionally organized. My deepest gratitude goes to the late J. Frank Dobie, for his kindness in turning over to me his files on Negro cowboys.
[1] May Davison Rhodes, *The Hired Man on Horseback: A Biography of Eugene Manlove Rhodes* (Boston, 1938), ix-xiii.

KENNETH W. PORTER *is Professor of History at the University of Oregon.*

thousand "cow critters." But he also needed the inborn courage and quick thinking to use these skills effectively while confronting an enraged bull, swimming a milling herd across a flooded river, or trying to turn a stampede of fear-crazed steers.

But the general public, under the influence of decades of "Western" movies and, more recently, television shows has come to regard the cowboy's workaday activities as altogether secondary to fighting off hostile Indians, pursuing rustlers and holding "necktie parties" for them, saving the rancher's daughter from Mexican raiders, and engaging in quick-draw gunfights in dusty streets. From similar sources this same public has also learned that cowboys, with the exception of an occasional low-browed villain or exotic and comic-accented *vaquero*, were all of the purest and noblest Anglo-Saxon type, as in Owen Wister's *The Virginian*.

In reality, as George W. Saunders of the Texas Trail Drivers Association has authoritatively estimated, of the fully 35,000 men who went up the trail from Texas with herds during the heroic age of the cattle industry, 1866-1895, "about one-third were Negroes and Mexicans."[2] This estimate is closely confirmed by extant lists of trail-herd outfits which identify their members racially. These lists also demonstrate that Negroes out-numbered Mexicans by more than two to one—slightly more than 63 percent whites, 25 percent Negroes, and slightly under 12 percent Mexicans.

The racial breakdown of individual outfits, of course, varied widely. Some were nearly all of one race, such as the 1874 outfit which was all-Negro, except for a white boss, or the 1872 outfit which consisted of a white trail-boss, eight Mexicans, and a Negro; but more typical were the two 1877 outfits composed, respectively, of seven whites and two Negro cowboys, and a Negro cook; and seven whites, two Negroes, and a Mexican hostler. Many outfits had no Mexicans at all, but it was an exceptional outfit that did not have at least one Negro and enough outfits were nearly all Negro, or a third or more Negro, to bring the number up to the estimated twenty-five percent of the total.[3] A trail-herd outfit of about a dozen men would on the average consist of seven or eight whites, including the trail boss, three Negroes—one of whom was probably the cook, while another might be the horse wrangler,

[2] John Marvin Hunter (ed.), *The Trail Drivers of Texas* (Nashville, 1925), 453.
[3] *Ibid.*, 987, 255, 717, 157, 505, 472, 817, 138-139, 805, 718-719; R. J. (Bob) Lauderdale and John M. Doak, *Life on the Range and on the Trail*, Lela Neal Pirtle, editor (San Antonio, 1936), 169.

and the third would simply be a trail hand—and one or two Mexicans; if a Negro was not the wrangler, then a Mexican often was. Needless to say, this is not the typical trail outfit of popular literature and drama.

The racial make-up of ranch outfits, with their seasonal and day-by-day fluctuations, was not so well recorded as that of the trail-herd outfits, but available information indicates that ranch hands, in Texas at least, were white, Negro, and Mexican in proportions varying according to locality and to ranchowner tastes; probably the overall proportions differed little from those of trail outfits. A ranch in the Indian Territory during the late 1890s, for example, was staffed by eight cowhands, two of whom were Negroes.[4] Negro cowhands were particularly numerous on the Texas Gulf Coast, in the coastal brush east of the Nueces and at the mouth of the Brazos and south of Houston, and parts of the Indian Territory; in some sections they were in the majority, and some ranches worked Negroes almost exclusively.[5]

Negro trail drivers swarmed west and north with herds from the Texas "hive" and, though most returned, a few remained as ranch hands as far north as Wyoming, the Dakotas, and even Canada and as far west as New Mexico, Arizona, and even California and Oregon.[6]

WRANGLERS

Negroes occupied all the positions among cattle-industry employees, from the usually lowly wrangler through ordinary hand to top hand and lofty cook. But they were almost never, except in the highly infrequent case of an all-Negro outfit, to be found as ranch or trail boss.

Negroes and also Mexicans were frequently wranglers, or *remuderos*[7] —in charge of the saddle horses not immediately in use—usually regarded as the lowliest job in the cattle industry, except for the boy who sometimes served as wrangler's assistant.[8] There were exceptions, how-

---

[4] John Hendrix, *If I Can Do It Horseback* (Austin, 1963), 205.
[5] John M. Hendrix, "Tribute Paid to Negro Cowmen," *The Cattleman*, XXII (Feb., 1936), 24. See also J. Frank Dobie to KWP, Jan. 30, 1953, J. Frank Dobie, *The Longhorns* (Boston, 1941), 309.
[6] William A. Keleher, *The Fabulous Frontier: Twelve New Mexico Items* (Albuquerque, 1962), 162-163, 245, 271; Theodore Roosevelt, *Ranch Life and the Hunting Trail* (N. Y., 1920; 1st ed., 1888), 10-11. See also Floyd C. Bard as told to Agnes Wright Spring, in *Horse Wrangler: Sixty Years in the Saddle in Wyoming and Montana* (Norman, 1960), 12-13; Sir Cecil E. Denny, *The Law Marches West* (Toronto, 1939), 187.
[7] J. Frank Dobie, *A Vaquero of the Brush Country* (Dallas, 1929), 12-13; Lauderdale and Doak, *op. cit.*, 11; Hunter, *op. cit.*, 679, 204.
[8] Douglas Branch, *The Cowboy and His Interpreters* (N. Y., 1926), 42-43; Ross Santee, *Men and Horses* (N. Y., 1926); Agnes Morley Cleaveland, *No Life for a Lady* (Boston, 1941), 111; William T. Hornaday, "The Cowboys of the Northwest," *Cosmo-*

ever, including some expert wranglers who became "second in authority to the foreman" in a few camps.[9] Such wranglers were "horse men" in the highest sense: capable of detecting and treating illness and injury, selecting the proper horse for each job, and taking the ginger out of unruly animals. Among these wranglers-extraordinary were Nigger Jim Kelly, the horsebreaker, horsetrainer, handyman, and gunman of the notorious Print Olive; and the famous John Chisum's "Nigger Frank," "who spent a lifetime wrangling Long I horses" and whom a white cattleman declared "the best line rider and horsewrangler I ever saw."[10]

COWBOYS

The majority of Negroes on the ranch or "long drive" were neither wranglers nor yet authoritative cooks (of whom more later). They were top hands or ordinary hands who, on the long drive, rode the point, the swing, the flank, or the drag, according to their experience and ability. The point—the position of honor—was at the front of the herd where the steers were strongest, most restless, and most likely to try to break away. There the most experienced top hands rode. Farther back, the cattle were somewhat less troublesome, while in the rear, where the tired beasts were comparatively easy to manage, could be found the fledgling cowboys of the drag, "eating the dust" of the entire herd. Negroes rode in all these positions.[11]

These Negro cowboys, whether on ranch or trail, were generally regarded as good workers, who got along well with others and who took pride in their work. A white Texan, a former cowboy and rancher, went so far as to write that "there was no better cowman on earth than the Negro."[12]

---

politan, II (Dec., 1886), 226; Edward Everett Dale, *Cow Country* (Norman, 1942), 46-47.

[9] Branch, *op. cit.*, 42-43. "For my money he [the wrangler] was one of the most capable fellows around an outfit." Hendrix, *If I Can Do It Horseback*, 185-186.

[10] Harry E. Chrisman, *The Ladder of Rivers: The Story of I. P. (Print) Olive* (Denver, 1962), 34-35, 77, 102, 147, 217, 378; Dane Coolidge, *Fighting Men of the West* (Bantam Books, 1952; 1st ed., 1932), 14, 32, 41; Frank Collinson, *Life in the Saddle*, Mary Whatley Clarke, editor, (Norman, 1963), 145.

[11] Charles A. Siringo, *Riata and Spurs: The Story of a Lifetime Spent in the Saddle as Cowboy and Ranger* (Boston, 1931; 1st ed., 1927), 27.

[12] Ramon F. Adams to KWP, Feb. 6, 1953; Roosevelt, *op. cit.*, 10-11; Ellsworth Collings, "The Hook Nine Ranch in the Indian Territory," *Chronicles of Oklahoma*, XXXIII (Winter, 1955-56), 462; Angie Debo, editor, *The Cowman's Southwest, being the Reminiscences of Oliver Nelson, Freighter, Camp Cook, Frontiersman, in Kansas, Indian Territory, Texas, and Oklahoma, 1876-1893* (Glendale, 1963), 98-99, 107-108; Hendrix, *If I Can Do It Horseback*, 161, 205.

Old, experienced Negro cowhands frequently served as unofficial, one-man apprentice systems to white greenhorns. This was particularly true, of course, when the fledgling was the employer's son or relative. Will Rogers, for example, got his first lessons in riding and roping from a Cherokee Negro employee of his father.[13] Almost any young would-be cowboy who showed the proper spirit, however, might have the good fortune to be "adopted" and "showed the ropes" by one of these black veterans, who would sometimes take on the inexperienced boy as partner when white cowboys were unwilling to do so.[14] Charles Siringo, later famous as a cowboy-detective-author, recalled that Negro cowboys again and again came to his rescue when, in his reckless cowboy youth, his life was threatened by a mad steer, a wild bronc, and even a hired assassin.[15]

Negro cowhands confronted all the dangers and met all the tests of the long trail. One poorly clad cowboy froze to death in his saddle during a "Norther" rather than give up and go in to the chuckwagon.[16] Stampedes were an ever-present danger, and experienced Negroes were frequently prominent in attempting to prevent or control them. Indeed they were also often among the few cowboys who stayed with the herd when others threw in their hands.[17]

Crossing the wide, deep, frequently flooded rivers was even more dangerous than stampedes. According to a white ex-cowboy, "it was the Negro hand who usually tried out the swimming water when a trailing herd came to a swollen stream"[18]—either because of his superior ability or because he was regarded as expendable. But whether or not this statement is valid, it probably would not have been made had not Negroes frequently demonstrated their ability to cope with the problems of river crossings. Numerous anecdotes about such crossings tell of Negro cowhands saving themselves by their own efforts, being assisted

---

[13] Homer Croy, *Our Will Rogers* (N. Y. and Boston, 1953), 19-20, 250, 334; Donald Day, *Will Rogers: A Biography* (N. Y., 1962), 11-16, Chrisman, 77; John Rolfe Burroughs, *Where the West Stayed Young: The Remarkable History of Brown's Park* . . . (N. Y., 1962), 109.

[14] Collinson, *op. cit.*, 25-26; James Emmit McCauley, *A Stove-Up Cowboy's Story*, with an introduction by John A. Lomax (Dallas, 1956; 1st ed., 1943), 12.

[15] Siringo, *A Texas Cowboy* (Signet Books, 1955; 1st ed., 1886), 38; Siringo, *Riata and Spurs*, 17, 18.

[16] Dobie, *Vaquero*, 100-101.

[17] Hunter, *op. cit.*, 112, 417-418; James C. Shaw, *North from Texas: Incidents in the Early Life of a Range Cowman in Texas, Dakota, and Wyoming 1852-1882*, Herbert O. Brayer, editor (Evanston, 1952), 46-47.

[18] Hendrix, "Negro Cowmen," 24.

to dry land by white cattlemen[19] and, on more than one occasion, saving their lives.

Negroes not only often showed courage and quick thinking in extricating themselves and others from the danger of swollen rivers, but in at least one case also displayed ingenuity superior to that of a great trail boss. In 1877 Ab Blocker, "the fastest driver on the trail," had reached the Platte River, which was spanned by a bridge of sorts, but the wild longhorns had never seen a bridge and refused to cross it. It looked as if, after all, they would have to swim the herd when a Negro hand suggested—and his suggestion was adopted—that they should drive the chuckwagon slowly across, followed by old Bully, an ox; the lead steers would follow Bully and the rest of the herd would trail them.[20]

RIDERS AND ROPERS

Although every top hand had to be a skillful rider and roper, some were so outstanding as to be considered "bronco busters" and/or ropers *par excellence* rather than as merely uncommonly able cowboys. Numerous references suggest that Negroes and Mexicans were widely regarded as particularly expert in both these capacities—the Mexicans especially noted for their prowess with the *reata* (or lasso). Mexicans were also, correctly or not, blamed for cruelty toward animals and consequently fell into disrepute as horsebreakers,[21] whereas the Negroes maintained and even advanced a reputation which went back to antebellum days.

A white ex-cowpuncher-writer states that Negroes were hired largely for their ability to cope with bad horses which the white cowhands did not want to tackle. "The Negro cow hands of the middle 1880s . . . were usually called on to do the hardest work around an outfit. . . . This most often took the form of 'topping' or taking the first pitch out of the rough horses of the outfit. . . . It was not unusual for one young

---

[19] Hunter, *op. cit.*, 47-48, 987-988; A. J. Sowell, *Early Settlers and Indian Fighters of Southwest Texas* (Austin, 1900), 757-758; J. Frank Dobie, interview with Joe McCloud, Beeville, Texas, *ca.* 1928, in letter to KWP, Feb. 16, 1953.

[20] Dobie, *Longhorns*, 246-247; E. C. Abbott ("Teddy Blue") and Helena Huntington Smith, *We Pointed Them North: Recollections of a Cowpuncher* (N. Y., 1939), 263.

[21] Emerson Hough, *The Story of the Cowboy* (N. Y., 1934; 1st ed., 1897), 91; James W. Freeman (ed.), *Poetry and Prose of the Live Stock Industry* (Denver and Kansas City, 1905), I, 13; Louis Pelzer, *The Cattleman's Frontier . . . 1850-1890* (Glendale, 1936), 48; Roosevelt, *op. cit.*, 10-11; Stanley Walker, "Decline and Fall of the Hired Man," *The New Yorker*, Sept. 12, 1953, p. 110; Clifford P. Westermeier, *Man, Beast, Dust: The Story of Rodeo* (n.p., 1947), 173.

Negro to 'top' a half dozen hard-pitching horses before breakfast." Andy Adams, the cowboy-author and a man who was far from being a Negrophile, declared that the "greatest bit of bad horse riding" he ever saw was performed by a dozen Negro cowboys who were assigned to ride a dozen horses which the white cowpunchers of their outfit were afraid to tackle. But each of the Negroes stayed on his horse till the animal was conquered.[22]

The list of Negro bronc riders—the comparatively few whose names have survived—is still a long one. A few of the better known, partly because they attracted the attention of published writers, were the following: Isam, Isom, or Isham Dart of Brown's Hole, "where Colorado, Wyoming, and Utah cornered," who, although now remembered principally as a reputed rustler, was also "numbered among the top bronc stompers of the Old West";[23] Nigger Jim Kelly, whom oldtime cowboys considered the peer of any rider they had seen in the United States, Canada, or the Argentine;[24] a mulatto named Williams in the Badlands of South Dakota, who was a horse-trainer rather than a horsebreaker and whose methods won the admiration of Theodore Roosevelt;[25] and Jim Perry, the famous XIT cook, who was even better known as "one of the best riders and roper ever to hit the West."[26]

While most of the famous riders were bronco busters only as one aspect of their work as cowhands, some, including a number of Negroes, were officially recognized as ranch horsebreakers, and a few were full-time or nearly full-time professionals. Perhaps the most famous of the professionals was Matthew (Bones) Hooks of the Panhandle—remembered, after his retirement from horsebreaking to Pullman-portering, for having once taken off his jacket and cap and laid aside his clothes brush, to mount and break an outlaw which no one had been able to ride, while his train stood in the station.[27]

---

[22] Hendrix, "Negro Cowmen," 24; Elmo S. Watson, "Tales of the Trail," probably in a Colorado Springs newspaper in 1916, and Arthur Chapman, interview with Andy Adams, *Denver Times*, Aug. 18, 1915, p. 2. See also Wilson M. Hudson, *Andy Adams: His Life and Writings* (Dallas, 1964), 184, 251. To Professor Hudson's kindness I owe copies of the two newspaper items, *supra*.

[23] Burroughs, *op. cit.*, 192-195; Coolidge, *op. cit.*, 79; Dean Krakel, *The Saga of Tom Horn: The Story of a Cattlemen's War* (Laramie, 1954), 9-12.

[24] Chrisman, *op. cit.*, 34-35, 77, 217, 378; Harry E. Chrisman, Denver, to KWP, Oct. 23, 1965.

[25] Lincoln A. Lang, *Ranching with Roosevelt* (Philadelphia, 1926), 286.

[26] Lewis Nordyke, *Cattle Empire: The Fabulous Story of the 3,000,000 Acre XIT* (N. Y., 1949), 138.

[27] Jean Ehly, " 'Bones' Hooks of the Panhandle," *Frontier Times*, XXXVI (June-July, 1963), 20-22, 54-55 (illustrated).

Other Negro cowhands were particularly renowned as ropers, such as Ab Blocker's Frank, who was, according to a white cowboy, "the best hand with a rope I ever saw," and whose roping skill once saved his employer from an angry steer;[28] Ike Word, according to Charles Siringo, "the best roper" at a roundup near Beeville, Texas;[29] Jim Simpson, "about the best roper" on his part of the Wyoming range;[30] and, more recently, the Negro rancher Jess Pickett who, according to a white neighbor, was "the world's best roper."[31]

Naturally enough, many of the famous Negro riders, such as Isom Dart and Jim Perry, were almost or quite as renowned as ropers. One of the most spectacular at both riding and roping was "Nigger Add," "one of the best hands on the Pecos," who would as a matter of course "top off" several bad horses of a morning. Walking into a corral full of tough broncs, he would seize any one he chose by the ear and nose, lead him out of the bunch, and then show him who was boss. As a roper he was even more sensational, and had the unusual technique of roping on foot, a practice which would have killed an ordinary man. He would tie a rope around his hips, work up to a horse in the corral or in the open pasture, rope him around the neck as he dashed by at full speed, and then, by sheer strength and skill, flatten the horse out on the ground where a lesser man would have been dragged to death.[32] Indeed, the prowess of such Negro riders, horsebreakers, and horse-trainers was so outstanding as to contribute to the commonly held belief of the time that there was some natural affinity between Negroes and horses.[33]

SINGING TO THE CATTLE

Riding, roping, and branding were not the only skills required of a top cowhand. Singing to the cattle, particularly on night herd but sometimes during the day's march, was not only a practical necessity for calming the animals and reducing the danger of a stampede, it also had recreational and esthetic values for the drivers. Negro trail hands were conspicuous in this practice, although Negro chuckwagon cooks were the most noted cow-country musicians, singers, and composers.

---

[28] Edward Seymour Nichols, *Ed Nichols Rode a Horse,* as told to Ruby Nichols Cutbirth (Dallas, 1943), 8-9.

[29] Siringo, *Texas Cowboy,* 82-83.

[30] Bard, *op. cit.,* 67.

[31] Fred Herring, Lometa, Texas, to KWP, July 20, 1965.

[32] J. Evetts Haley, *George W. Littlefield, Texan* (Norman, 1943), 181-186.

[33] Frederic Remington, "Vagabonding with the Tenth Horse," *The Cosmopolitan,* XXII (Feb., 1897), 352.

"Nigger" Jim Kelly, the Olives' versatile horsebreaker and gunman, is also credited with composing a humorous song, "Willie the Cook," which he sang to accordion accompaniment furnished by a white trail hand. "Teddy Blue," a white cowhand whose autobiography is a cow-country classic, tells movingly of his first memory of the "Ogallaly song," which had a verse for every river on the trail, beginning with the Nueces and ending in 1881, when he first heard it, with Ogallala.

> There were [he recalled] thirteen herds camped on the Cimarron that night and you could count their fires. A Blocker herd was bedded close to ours; it was bright starlight, and John Henry was riding around the herd singing the Ogallaly song. John Henry was the Blocker's [sic] top nigger. . . .
>
> 'We left Nueces River in April eighty-one
>
> With three thousand horned cattle and all they knowed was run
>
> O-o-o-o-oh!'
> and so on.[34]

The special quality which these Negro cowhands gave to the cattle country is epitomized in an episode at Doan's store on the Red River, which was the last place where a trail herd hand could receive mail and purchase supplies before reaching the Kansas cattle towns. One night a crowd sitting around the little adobe store heard the strains of "a lively air on a French harp." The door opened and in sailed a hat, closely followed by a big Negro who began to dance to his own accompaniment. "It was one of Ab Blocker's niggers"—perhaps John Henry himself— "who had been sent up for the mail, giving first notice of the herd's arrival."[35] The ranch or cattle trail, without its many Negroes, would not only have suffered from a lack of expert riders, ropers, and cooks, but would also have lacked much of its vitality and vivacity and spontaneous gaiety, and ranching and trail-driving would have been duller occupations.

COWBOY COOKS—MEN OF PARTS

High in the hierarchy of cow-country employees was the ranch or trail cook,[36] who ranked next to the foreman or trail boss and, in camp,

[34] Abbott and Smith, *op. cit.,* 261-264.
[35] Hunter, *op. cit.,* 778.
[36] The standard work on the cow-country cook is, of course, Ramon F. Adams, *Come an' Get It: The Story of the Old Cowboy Cook* (Norman, 1952). Almost every general work on the cowboy or the cattle country, and many reminiscences and special studies, also contain useful information.

ruled supreme over an area of sixty feet around the chuckwagon. In addition to culinary skill—including the ability to prepare a meal in a blizzard, cloudburst, or high wind—the cook also had to be an expert muleskinner or bullwhacker, capable of driving two or three yoke of oxen or a four-mule team attached to the chuckwagon over the most difficult terrain, including flooded rivers. He could do more than any-one else to make life pleasant and many a cowboy selected an outfit because of the reputation of its cook. In compensation for duties which few men could satisfactorily perform, the cook normally was paid from $5 per month more than the ordinary cowhand up to even twice as much.

The cowboy cook was also commonly credited with other qualities less essential and certainly less endearing than the ability to cook and drive the chuckwagon. He was frequently something of a despot; bad-tempered, hard-featured, and unlovely. "As tetchy as a cook" is still a ranch byword. He was often an old "stove-up" cowpuncher who re-sented having to "wait on" cowboys still in their prime, "just kids" in his opinion. He often was also a "hard character," and frequently had a drinking problem. Finally, as one authority has stated, cooks were seldom good riders.

The above description of the cowboy-cook is synthesized from the reports of numerous observers on cooks of all races and backgrounds in all parts of the cow-country. Some of these qualities doubtless applied to most of them, and all to some of them. But numerous accounts of Negro cow-country cooks suggest that the traditional "hard character" pattern fitted them much less than it did whites. The cow-country cook of the Texas and Texas-influenced range, if not typically a Negro, was at least very frequently one.[37] To be sure, the historian of the cowboy-cook writes: "Most bosses preferred a native white cook. . . . Some Negroes were good cooks, but were usually lazy, and, too, white cow-boys refused to take orders from them." This statement, however, is not confirmed by the literature of the cattle country, which strongly sug-gests that many if not most cattlemen were in agreement with the trail boss who wrote: "For cooks I always preferred darkies."[38]

[37] Rufus Rockwell Wilson, *Out of the West* (N. Y., 1933), 377; Hough, *op. cit.*, 138-139; J. Frank Dobie, *Cow People* (Boston, 1964), 132; Hunter, *op. cit.*, 485, 43, 307, 535, 295-303, 416-417, 981, 688, 231, 606-607, 81, 679.
[38] R. F. Adams, *op. cit.*, 21-22; Lauderdale and Doak, *op. cit.*, 183-185.

The primary reason for this preference is probably that Negroes simply were on the average better workers than the available whites. They could, of course, occasionally be lazy, stupid, careless, dishonest, and many whites were excellent cooks, but the cow-camp menus on record seem to have been disproportionately the work of Negro cooks. Good cooks occasionally supplemented the filling but somewhat monotonous diet of biscuits, "sowbelly," beef, molasses, and coffee by carrying a gun in the wagon and, between dishwashing and starting the next meal, hunted deer, turkey, and other game. An extraordinary cook who took full advantage of such opportunities was a thirty-year-old Negro named Sam who, in 1878, prepared for an outfit on Pease River what one of its members years later described as "about the most luscious eating. . . . I have ever enjoyed . . . an oven of buffalo steaks, another . . . of roast bear meat, better than pork, a frying pan full of the breast of wild turkey in gravy of flour, water, and grease, . . . antelope ribs barbecued on a stick over the coals." Sometimes he would roast a turkey in its feathers in a pit. He also cooked wild plums, stewing them or making them into a cobbler. Small wonder that the cowboys of his outfit always saw to it that he had plenty of wood.[39] Sam was merely one of a galaxy of Negro cow-country cooks, each with his specialty— Dutch oven-baked peach pies, "cathead biscuits," son-of-a-gun stew," etc.

The cook was frequently in sole charge not merely of the kitchen but of the ranch house itself, and on the long drive was of course frequently left alone to protect the chuckwagon and its contents in any emergency, whether crossing a river or encountering Indians. A Negro cook distinguished himself in an episode of 1877 in which the other members of his outfit played no very heroic roles. Four white men and three Negroes were working cattle in Coleman County, Texas, when Indians suddenly swooped down upon them. All took refuge in a cave except "old Negro Andy, the cook," who stayed by the wagon, fought off the Indians, and saved the supplies.[40]

By and large, Negro cooks managed their kitchens or chuckwagon, dealt with Indians, and accomplished their culinary feats without the "crankiness" which was almost as much standard equipment for cow-country cooks as was their "starter" for salt-rising bread. Some white

[39] Dobie, *Vaquero,* 137-139; Dobie, *Cow People,* 140.
[40] J. S. Hart, "Jesse Hart, Callahan County Pioneer," *Frontier Times* (Jan., 1953), 86.

cooks manifested such behavior to an almost psychopathic extent, and some Negro cooks lived up to the tradition, to be sure, but more typical were those remembered for opposite qualities.[41] Jim Perry was not only a fine cook but also "the best Negro who ever lived"; Sam "always had a cheerful word or a cheerful song"; etc. Frank Dobie believes that Negro and Mexican cooks were notably above average in their tendency to be "providers by nature" and in their readiness to go out of their way to furnish extra services, from medicinal supplies to home-made remedies. When, for example, a young cowboy drank alkali water, and "wasn't feeling too good," Jim Simpson, the Negro cook, told him to roll a can of tomatoes in his slicker for both food and drink; the acid from the tomatoes would help neutralize the alkali.[42]

The Negro cook often possessed other skills beyond the culinary. So many Negro cooks, in fact, were noted riders and ropers that something of a pattern emerges. The wild-game cook extraordinary, Black Sam, was such a good rider that "frequently one of the boys would get him to 'top' a bad horse." Jim Perry of the XIT was not only the best cook that ever lived, according to a white hand, but he was also the best rider as well. Jim Simpson, roundup cook and fiddler, who had come up from Texas in the 1880s with a herd of longhorns, was at one time also "about the best roper" in that part of the Wyoming range.[43] When an associate of one of the famous Blockers expressed some doubt about his roping ability, Blocker told his Negro cook, "Goat," to wipe the the dough off his hands and get a rope and a horse. Blocker swung a regular "Blocker loop" on the first cow, which picked up her front feet, and the cow pony did the rest. "Goat" similarly roped and threw the next cow, Blocker the third, and so on, until they had roped about twenty, never missing.[44]

Negro cooks often left the chuckwagon for the saddle in an emergency. "Doc" Little, who had risen from cowboy to volunteer cook's assistant to full-time cook, "always remained the good cowboy" and in the event of a stampede was usually the first on a horse. The same was said of the Slaughter cook, "Old Bat." When a drove of 500 horses

---

[41] Cordia Sloan Duke and Joe B. Frantz, *6,000 Miles of Fence: Life on the XIT Ranch of Texas* (Austin, 1961), 172n.; Dobie, *Vaquero*, 137-139; Frazier Hunt, *The Long Trail from Texas: The Story of Ad Spaugh, Cattleman* (N. Y., 1940), 141-145; Bard, *op. cit.*, 145-146.

[42] Dobie, *Cow People*, 139-140; Bard, *op. cit.*, 82.

[43] Dobie, *Vaquero*, 137-139; Duke and Frantz, *op. cit.*, 172n, 84; Bard, *op. cit.*, 67.

[44] J. Evetts Haley, *The XIT Ranch of Texas and the Early Days of the Llano Estacado* (Norman, 1953), 77-78.

stampeded, taking the *remuda* with them, including the *remudero's* own picketed horse, the Negro cook threw himself on the trailing rope and "went bumping along for about a hundred yards" before he could stop the animal. He then mounted and took the lead in rounding up the herd.[45]

All cowboys, we have noted, were expected to be able to "sing" in order to soothe the restless cattle. Just as they were expert riders and ropers, Negro cooks were frequently singers, musicians, and even composers. Although hard-worked, they were about the only men in an outfit with the opportunity to carry and play a musical instrument. "The Zebra Dun," a song about a supposed greenhorn who surprised everyone by riding an outlaw horse, is said to have been composed by Jake, who worked for a Pecos River ranch.[46] One chuckwagon cook who supplemented his menu with deer and turkey which he shot himself, also sang and played the guitar.[47] Another, Old Bat, the Slaughter cook, played both the fiddle and the fife. Jim Perry, the XIT cook, was not only the best cook, the best rider, and the best Negro in the world, but also the best fiddler. Jim Simpson, Negro cook and roper of the Wyoming range, was also the regular fiddler for the Saturday night dances. Big Sam, cook and rider, played the banjo and sang until someone stepped on the instrument, whereupon the bunch bought him a fiddle on which he would play such songs as "Green corn, green corn, bring along the demijohn."[48] But the Negro cook-musician who made the most spectacular appearance on the cow-country stage was Gordon Davis, who led Ab Blocker's trail herd through Dodge City while mounted on his left wheel ox, fiddle in hand, playing "Buffalo Gals."[49]

Negro cooks, in addition to riding and roping, singing and playing, sometimes possessed skills so various as to be unclassifiable. The Negro cook, "Old Lee," was "handy as a pocket shirt, ready to do anything, and with the 'know-how' for almost anything that showed up, from cooking to horsewrangling to mending saddle leathers and boots." One of the most versatile of Negro cooks was John Battavia Hinnaut ("Old Bat"), probably the most useful man on the Slaughter spread. Although

[45] Lauderdale and Doak, 183-185; Allen A. Erwin, *The Southwest of John H. Slaughter* (Glendale, 1965), 147-149; Hunter, *op. cit.*, 272.
[46] John A. and Alan Lomax, *Cowboy Songs* (N. Y., 1938), 78-81, xvii-xix.
[47] Max Krueger, *Pioneer Life in Texas* (San Antonio, 1930), 58-71.
[48] Erwin, *op. cit.*, 147-149, 159; Dobie and Frantz, bet. 102 and 103; Bard, *op. cit.*, 102; Dobie, *Vaquero*, 137-139.
[49] Colonel Jack Potter, *Cattle Trails of the Old West* (Clayton, N. M., 1939), 75.

primarily and officially a roundup cook, he was a first-class ranch-hand, a musician, an expert teamster and coachman, an Indian fighter, a mighty hunter, and also served as the boss's valet, practical nurse, and bodyguard.[50]

That the Negro cow-country cook frequently possessed unusual abilities was due in part to limitations imposed because of racial discrimination. He was much more likely than the average white man to have been brought up about the kitchen and stables of a plantation or ranch and there, at an early age, to have become acquainted with cooking and horses. He was less likely to regard kitchen chores as somehow beneath him. The unusually able and ambitious white cowboy could look forward to possible promotion to foreman or trail boss; the Negro of equal ability knew he had little chance of attaining such a position. To become a ranch or roundup cook was about as much as could be expected. Age, inexperience, or physical handicap might preclude a white man from any ranch job outside of the kitchen; but for the superior Negro cowboy to preside over a chuckwagon or ranch kitchen meant an increase in pay and prestige.

FOREMEN AND TRAIL BOSSES

The Negro cowhand, however able, could, as we have seen, rarely rise to a position higher than chuckwagon or ranch-house cook. The principal obstacle to his becoming a ranch foreman or trail boss was a general belief that a Negro simply did not possess the qualities necessary for such a position. But even if a ranch owner or group of cattlemen were confident that a Negro had the necessary intelligence, initiative, and general capacity, there was always the practical consideration that such a man, even if in charge of an all-Negro outfit, would on occasion have to deal with white foremen and trail bosses who might refuse to recognize his authority, and that expensive trouble might ensue. A Negro, however great his ability, thus had difficulty in attaining greater authority than could be exercised over a chuckwagon or kitchen. The phenomenal success of Ora Haley, who for three decades was the dominant figure in the range-cattle business of Northwestern Colorado, is said to have been partly due to his Negro top hand Thornton Biggs, who although he "taught a whole generation of future range managers, wagon bosses, and all-round cowpunchers the finer points of the range-

---

[50] Potter, *op. cit.*, 79-80; Erwin, *op. cit.*, 102, 147, 150, 159, 307-308, 317, 323.

cattle business," himself "never became a range manager or even a foreman." The fairer-minded recognized the handicaps under which their Negro cowhands labored. Jim Perry, redoubtable cook, rider, and fiddler of the XIT ranch, once wryly remarked: "If it weren't for my damned old black face I'd have been boss of one of these divisions long ago."[51] "And no doubt he would have," a white employee commented.

And yet a very few Negroes of exceptional ability, and sometimes under unusal circumstances, did make the grade. There was the master West Texas rider and roper, "Nigger Add" or "Old Add" who, by 1889 if not earlier, was the LFD's range boss, working "South Texas colored hands almost entirely." One of his qualifications was that he was a "dictionary of earmarks and brands" but probably more important was his universal popularity among cattlemen from Toyah, Texas, to Las Vegas, New Mexico.[52] Nigger Add's outfit consisted "almost entirely" of Negroes—and one wonders who the exceptions were. Probably they were Mexicans.

But did any Negro break through the color line to direct outfits including at least some whites? A leading authority on the cow country doubts that it could have happened.[53] Nevertheless at least one Negro, it seems, through sheer ability and force of character was able to defy the tradition that the white man always gives the orders and the black man obeys. Al Jones was a six-footer with a proud carriage and finely chiseled features of a somewhat "Indian" type. He went up the trail no less than thirteen times, and four times—once was in 1885—he was trail boss, directing Negroes, Mexicans, and sometimes white men. As a trail boss he was resourceful and decisive, but probably needed an abundance of tact to get the job done.[54]

Paradoxically, the race prejudice which prevented more than a very few Negro cowhands from rising to the status of foreman or trail boss may have spurred able and ambitious Negroes into taking up land, acquiring cattle, and setting up as independent small ranchers, whereas, lacking the incentive such an obstacle provided, they might have re-

---

[51] Burroughs, *op. cit.*, 71; Duke and Frantz, *op. cit.*, 171-172.
[52] N. Howard (Jack) Thorp, *Songs of the Cowboys* (Boston, 1921), 166-168; Thorp, "Banjo in the Cow Camps," *Atlantic*, CLXVI (Aug., 1940), 195-196; Thorp, *Pardner of the Wind* (Caldwell, Ida., 1945), 22, 285.
[53] Ramon F. Adams, Dallas, to KWP, Feb. 6, 1953.
[54] Frank Dobie, "Notes on Meeting of Trail Drivers of Texas, San Antonio, *ca.* October 1924"; Dobie, "The Old Trail Drivers," *Country Gentleman*, XC (Feb., 14, 1925), 8, 28 (photograph); Dobie to KWP, Feb. 16, 1953; Dobie, *Cow People*, 222-223 (photograph); Hunter, *op. cit.*, 378.

mained satisfied with a position as ranch foreman. But the story of the Negro rancher belongs to the history of petty capitalism rather than to labor history.

HENCHMEN, BODYGUARDS, "BANKERS," AND FACTOTUMS

Some especially able and trustworthy cow-country Negroes fulfilled roles for which there was no equivalent among white cowhands; as confidential assistants, factotums and, when it was necessary to transport large sums of money, bodyguards and "bankers."

Colonel Charles Goodnight wrote of Bose Ikard, his right hand man: "I have trusted him farther than any living man. He was my detective, banker, and everything else." Bose would sometimes have on his person proceeds from his employer's cattle sales amounting to as much as $20,000, since it was reasoned that a thief would be unlikely to search a Negro's belongings.[55]

John Slaughter's "Old Bat" played a similar role. Officially a roundup cook, he could also do almost any ranch work, but his major importance was as a general factotum in anything connected with Slaughter's personal needs—valet, practical nurse, and, above all, bodyguard. When Slaughter was on a cattle-buying trip, Bat always went along to guard the approximately $10,000 in gold which Slaughter usually carried in his money belt, watching while his employer slept. When Slaughter went into Mexico, where silver was preferable, Bat had charge of a mule loaded with "dobe" dollars. His fitness as bodyguard was demonstrated in action against the Apache and when, with another Negro, he stood at Slaughter's side and helped beat off an attack by Mexican bandits.[56]

Print Olive's handyman and bodyguard was Nigger Jim Kelly—wrangler, horsebreaker, gunman—who in the fall of 1869 accompanied his boss back from Fort Kearney, Nebraska, their saddlebags stuffed with currency and gold, and who in 1872, with a quick well-aimed bullet, saved Print's life after he had been shot three times and was about to be killed.[57]

Still another formidable Negro henchman was Zeke, a giant "two-knife" Negro, who in 1879 accompanied Colonel Draper to

---

[55] J. Evetts Haley, *Charles Goodnight: Cowman & Plainsman* (Boston and N. Y., 1936), 166-167, 207, 215, 242-243; *The West Texas Historical Association Year Book* (Oct., 1942), 127.
[56] Erwin, *op. cit.*, 102, 147-150, 159, 307-308, 317, 323.
[57] Chrisman, *op. cit.*, 93, 124, 321, 358-359, 401.

Dodge City on a cattle-buying trip with a paper-wrapped bundle of
$5,000 in currency.[58] Finally, there was "Old Nep." The famous
"Shanghai" Pierce may have thought more of him, according to Frank
Dobie, than of anyone else; for thirty five years Neptune Holmes used
to accompany Shanghai on his cattle-buying expeditions, leading a mule
loaded with saddlebags which bulged with gold and silver and on which
he would pillow his head at night.[59]

Where large sums of money were involved, and courage and loyalty
in protecting and defending it was needed, prominent cattlemen such
as Goodnight, Slaughter, Olive, and Pierce, characteristically preferred
to depend on Negro bodyguards.

WAGES

For a generation and more, cow-country Negroes distinguished themselves as riders and ropers, cooks and bodyguards, as well as in the
more common and still highly necessary positions of wranglers, ordinary cowboys, and top hands. What compensation, financial and psycho-
logical, did they receive for their services? And how did their wages,
working, and living conditions, and opportunities for advancement and
a "good life," compare with those of white hands of corresponding
abilities and of Negroes outside the cattle country?

In view of the racial situation which then prevailed throughout the
United States, particularly in the South and West, it can be assumed that
Negro cowmen encountered discrimination and segregation. The question therefore is not: Did discrimination and segregation exist? But
rather: What was their extent and character? And how uniform were
they? For although racism was general, it did vary from region to region, from state to state, and even from community to community. It
also varied from period to period, probably increasing rather than di-
minishing during the years in question.

Racial discrimination in the cattle country falls into several categories: wages and working conditions on the job; personal and social
relations on the ranch or on cattle trails; and in town or at the end of
the cattle trail.

Discrimination was probably least evident on the job. As to wages,

---

[58] George Bolds, *Across the Cimarron: The Adventures of "Cimarron" George Bolds, Last of the Frontiersmen,* as he related his life story to James D. Horan (N. Y., 1956), 48-49.
[59] Dobie, *Cow People,* 47; Chris Emmett, *Shanghai Pierce: A Fair Likeness* (Norman, 1953), viii, 4, 10, 47, 51-52, 101, 127, 130, 133, 265-266.

cow-punching was, of course, by no means a highly paid occupation, regardless of race. Wages of various categories of cowhands varied widely not only from year to year and from region to region, but even within the same year and region and sometimes within the same outfit as well. Wages were generally low, but increased somewhat from the 1860s into the 1890s and were higher on the Northern Range than in Texas and Kansas. An ordinary hand in the South received from a minimum $15 per month immediately after the Civil War, to $20-$30 through the late 1860s, 1870s, and into the 1880s, to as much as $45 in the 1890s. An experienced top hand would receive $5 or $10 per month more than a less experienced man, and trail hands were paid somewhat more than ordinary ranch hands. Especially experienced trail hands, below the rank of trail boss, occasionaly drew double wages of as much as $60 or even $75; but a "green" boy would receive half-wages of $10-$15. The wages of trail bosses and foreman normally ranged during this period from $100 to $150. Cooks' salaries, as we have seen, might be as little as that of a top hand or as much as double an ordinary cowhand's, but customarily were $5 or $10 more than those of the best-paid cowhand in the outfit. In the North, cowhands usually got about $10 a month more than those in the South. In all cases compensation included food and, in the case of ranch hands, sleeping accommodations, such as they were.[60]

Strange though it may seem, there is no clear-cut evidence that Negro cowhands were generally or seriously discriminated against in the matter of wages, though this was obviously so with Mexicans, who sometimes received one half to one third that of white cowboys earning $20-25.[61] "Teddy Blue," to be sure, says of the Olive outfit, for which he worked in 1879, that they hated Mexicans and "niggers" but "hired them because they worked cheaper than white men." He gives no details, however, and the notoriously violent Olives may have been no more typical in their wage policy than in their conduct generally. On the other hand, one trail boss stated: "I have worked white Americans, Mexicans, and Negroes and they all got just the same salary."[62] Wages were so much under the control of the individual employer that no doubt Negroes

[60] All the general works on the cattle industry and most of the personal reminiscences give more or less attention to wages. Perhaps most generally useful is Louis Pelzer, *op. cit.*, 166, 246.

[61] Freeman, I. *op. cit.*, 559; James Henry Cook, *Fifty Years on the Old Frontier as Cowboy, Hunter, Guide, Scout, and Ranchman* (New Haven, 1925; 1st ed., 1923), 8-9.

[62] Abbott and Smith, *op. cit.*, 39; Lauderdale and Doak, *op. cit.*, 183-185.

were sometimes discriminated against; but such discrimination seems
not to have been characteristic and, when it occurred, was never nearly
as serious as that to which Mexicans were subjected.

COWBOY STRIKES

The question of wages naturally brings up the further question: Did
cowboys, through united action, ever endeavor to raise their low wages?
The general impression is that the happy, carefree, independent-spirited
cowboy could not have cared less about wages, so long as they were
sufficient to keep him in smoking tobacco and to finance a spree on
pay day at the trail's end. The late Stanley Vestal—a better authority on
the Northern Plains Indians than on the cattle industry—was writing
in this spirit when he enquired, rhetorically and contemptuously, "What
cowboy ever wished to join a union?"[63] The answer could have been
supplied by anyone acquainted with the cattle industry of the Texas
Panhandle and of the Powder River region of Wyoming during the
1880s.

In 1883, just before the spring roundup, cowboys on a number of big
Panhandle ranches issued an ultimatum to their bosses demanding
higher wages—$50 per month instead of the $25-35 they were then
receiving. Better food, particularly more vegetables, is said to have been
another objective, but there was apparently no demand for shorter
hours than the usual 105 for a seven-day week—15 hours a day! According to the official record of the Federal Bureau of Labor Statistics,
the strike was a prompt and unequivocal success, but all other evidence
indicates that, though from five to seven large ranches and over 300
cowboys were involved, the strike dragged on for over a year and finally
"petered out." Texas Rangers, hired gunmen, and dancehall girls, who
soon consumed the strikers' savings, are all credited with responsibility
for the failure of this first cowboy strike.[64]

The Panhandle cowboy strike, though the first, was not the last. The
Wyoming cattle industry was largely in the hands of absentee ranch
owners from Great Britain and the Eastern states, and early in 1886

---

[63] Stanley Vestal, *The Missouri* (N. Y., 1945), 163.
[64] The only treatment of this strike in any detail is by Ruth Allen, *Chapters in the History
of Organized Labor in Texas* (Austin, 1941), 33-42. Excellent as is this pioneer
study, the "cowboy strike" deserves still further attention. Other accounts of, or
references to, this strike—not mentioned in the Allen article—are in Charles A.
Siringo, *A Lone Star Cowboy* (Santa Fe, 1919), 268-269; and Lewis Nordyke, *Great
Roundup: The Story of Texas and Southwestern Cowmen* (N. Y., 1955), 109-111.

they ordered a general cut of at least $5 in the prevailing monthly wage of $35-40. Just before the spring roundup the cowboys on the south fork of Powder River struck for $40 a month all around; the strike was led by men who were themselves getting $40, but who objected to working beside men who were getting only $35 and even $30. The strike, which spread to the Sweetwater-Platte area, was generally successful, though its leader was later blackballed.[65]

Negro cowboys could hardly have played any important part in these strikes, as there were not many in the Panhandle and very few in Wyoming. The only Negro cow-country employee in the Panhandle strike about whom we have clear-cut evidence was loyal to his employer rather than to his fellow workers. When it was rumored that a delegation of strikers was descending on the T-Anchor ranch, its owner planted a black-powder mine in an outbuilding—in case strikers should attempt to use the structure as cover for an attack on the ranch house. He commissioned "Gus Lee, the faithful and later famous Negro cook," in the event of such an attack, to crawl out and light the fuse. But the strikers, after a few bullets had kicked up dirt about their horses, advanced no farther and thus relieved Lee of this responsibility.[66]

A Negro or two may, however, have been among the Panhandle strikers. Both in the Panhandle and on Powder River the cowboy strike against the big ranches was followed within a few years by a bloody feud between the big ranchers and the "nester ranchers and little men," with the big ranchers hiring cowboy-gunmen and their opponents drawing support from disgruntled and sometimes blackballed cowboys. The little town of Tascosa in the Panhandle was headquarters for both the striking cowboys in 1883, and for the "nester ranchers" and their supporters in 1886. Among the cowboy partisans of the "little men" was "Nigger Bob" who, when cowboy-gunmen about 2 a.m. on March 21 invaded Tascosa, was "sleepin' on a hot roll" between a woodpile and a small adobe. As the gunmen advanced, firing, rifle shots apparently from the woodpile, drilled one of them through the chest. "Nigger Bob" claimed that, when the bullets got too close, he prudently left

---

[65] Helena Huntington Smith, *The War on Powder River* (N. Y., 1966), 31-33, 289; John Clay, *My Life on the Range* (Chicago, 1924), 123, 125 (Clay mistakenly places this strike in 1884 rather than 1886; he also mentions another strike in the fall).

[66] John L. McCarty, *Maverick Town: The Story of Old Tascosa* (Norman, 1946), 112-113; Boone McClure, "A Review of the T Anchor Ranch," *Panhandle Plains Historical Review*, III (1930), 68-69.

the scene, but his "tough hombre" reputation raised the suspicion that he might have done more shooting than he was willing to admit. If "Nigger Bob" and others like him were around during the strike, they probably supported it.[67]

WORKING CONDITIONS

Negroes were not discriminated against in the work permitted them—below the rank of foreman and trail boss. An experienced Negro would not be told to help the wrangler or to "eat dust" on the drag while a white greenhorn rode at point. On the other hand, Negroes may have been worked harder and longer than whites. John M. Hendrix, a white former cowpuncher and rancher, writing in the middle 1930s, approvingly presented the most extreme picture of discrimination. Negroes, he says, "were usually called on to do the hardest work around an outfit," such as "taking the first pitch out of the rough horses," while the whites were eating breakfast. "It was the Negro hand who usually tried out the swimming water when a trailing herd came to a swollen stream, or if a fighting bull or steer was to be handled, he knew without being told that it was his job." On cold rainy nights, moreover, Negroes would stand "a double guard rather than call the white folks" and would even launder everyone's clothes when the opportunity offered. "These Negroes knew their place, and were careful to stay in it."[68]

Their "place," according to this white Texan, was to do the most dangerous and difficult work, and more of it than any white hand, and in addition to serve as *valets de chambre* to the white hands..

But such a picture cannot be accepted as generally valid. There may have been some outfits to which this description applied and some Negro hands who endeavored to win favor by such works of supererogation, but firsthand accounts of the cattle industry in its heyday—Hendrix's own experiences belonged entirely to the twentieth century—hardly seem to confirm this picture. Negroes were frequently expert riders and did "top" horses for less able wranglers, but contemporaries indicate that such work was regarded as a favor, not as a duty, and its beneficiaries were grateful for it. That Negroes were usually sent to test a swollen stream or handle a dangerous animal cannot be confirmed. There is a similar lack of information about Negroes gratuitously acting

---

[67] McCarty, *op. cit.*, 141-149, esp. 144 and 149.
[68] Hendrix, "Negro Cowmen," 24.

as valets. The only Negro trail hand so described did it exclusively for the trail boss and even this was regarded as unprecedented.[69]

The Negro, to be sure, was occasionally given unpleasant chores, but due to individual unfairness rather than to accepted custom. They might be given jobs which no one else would do—such as killing the calves dropped during the night on a cattle drive.[70] They were sometimes tricked or bullied into doing more than their share of work.[71] But there is no evidence that Negroes were normally expected to do double night-herding duty or guard the cattle while the whites went on a spree—merely that some cowboys were cheats or bullies who were ready to take advantage of Negroes or, for that matter, of inexperienced white cowhands.

LIVING CONDITIONS

Discrimination and segregation off the job, whether on the ranch or the cattle trail, would have been difficult. Hendrix insists on at least partially segregated eating facilities when he describes the Negroes as "topping" the white hands' horses while the whites ate breakfast—presumably the Negroes ate at the "second table"—and he also states that the Negroes "had their own dishes"! But one can hardly imagine the independent and even cranky chuckwagon cook actually taking the trouble to segregate the dishes! Hendrix may have been reading back into the 1870s and 1880s the pattern of race relationships which he considered proper in his own times.[72]

Actually, firsthand accounts of ranch and cattle-trail life indicate about as much segregation as prevailed on Huckleberry Finn's and the "Nigger Jim's" raft before the appearance of "The King" and "The Duke." The sleeping arrangements were usually such as to defy any idea of racial segregation. Ranchowner, trail boss, Negro and white cowhands—particularly in bad weather—frequently not only slept in the same shack or tent but also shared the same blankets.[73] The one case of such segregation I have encountered occurred on a Wyoming ranch in 1885 when an Irish cook (sex not specified) refused to allow a Negro

[69] Dobie, *Cow People*, 233.
[70] Haley, *Goodnight*, 136.
[71] Dobie, *Vaquero*, 97, 34-36, 46-47; Shaw, *op. cit.*, 34-36, 46-47.
[72] C. Vann Woodward, *The Strange Career of Jim Crow* (N. Y., 1955), presents the thesis that segregation in the extreme form which it had assumed by the early 1900s was a comparatively recent development.
[73] Siringo, *Riata and Spurs*, 27; Haley, *Littlefield*, 55, 90, 93, 100-101, 114, 134; J. Evetts Haley, *Jeff Milton: A Good Man with a Gun* (Norman, 1948), 19.

bronc buster to sleep in the bunkhouse.[74] But when white women began to appear, those extreme manifestations of racial 'integration" belonging to the womanless world of the cattle trail and the wintering camp yielded to a more formal and conventional pattern of conduct. When a highly respected Negro cowboy, in the midst of a blizzard, was permitted to sleep on the kitchen floor of a shack in which a camp manager was living with his wife it was regarded by the Negro as an example of extreme condescension or of humanity or both.[75]

HAZING AND ILL TREATMENT

A good deal of hazing and practical joking is inevitable in a community made up largely of rough and uneducated men. Negro hands, particularly those who were young, inexperienced, or timid, probably were subjected to more than their share of such horseplay. But no one in the cattle country—Negro or white, tenderfoot or old timer—was entirely immune to such treatment.[76] In the case of rough treatment which went beyond hazing and became grossly insulting or physically injurious, the Negro cowhand—nearly always a minority member of an outfit composed principally of whites—was in a difficult position. He was almost never a gunslinger. If he were, and if he succeeded in shooting a white opponent in a quarrel, it might have had very serious consequences for him. Negro cowhands rarely used, or attempted to use, a gun in a quarrel within their own outfit. One exception occurred in 1872, when Jim Kelly got the drop on a white cowboy with whom he had had words; but the boss, Print Olive, finally intervened on behalf of the threatened man.[77] Kelly, however, was not only a gunman; he was Print Olive's gunman as well, so nothing happened to him. In 1880 a Negro cowhand, who also served as the trail boss's flunky, attempted to draw on a recently-hired white cowboy who had "cussed him out" for taking his horse's hobbles after repeated warnings, but fell dead with three bullets through the heart.[78] In both these cases the Negro had a special relationship with his employer which encouraged him to stand up to a white man.

---

[74] Amanda Wardin Brown, "A Pioneer in Colorado and Wyoming," *The Colorado Magazine*, XXXV (Oct., 1958), 274.
[75] Duke and Frantz, *op. cit.*, 163-164.
[76] Debo, *op. cit.*, 108; Dobie, *Longhorns*, 107-108; Hunter, *op. cit.*, 205; Ray M. Beauchamp, "The Town That Died Laughing," *Frontier Times* (Summer, 1960), 30-31, 50-52; Westermeier, *Trailing the Cowboy*, 202-203.
[77] Chrisman, *op. cit.*, 104, 201; Harry E. Chrisman, Denver, to KWP, Oct. 23, 1965.
[78] Dobie, *Cow People*, 233-237.

Cowboys seldom engaged in fisticuffs and I have found only one case of a fist fight between a Negro cowhand and a white: this involved the later famous "80 John" Wallace, then a youthful wrangler, and a white boy from another outfit, during a roundup. Wallace claimed the victory. But both participants were mere boys, who were encouraged by the older cowhands;[79] an inter-racial fight between adults probably would not have been so favorably regarded.

Negro cowhands normally depended for protection against insult or injury—whether from members of their own outfits or outsiders—not on fists or weapons but on good conduct, tactful behavior, and their standing among the better element of whites. Negro cooks, though supported by their traditional prestige and real power, were always in danger of encountering violently prejudiced white cowhands who would challenge their authority. For the most part, Negro cooks avoided such a challenge (or insured that, should it materialize, they would have the support of other white cowhands) by a policy of tact and good management—by means of their excellent cookery and, when they were exceptionally good riders, as they often were, by occasionally "topping" a difficult horse. Black Sam of Pease River was particularly skillful in maintaining his prestige without causing ill-feelings. He was an exceptional cook and rider and a popular musician, as well as the biggest and most powerful man in camp. One day when a cowboy jokingly said that he was "too big for a man but not big enough for a horse," he promptly replied that he *was* a horse and would give a dollar to any man who could ride him without spurs. Sam then stripped, with only a bandanna around his neck to hold on by, and one by one he hurled his would-be riders to the ground—thereby demonstrating, but in a friendly and tactful fashion, his ability to take care of himself. He never had any trouble.[80]

White cowhands repeatedly came to the support of Negro members of their outfits. When a drunken cowpuncher in Dodge City began to abuse a Negro cook, for no reason except that he was colored, a sixteen-year-old boy belonging to the Negro's outfit promptly sailed in—carrying guns was banned in Dodge at this time—and soon had the best of the fight. Potentially, a much more serious occasion arose in 1879. It involved the Olive brothers' trail boss, Ira Olive, who had killed a

[79] Hettye Wallace Branch, *The Story of "80 John": A Biography of the Most Respected Negro Ranchmen in the Old West* (N. Y., 1960), 17-18.
[80] Dobie, *Vaquero*, 137-139.

Mexican cowhand a year or so before and who for some reason now began to abuse Jim Kelly—with the aim, E. C. Abbott believed, of getting Kelly to go for his gun so that he could kill him. Kelly, himself a gunman, later claimed that he would have drawn and killed Ira except for the knowledge that he would have to reckon with his brother Print if he did; this he wished to avoid, since Print was his friend. So he took the abuse until Ira struck him in the mouth with his gun, knocking out two teeth. What might have happened next will never be known for at this point the nineteen-year-old Abbott brashly intervened. "If you hit that boy again," he warned ("that boy" was forty years old) "I'll shoot your damn eyes out."[81]

But such protection was not always available. In 1878 a Negro was hired to work on the 22 Ranch, but a member of the outfit—a "nigger killer" type—set out to run him off and one morning began shooting at him. In desperation, the Negro scrambled onto a horse and fled, with the white man in pursuit. Only the white man returned to camp and the Negro's horse showed up the next day with the saddle still on; a few years later a human skeleton, believed to be the Negro's, was found in the neighborhood. The Negro, during this fracas, apparently never attempted to defend himself nor did any member of the outfit lift a finger or even his voice on behalf of the man, or venture to question the white man's conduct. Possibly, had the Negro been with the outfit long enough to establish himself, someone would have intervened, but this is speculation: the outfit stands condemned, with not a single man of the calibre of young Abbott or the sixteen-year-old boy in Dodge City.[82]

RECREATION AND SOCIAL LIFE

The Negro cowboy engaged in the same amusements as the white— on a basis ranging from apparently complete integration to rigid separation. The extent of this segregation depended upon how well the parties knew one another and, more important, upon whether or not the whites included women.

To understand the character and degree of this segregation, and the way in which it was regarded by both whites and blacks, one must remember that the white men and women of the cow country were largely

---

[81] Hendrix, "Negro Cowmen," 24; Ross Santee, *Lost Pony Tracks* (Bantam Books, 1956; 1st ed., 1953), 202-203; Abbott and Smith, *op. cit.*, 38-40; Chrisman, 201.
[82] William Joseph Alexander Elliot, *The Spurs* (Spur, Texas, 1939), 209-210.

Southerners, or Westerners with a Southern exposure, while the Negroes, if not former slaves, were usually the children of ex-slaves. Both whites and Negroes were thus acquainted, by personal experience or recent tradition, with racial *discrimination* far more severe than anything practiced in the post-bellum cow country, even though racial *segregation* under slavery was less rigid than it became during the late nineteenth century.

When ranch work was slack, particularly in the winter, the hands sometimes held a dance, either a "bunkhouse 'shindig' " in which the participants were all males or a "regular dance" with girls from neighboring ranches or from town if one was close enough. On these occasions the Negro hands had the opportunity to shine, as musicians or dancers or both. Although serving as musicians at either type of dance, they were more conspicuous as dancers in the womanless bunkhouse affairs. Indeed, they might not appear on the dance floor with white women, though, singly or in groups, they might present dancing exhibitions as part of the entertainment.[83]

Segregation in a cattle town, where the Negro cowhand was more of a stranger and white women were present, was much more clearcut than on the familiar ranch. But even here the restrictions were not always as rigid as one might perhaps expect. On the town's streets and among members of the same outfit, segregation might be non-existent. A French baron, returning in 1883 from a visit to the Black Hills, was astonished to see a group of cowboys throwing the lasso and wrestling in front of the door to the hotel bar, with a Negro participating "on a footing of perfect equality." Consequently, he naively assumed that race prejudice had disappeared,"[84] but had the cowboys *entered* the bar this illusion would probably have vanished, even though the region was the Northern Range, not Gulf Coast Texas.

Even in Texas, however, segregation in the saloons was apparently informal. Whites, it seems, were served at one end of the bar, Negroes at the other. But should a white man and a Negro choose to drink and converse together in the "neutral zone" between the two sections probably no objection would be raised. The gunman and gambler Ben Thompson once undertook to "integrate" a San Antonio saloon at the

[83] Duke and Frantz, *op. cit.*, 102-103, 189-190; Santee, *op. cit.*, 158-159.
[84] Edmond Mandat-Gracey, *Cow-Boys and Colonels: Narrative of a Journey across the Prairie and over the Black Hills of Dakota*, translated by William Conn (Philadelphia and N. Y., 1963), 325-326.

point of a revolver, forcing the bartender to permit the Negroes to "spread out" from their crowded corner into the vacant space at the "white" end of the bar. His friends charitably assumed that he was suffering from a nervous breakdown, but since, upon an earlier occasion, Thompson had shot a white bully who was trying to force a Cherokee-Negro cowboy to down a beer mug full of whiskey, he may actually have been in part influenced by a fleeting impulse to defend the underdog.[85]

If the Negro moved from the saloon to a restaurant, he would normally encounter a completely segregated situation, partly because of the symbolic value attached to sitting down and eating together—as opposed to standing up at the same bar[86]—but principally because women might be guests in the dining room or cafe. In a town without a colored restaurant, the Negro might have food handed to him at the back door of a cafe—perhaps he might even be permitted to eat in the kitchen—but more probably would, like many white cowboys, prefer to purchase groceries and eat sitting on a hitching rail.[87]

Negroes, of course, were rarely lodged in "white" hotels—unless they were in attendance on prominent white cattlemen—but cowboys, black and white, usually felt that they had better use for their money than to spend it on hotel rooms. They preferred to spread their "hot rolls" in a livery stable or some other sheltered spot.[88]

The most rigorously segregated cow-town establishments, at least so far as Negro cowhands were concerned, were brothels staffed with white prostitutes. However, the larger cow-towns at least, such as Dodge City, were also equipped with *bagnios* occupied by "soiled doves of color," while smaller communities usually had a few "public women" of color who operated independently. The rule that Negroes must not patronize white prostitutes did not of course bar relations between white cowhands and colored women.[89]

---

[85] J. H. Plenn, *Texas Hellion: The True Story of Ben Thompson* (N. Y., 1955), 60, 142; Hendrix, "Negro Cowmen," 24; O. C. Fisher with J. C. Dykes, *King Fisher: His Life and Times* (Norman, 1966), 124-126.

[86] Harry Golden, *Only in America* (Permabooks, 1959; 1st ed., 1958), 105-107, presenting his "Vertical Negro Plan" for abolishing segregation, advances the theory that no Southerner objected to mingling with Negroes so long as neither party sat down!

[87] See Rhodes, *op. cit.*, 86-88, for the attempt of a Negro to eat in a white restaurant in a New Mexico cowtown.

[88] Bolds, *op. cit.*, 48-49; McCarty, *op. cit.*, 149.

[89] Nyle E. Miller and Joseph W. Snell, *Why the West Was Wild* (Topeka, 1963), 614-615, 127, 453; Burroughs, *op. cit.*, 71; William R. Cox, *Luke Short and His Era*

The cow-town gambling-house, on the other hand, was apparently entirely unsegregated. A gambler who intended to separate a Negro trail hand from his wages through the more than expert use of cards and dice could hardly do so without sitting down with him at the same card or crap table.[90]

The Negro cowhand was accustomed to a degree of segregation and apparently did not resent it—at least not to the extent of risking his life in defiance of the practice. Clashes between Negro cowhands and whites were exceedingly rare. When racial encounters occurred in cattle towns, the Negroes involved were almost always colord soldiers.

CONCLUSION

Without the services of the eight or nine thousand Negroes—a quarter of the total number of trail drivers—who during the generation after the Civil War helped to move herds up the cattle trails to shipping points, Indian reservations, and fattening grounds and who, between drives, worked on the ranches of Texas and the Indian Territory, the cattle industry would have been seriously handicapped. For apart from their considerable numbers, many of them were especially well-qualified top hands, riders, ropers, and cooks. Of the comparatively few Negroes on the Northern Range, a good many were also men of conspicuous abilities who notably contributed to the industry in that region. These cowhands, in their turn, benefitted from their participation in the industry, even if not to the extent that they deserved. That a degree of discrimination and segregation existed in the cattle country should not obscure the fact that, during the halcyon days of the cattle range, Negroes there frequently enjoyed greater opportunities for a dignified life than anywhere else in the United States. They worked, ate, slept, played, and on occasion fought, side by side with their white comrades, and their ability and courage won respect, even admiration. They were often paid the same wages as white cowboys and, in the case of certain horsebreakers, ropers, and cooks, occupied positions of considerable prestige. In a region and period characterized by violence, their lives were probably safer than they would have been in the Southern cotton regions where between 1,500 and 1,600 Negroes were lynched in the

(Garden City, N. Y., 1961), 54-55; Westermeier, *Trailing the Cowboy*, 209, 213; Walker D. Wyman and Bruce Sibert, *Nothing But Prairie and Sky: Life on the Dakota Range in the Early Days* (Norman, 1954), 142-143.
[90] Lauderdale and Doak, *op. cit.*, 161; Haley, *Jeff Milton*, 95; Rhodes, *op. cit.*, 86-88; W. M. Hutchinson, editor, *A Bar Cross Man: The Life & Personal Writings of Eugene Manlove Rhodes* (Norman, 1956), 3-5.

two decades after 1882.[91] The skilled and handy Negro probably had a more enjoyable, if a rougher, existence as a cowhand then he would have had as a sharecropper or laborer. Bose Ikard, for example, had a rich, full, and dignified life on the West Texas frontier—as trail driver, as Indian fighter, and as Colonel Goodnight's right-hand man—more so undoubtedly than he could ever have known on a plantation in his native Mississippi.

Negro cowhands, to be sure, were not treated as "equals," except in the rude quasi-equality of the round-up, roping-pen, stampede, and river-crossing—where they were sometimes tacitly recognized even as superiors—but where else in post-Civil War America, at a time of the Negro's nadir, did so many adult Negroes and whites attain even this degree of fraternity? The cow country was no utopia for Negroes, but it did demonstrate that under some circumstances and for at least brief periods white and black in significant numbers could live and work together on more nearly equal terms than had been possible in the United States for two hundred years or would be possible again for nearly another century.

[91] Walter White, *Rope & Faggot: A Biography of Judge Lynch* (N. Y., 1929), *passim;* Jessie Parkhurst Guzman, editor, *Negro Year Book, 1941-1946* (Tuskegee, Ala., 1947), 306-307.

3

Black Workers and
Labor Unions in
Birmingham, Alabama,
1897-1904

PAUL B. WORTHMAN

Southern industrial development at the end of the nineteenth century drew thousands of black workers to the region's cities and towns, where many of the migrants became an integral part of the South's industrial labor force. Historians have drawn attention to the organization of these and Northern black workers by the Knights of Labor and other unions during the 1880s and early 1890s.[1] Later efforts to organize black workers, especially in the South, have too often been ignored, however, because most historians dealing with relations between black workers and trade unions have concentrated on the racial hostility of white workers, and the exclusionary and racially restrictive policies of various trade unions.[2] Exclusive emphasis on the labor move-

The author is indebted to Yale University for a travel grant which made much of the research for this article possible. I am also grateful to C. Vann Woodward, Mark Leiserson, and Edwin Redkey for their critical reading of an earlier version.

[1] Sidney Kessler, "The Negro in Labor Strikes," in *Midwest Journal*, VI:2 (Summer 1954), 16-35; Frederic Myers, "The Knights of Labor in the South," in *Southern Economic Journal*, VI:2 (April 1940), 479-485; C. Vann Woodward, *Origins of the New South, 1877-1913* (Baton Rouge, 1951), 229-234; Sterling D. Spero and Abram L. Harris, *The Black Worker: The Negro and the Labor Movement* (New York, 1931), 40-45; Roger W. Shugg, "The New Orleans General Strike of 1892," in *Louisiana Historical Quarterly*, XXI:2 (April 1938), 559-563; Robert Ward and William Warren Rogers, *Labor Revolt in Alabama: The Great Strike of 1894* (University, Alabama, 1965); F. Ray Marshall, *Labor in the South* (Cambridge, Mass., 1967), 21-24, 60-70; W.E.B. Du Bois, *The Negro Artisan* (Atlanta, 1902), *passim;* Herbert Gutman, "The Negro and the United Mine Workers," in Julius Jacobson, ed., *The Negro and the American Labor Movement* (Garden City, N. Y., 1968), 49-127.

[2] A vast amount of literature examining the failure of the American Federation of Labor and national trade unions to organize black workers at the beginning of the twentieth century is available. Herman D. Bloch, "Labor and the Negro, 1866-1910," in *Journal of Negro History*, L:3 (July 1965), 163-184; Philip S. Foner, *History of the Labor*

PAUL B. WORTHMAN *is an instructor in history at Wellesley College.*

ment's abandonment of black workers during the early years of the twentieth century has obscured the complex relationships which existed among black workers, white workers, and trade unions, and has led to the neglect of tensions and conflicts in the labor movement and in the South which helped shape those relationships.[3] Within trade unions no monolithic attitude towards black workers existed. While some national labor leaders opposed organizing Negroes, others favored such a policy. In addition, since most black workers labored in unskilled jobs, union relations with them were determined not merely by racial attitudes, but also by a particular union's outlook towards organizing the unskilled. As C. Vann Woodward pointed out in *Origins of the New South,* moreover, the evolution of post-Civil War Southern society involved a tangled web of economic and political conflicts and alliances with industrial laborers as well as agrarian Populists often seeking to overcome racial animosities in order to challenge the hegemony of Southern industrialists.[4] Evidence from Birmingham, Alabama, indicates that despite the rapid spread of racial conflict at the beginning of the twentieth century, the heritage of interracial cooperation in the Knights of Labor and in Populist campaigns lingered among many white and black workingmen. Between 1897 and 1904, in the face of mounting racial segregation and discrimination in Alabama, Birmingham's labor movement encouraged organization of the district's black workers and made new efforts to establish interracial workingmen's cooperation.

Exploitation of the rich coal and iron reserves of northern Alabama, which began after the Civil War rapidly transformed this agrarian region into one of the most important industrial centers in the United

---

Movement in the United States, II (New York, 1955), 347-361, and III (New York, 1964), 233-255; Gerald Grob, "Organized Labor and the Negro Workers, 1865-1900," in *Labor History,* I:1 (Spring 1960), 164-176; Herbert Hill, "In the Age of Gompers and After: Racial Practices of Organized Labor," in *New Politics,* IV:2 (Spring 1965), 26-46; Marc Karson and Ronald Radosh, "The American Federation of Labor and the Negro Worker, 1894-1949," in Jacobson, ed., *Negro and the Labor Movement,* 155-187; Bernard Mandel, "Samuel Gompers and the Negro Workers, 1886-1914," in *Journal of Negro History,* XL:1 (January 1955), 34-60; F. Ray Marshall, *The Negro and Organized Labor* (New York, 1965), 14-33, and *Labor in the South,* 3-19, 29-36; Herbert Northup, *Organized Labor and the Negro* (New York, 1944), *passim;* Spero and Harris, *The Black Worker, passim;* Philip S. Taft, *The AF of L in the Time of Gompers* (New York, 1957), 308-317, and *Organized Labor in American History* (New York, 1964), 665-670; French E. Wolfe, *Admission to American Trade Unions* (Baltimore, 1912), 117-134.

[3] As Herbert Gutman recently suggested, where a particular national or local union did not explicitly exclude black workers, "local 'traditions,' particular notions of 'self-interest,' the conflict between racial attitudes and the egalitarian emphasis of much trade union ideology, and numerous other influences as yet unstudied shaped the behavior and the attitudes of Negro and white workers." Gutman, *op. cit.,* 117.

[4] Woodward, *op. cit.,* 175-290.

States.[5] Delayed by the depression of the 1870s and harassed during the remainder of the century by periodic economic setbacks, the growth of Alabama's mineral district was nothing short of phenomenal. In 1870 only eighty-one manufacturing establishments employing 500 people existed in the area. One mine had seven workers who irregularly turned out coal for local use. By 1900 almost 700 manufacturing establishments, capitalized at more than $25 million, employed 16,000 workers and made products valued at $30 million. Three hundred mines employing 18,000 miners produced over ten million tons of coal and iron ore. The district's coke ovens, first built during the 1870s, turned out more than two million tons of coke, and blast furnaces produced over one million tons of pig iron. Subsidiary industries like iron foundries, machine shops, rolling mills, cast-iron pipe factories, and a newly-erected steel plant added to the industrial production of the region. As a result of consolidation, expansion, and diversification, by the end of the nineteenth century several large firms, led by the giant Tennessee Coal, Iron and Railroad Company, controlled the district's economy. The return of prosperity in 1897 sparked an economic boom for these firms and for the region which lasted seven years, reducing labor conflict and leading many people to look forward confidently to the city's emergence as the nation's iron and steel capital.[6]

Alabama's coal and iron production gave birth to numerous mining villages and industrial communities. The largest of these new towns was Birmingham, laid out in 1871 in an old cornfield at the anticipated junction of two railroads. By 1880 the young city had a population of 3,800. Twenty years later the population had increased ten times, and by 1910, with further migration and the incorporation of surrounding suburbs, Birmingham's population exceeded 130,000. Jefferson County, the heart of Alabama's mineral district, contained only 12,345 people

[5] Ethel Armes, *The Story of Coal and Iron in Alabama* (Birmingham, 1910) is still the best account of Alabama's industrial development before World War I. The "Birmingham District" consists of Jefferson, Walker, Bibb, and parts of Tuscaloosa and Shelby counties. Before and during the Civil War coal mining and manufacturing developed in the southern part of Shelby County, which is not really a part of the "district." Statistical information about the district is based on Jefferson, Walker, and Bibb counties.

[6] Armes, *op. cit.*, 461-472; U. S. Census: *Manufactures: Ninth Census, 1870*, Vol. III, 392, *Tenth Census, 1880*, Vol. III, 88-89, *Eleventh Census, 1890*, Part I, 334-339, *Twelfth Census, 1900*, Part II, 8-13, Part IV, 39-78, *Mining: Tenth Census, 1880*, Vol. V, 642-644; American Iron and Steel Association, *Statistics of the Foreign and American Iron Trade, 1874, . . . -1910* (Philadelphia, 1874-1910); Alabama Inspector of Mines, *Report, 1910* (Montgomery, Alabama, 1910), 3.

in 1870; within ten years the figure had doubled. By 1900 it approached 150,000 and by 1910 more than 226,000 people lived in Jefferson County.[7] The steady migration of new people, and the region's rapid transition from agriculture to industry, destroyed the area's social fabric, forcing people to adjust almost overnight to a complex urban and industrial environment.[8]

Birmingham's growing industrial labor force dramatically altered the composition as well as the size of the district's population. For the first time large numbers of foreign-white and black workers came to the region. In 1870 only one percent of the white population in the district and in Jefferson Country was foreign-born or of foreign parentage. Twenty years later, however, the proportion of first- and second-generation immigrants in the total white population had increased to fourteen percent in the district, eighteen percent in Jefferson County, and twenty-five percent in Birmingham.[9] In industrial occupations the proportion was even greater. As indicated in Table 1, forty-two percent of the white miners in the state and thirty-eight percent of the white iron and steel

TABLE I

Employment in Mining and Iron and Steel Industries in Alabama,
by Race and Nativity, 1890 and 1900[10]

	Mining				*Iron and Steel*			
	1890		1900		1890		1900	
Total White	4279	100%	8163	100%	1410	100%	2440	100%
Native White: Native Born	2487	58%	5984	73%	877	62%	1717	70%
Foreign Born White	1492	35%	1573	19%	321	23%	351	15%
1 or Both Parents For. Born White ..	300	7%	606	7%	212	15%	372	15%
Colored	3687	46%	9735	55%	1749	55%	4439	65%
Total Workers	7966	100%	17898	100%	3159	100%	6879	100%

[7] U. S. Census, *Population: Ninth Census, 1870*, Vol. I. 11, *Tenth Census, 1890*, Part I, 451, *Twelfth Census, 1900*, Part I, 573.

[8] The impact of the rapid development of industrial and mining communities in Alabama during the last quarter of the nineteenth century can profitably be compared with similar developments and their impact in the middle-west and mountain west. See Herbert Gutman, "The Worker's Search for Power: Labor in the Gilded Age," in H. Wayne Morgan, ed., *The Gilded Age: A Reappraisal* (Syracuse, 1963), 38-68, and Melvin Dubofsky, "The Origins of Western Working Class Radicalism, 1890-1905," in *Labor History*, 7:2 (Spring 1966), 131-155.

[9] U. S. Census, *Population: Ninth Census, 1870*, Vol. I, 303, *Eleventh Census, 1890*, Part I, 480, 610, *Twelfth Census, 1900*, Part I, 647. While the proportion of the foreign-born in the *total* population was low, an assessment of the role of the European immigrants in Birmingham society can more properly be understood by considering the proportion of first and second generation immigrants in the *white* population.

workers were of immigrant stock in 1890. Even though the depression of the 1890s slowed the migration of foreign-born workmen into Alabama and intensified the migration of Southern whites to the mineral district, in 1900 first- and second-generation immigrants still made up twenty to thirty percent of the white population in the city and county, and in the mining and iron and steel industries. These large numbers of foreign workers, an ever-increasing number of whom came from Southern European countries after 1897, did not share traditional Southern habits and patterns of thought and complicated the problems of adjusting to industrialism and rapid population growth. Often difficult to control, less moved by appeals to white solidarity, and sometimes linked to Northern-based trade unions, they were an important influence in the development of new social and industrial relationships among the district's growing population.[11]

Even more important than the migration of foreign workers for such relationships was the influx of black labor into the district during the last quarter of the nineteenth century. Before the founding of Birmingham only ten percent of the district was black. By the end of the century, Negroes made up thirty-five percent of the population in the district, and forty percent in Jefferson County and in the city of Birmingham.[12] In 1870 fewer than 2,500 black people lived in Jefferson County, and only 5,000 in the district. Thirty years later, however, 67,000 blacks lived in the Birmingham district—57,000 of them in Jefferson County and 16,500 within the city limits of Birmingham. As the economy expanded, the black worker's role in the industrial labor force expanded with it. In 1880 only 163 of the district's 389 miners were black.[13] As Table 1 points out, despite the influx of white miners, by 1900 the number of black miners had increased 600 percent and more than one-half of the state's miners were black. In the iron and steel industry black workers were even more dominant, making up

[10] U. S. Immigration Commission, *Immigrants in Industries: Bituminous Coal Mining & Iron and Steel* (Washington, 1911), IV, 142-161, VII, 125-126.

[11] Foreign-born and second-generation immigrants, particularly coal miners, were often leaders in the labor movement in Alabama. In addition, several contemporary commentators noted that foreign workers in Alabama were often less hostile to cooperation with Negroes than native whites. Richard L. Davis to Editor, *United Mine Workers' Journal*, November 25, 1897 (hereafter *UMW Journal*), and *Immigrants In Industries: Bituminous Coal Mining*, IV, 196-200.

[12] U. S. Census, *Population: Ninth Census, 1870*, Vol. I, 11, *Twelfth Census, 1900*, Part I, 573.

[13] Compiled from U. S. Census, Tenth Census, 1880, Manuscript Census Schedules, Bibb, Jefferson, Walker Counties, Alabama.

sixty-five percent of the industry's workmen. The district's population thus had to answer not only questions about industrial relations, but also about race relations.[14]

Birmingham employers had never hesitated to hire black workers as a source of cheap, tractable labor. Testimony before a Senate committee investigating capital-labor relations in 1883 revealed that, despite complaints about the shiftlessness and irregularity of their black employees, industrialists were well-satisfied with their alleged docility and willingness to work for low wages.[15] After a series of strikes in the 1890s and the introduction of technological changes which made possible greater utilization of unskilled labor, Birmingham industrialists increased their use of black labor. Companies began to employ black craftsmen in preference to whites in the expansion and improvement of their plants.[16] The Tennessee Coal and Iron Company employed Negroes exclusively at several of its mines, promising them "a chance to demonstrate . . . whether there is intelligence enough among colored people to manage their social and domestic affairs . . . without the aid or interference of the white race."[17] The Louisville and Nashville Railroad, after a strike of white firemen in 1893 and of white switchmen, two years later, turned over almost all the brakemen, switchmen, and firemen jobs in its Birmingham division to non-union Negroes as a bulwark against the white railroad brotherhoods.[18] Except for the L&N, however, few firms during these years paid much attention to programs designed to obtain the loyalty of their black laborers. Although the high labor turnover reduced efficiency and increased labor costs, most companies merely relied on the ease with which they could recruit additional black labor, and depended on racial divisions which separated black workers from white to keep their employees from rebelling.[19]

---

[14] By 1900, forty-three percent of the males over twenty-one-years old in the district were black. U. S. Census, *Twelfth Census, 1900: Population,* Part I, 442.

[15] U. S. Senate Committee on Education and Labor, 49th Congress, 2nd Session, *Testimony Before the Committee to Investigate the Relations Between Capital and Labor* (Washington, 1885), III, 47, 290, 483.

[16] Birmingham *Labor Advocate,* August 21, 1897, March 19, 1898, June 3, 17, 1899 (Hereafter *Labor Advocate*).

[17] Birmingham *Daily News,* April 20, 1894; *Proceedings of Joint Scale Convention of Coal Operators and District 20, UMW, 1903, and Arbitration Proceedings* (Birmingham, 1903), 226-268.

[18] File #63298, "Re-examination of Employees on Train Service Rules: Colored Switchmen and Brakemen," General Manager's Office, Louisville and Nashville Railroad Archives, Louisville, Kentucky.

[19] Material in the file on "Colored Brakemen and Switchmen" in the L&N archives reveals

As race relations in Alabama deteriorated generally at the end of the nineteenth century, racial divisions between Birmingham's workingmen intensified. Efforts to use Negroes as scapegoats in order to reconcile whites estranged by the Populist crusade of the 1890s led to disfranchisement of the state's black population in 1901, and with it to an extension of segregation, discrimination, and racial violence.[20] When Richard L. Davis, a Negro member of the United Mine Workers' Executive Board, visited Birmingham in the winter of 1897-1898 to encourage organization of the district's coal miners, he reported that "The one great drawback is the division between white and colored." Racial segregation was so extensive, he observed, that at post offices "the white man and the colored man cannot get his [sic] mail from the same window." Even in coal mines, Davis found, "while white and colored miners worked in the same mines, and maybe even in adjoining rooms, they will not ride even on a work-train with their dirty mining clothes on together."[21]

Racial prejudice among Birmingham workers sometimes broke out into open conflict as white workingmen attempted to eliminate the economic competition from black workers by barring them from certain trades. Railroad firemen and trainmen unsuccessfully attempted to pressure the L&N and other Alabama railroads into eliminating Negroes from train crews.[22] Birmingham's white bricklayers, carpenters, machinists, and telephone linemen engaged in strikes against the employment of Negroes between 1899 and 1901.[23] In 1899 employees at a Walker County cotton mill drove black workmen out of town after they had begun work around the factory.[24] Even union membership did not insure acceptance from white workers. When a black bricklayer transferred from a Denver local to Birmingham in 1899 and began work on a union job, the white bricklayers struck against his employment.

some efforts to provide YMCA's and other social clubs for black trainmen. On the later establishment of welfare work by coal and iron companies see Spero and Harris. *op. cit.* 246-247.

[20] Woodward, *op. cit.*, 321-368, *Strange Career of Jim Crow* (New York, 1957), 49-95; Malcolm Cook McMillan, *Constitutional Development in Alabama, 1798-1901: A Study in Politics, the Negro, and Sectionalism* (Chapel Hill, 1955), 233-248.

[21] Richard L. Davis to Editor, *UMW Journal*, February 10, 1898.

[22] See for examples *Railroad Trainmen's Journal*, XVII:8 (August 1900), 678; *Locomotive Firemen's Magazine*, 33:3 (September, 1902), 428; File #63298, "Colored Switchmen and Brakemen," L&N RR Archives.

[23] *Labor Advocate*, June 3, 17, 1899, July 29, 1899, January 18, 1901; Birmingham *News*, April 6, 1901.

[24] Jasper *Mountain Eagle*, May 19, 1899.

When the Negro continued work, the local filed charges against him for strikebreaking and forced him out of the union.[25]

Antagonism of white workers, coupled with the lure of jobs provided by white employers, naturally left black workers suspicious of white workingmen and their labor organizations. Since the ante-bellum period many black men had looked to upper-class whites to protect them from the assaults of white workers. Despite the dislocations of freedom and industrialism this traditional alliance retained strong appeal. Negro spokesmen in the Birmingham district, supported by frequent appearances by Booker T. Washington and William H. Councill, denounced cooperation between white and black wage-earners and urged the district's black workers to "maintain peaceful and friendly relations with the best white people of the community . . . who give our race employment and pay their wages."[26] Reverend William McGill, editor of the Negro *Hot Shots,* probably spoke for several ministers in urging "every colored laborer [to] strive to make friends with his employer." If a dispute arose, the worker should "take whatever wages the company offered." The black worker who "puts in full time, saves his money, puts it to good use, has no cause to strike, nor sympathize with those that do strike," McGill insisted.[27] Labor organizers, another minister warned his followers, were "trifling, ungrateful soreheads who are going around poisoning the minds of the ignorant masses against wealth."[28]

In the midst of this climate of hostility and suspicion between Birmingham's black and white workingmen, the American Federation of Labor and national trade unions launched their Southern organizing campaigns.[29] The return of industrial prosperity in 1897 brought with

[25] "Case No. 6: Giddens vs. Union No. 1 Alabama," in *37th Annual Report of President and Secretary of the Bricklayers and Masons' International Union, 1902* (North Adams, Mass., 1902), 173-180.

[26] Birmingham *Hot Shots,* July 23, 1908. Washington and Councill often travelled into the Birmingham district to speak. Visits of Washington were reported in Birmingham *Age-Herald* (Hereafter *Age-Herald*) April 1, 1899, May 19, 1906, June 11, 1906, Birmingham *News,* September 20, 1902, January 31, 1903, *Negro Enterprise,* November 19, 1904. Visits of Council were reported in Birmingham *News* January 2, 1901, September 19, 1902, *Age-Herald* May 18, 1900, *Ensley Enterprise,* January 28, 1905. For an excellent analysis of both Washington's and Councill's attitudes toward labor unions and employers, see August Meier, *Negro Thought in America, 1880-1915* (Ann Arbor, 1966), 100-118, 209-210. For the close relations between prominent Birmingham ministers and industrialists see Horace Mann Bond, *Negro Education in Alabama: A Study in Cotton and Steel* (Washington, 1939), 168-170.

[27] *Hot Shots,* August 17, 1899, March 2, 1905, April 15, 1905, July 23, 1908.

[28] Birmingham [Negro] *Free Speech,* June 20, 1903.

[29] American Federation of Labor, *Report of Proceedings, Eighteenth Annual Convention, 1898* (n.p., 1898), 89-90, 93-100; Leo Wolman, *The Growth of American Trade*

it strong, stable, national trade unions and the revival and expansion of trade union activity. These unions undertook, directed, and financed organizing campaigns across the country, including the South, in an effort to minimize sectional wage differentials in various industries. Craft unions, as well as Knights of Labor locals, had existed in Birmingham since 1878 and had achieved enough strength by the early 1890s to form a city trades council with twenty-five locals and to host the 1891 A.F.L. national convention.[30] The depression of the 1890s decimated the labor movement in Birmingham. At the end of the nineteenth century, however, organizers from a number of unions, including the bricklayers, carpenters, machinists, molders, boilermakers, iron and steel workers, miners, as well as the A.F.L., appeared in Birmingham to revive locals which had collapsed during the depression and to found new ones.[31] Thirty-one locals with 6,000 members were represented in the Birmingham Trades Council by the end of 1900, and within two more years the number had grown to over sixty locals with more than 20,000 members, including District 20 of the United Mine Workers' of America representing 8,000 miners.[32]

Despite the general climate of racial hostility in Alabama, relations between trade unions and Birmingham's black workers were still undetermined at the end of the nineteenth century. While many national labor leaders ignored black workers or equivocated about organizing them, and several craft unions adopted racially restrictive membership policies which barred Negroes, in at least a dozen unions, including some of the exclusionary ones, officers and members argued that effectively organizing the South depended upon the inclusion of black workers.[33]

Unions, 1880-1923 (New York, 1924), 33; Taft, *The AF of L in the Time of Gompers*, 95-111.

[30] Holman Head, "The Development of the Labor Movement in Alabama Prior to 1900" (Unpublished Master's thesis, University of Alabama, 1955); See also *Journal of United Labor*, August 15, 1880 and *National Labor Tribune*, January 4, 1878.

[31] *American Federationist*, VI:3-VII:6 (May 1899-June 1900), lists activities of organizers in Birmingham. Also *Age-Herald*, May 14, 24, 1899; Birmingham *News*, February 26, 1900, October 17, 1901; *Labor Advocate*, August 5, 1899, April 8, 1901; *Iron Molders' Journal*, 38:9 (September 1902), 603.

[32] *Labor Advocate*, April 8, 1901, August 2, 1902.

[33] Appeals for the organization of Negroes fill union journals and the reports of proceedings of labor conventions. *Iron Molders' Journal*, 35:1 (November 1899), 590-592, 36:5 (May 1900), 283-284; *Machinists' Monthly Journal*, IX:21 (March 1897), 61-63; *Railroad Trainmen's Journal*, XV:11 (November 1898), 912-914, XVI:9 (September 1899), 620-621, XX:10 (October 1903), 790-791; *Locomotive Firemen's Magazine*, 31:1 (January 1901), 112; *Blacksmith's Journal*, IV:2 (February 1903), 11; *The Carpenter*, 23:1 (January, 1903), 3, 23:9 (September 1903), 5; *Bricklayer and Mason* V:1 (February 1902), 8, IX:1 (February 1906), 3; *37th*

Both the egalitarian principles of the labor movement and the self-interest of white workers, they insisted, dictated that Southern Negroes not be left unorganized. "We are banded together in our grand Brotherhood for the purpose of elevating the condition of our entire craft, regardless of color, nationality, race or creed," the editor of *The Carpenter,* the journal of the United Brotherhood of Carpenters and Joiners, asserted in 1903.[34] The Negro carpenter, he added, "must be brought into our fold in order that his hours of toil will be reduced and his wages raised, and thus his white brother will be given an opportunity to raise his own standing to the level of his brother in the East and West." The president of the Bricklayers and Masons' Union, disturbed that racial discrimination impeded the organization of Southern bricklayers, urged that "every opportunity [be] given our colored brothers to earn a livelihood as union members instead of driving them into the non-union ranks or a hostile organization to be used against us."[35] Although by 1900 Samuel Gompers accepted racially exclusive unions into the A.F.L. and sanctioned segregated city labor councils, he also insisted that unless black workers were organized and befriended by trade unions they would "not only be forced down in the economic scale," but would be "used against any effort made by us for our economic and social advancement, [and] race prejudice will be made more bitter and to the injury of all."[36] Rarely conscious of the needs of black workers and frequently racist in his public statements when referring to them, Gompers nevertheless warned Henry Randall, the Federation's Birmingham organizer, that "The Negro workers must be organized in order that they may be in a position to protect themselves and in some way feel an interest with our organized white workmen, or we shall unquestioningly have their undying enmity."[37] The failure of Southern railroad trainmen to

Annual Report . . . Bricklayers and Masons' International Union, 1902 (North Adams, Mass., 1902), 152-153; International Union of Hod Carriers and Building Laborers, 5th Annual Convention, *Proceedings, 1907* (Norfolk, Virginia, 1907), 41; Amalgamated Association of Iron, Steel and Tin Workers, *Amalgamated Journal,* May 11, 1905; *United Mine Workers' Journal,* February 7, 1895, and letters quoted in Gutman, "The Negro and the United Mine Workers", 49-127; American Federation of Labor, 17th Annual Convention, *Proceedings, 1897* (Nashville, 1897), 36; *American Federationist,* VIII:4 (April 1901), 118-120; International Car Workers, *Proceedings, 1905,* as quoted in Spero and Harris, *op. cit.,* 65.

[34] *The Carpenter,* 23:1 (January 1903), 3.
[35] *Bricklayer and Mason,* IX:1 (February 1906), 5.
[36] American Federation of Labor, 20th Annual Convention, *Proceedings, 1900* (Louisville, 1900), 12-13.
[37] Samuel Gompers to H. N. Randle [sic], March 19, 1903, Samuel Gompers Letterbooks, Library of Congress, Washington, D. C.

bar Negroes as job competitors even convinced the editor of the *Railroad Trainmen's Journal* that only by organizing black trainmen and committing them to the defense of common standards of wages and hours could white trainmen improve their working conditions. "It is humiliating, no one will take kindly to it, ..." he pleaded, "but unless the Negro is raised, the white man will have to come down."[38]

Implementing these views depended not merely on convincing union leaders of the desirability of organizing black workers, but also on the response to such proposals from white workingmen in the South. Railroad trainmen and many other white union members in Birmingham did not, in fact, take kindly to admitting Negroes to their unions. Some protested to their union journals that they would "never accept the Negro as their equal," and threatened that they could not "entertain the idea of complying with the oath we take if the Negro is admitted to our brotherhood."[39] A white fireman on the L&N who opposed any effort to improve black firemen's wages argued that "If he were getting our wages, he would then be on our plane."[40] The city's union bricklayers, as previously noted, refused to work with a black union bricklayer who transferred to the city in 1899, and Birmingham's union carpenters, despite their complaints about non-union Negro competition, ignored the request of black carpenters in the city for organization in 1902.[41] As will be discussed later, when national unions which supported the organization of black workers stood firm, they often found that they could overcome objections from white locals. More important, though, these protests did not represent the thinking of all of Birmingham's white unionists.

In spite of mounting hysteria by Alabama's white supremacists, there were white workingmen in Birmingham at the beginning of the twentieth century who not only supported organization of black laborers, but also encouraged such organization. The city's labor newspaper, the *Labor Advocate,* advised Birmingham unions to "Obliterate the Color Line," and to recognize that "the common cause of labor is more im-

[38] *Railroad Trainmen's Journal,* XVI:9 (September 1899), 880, and XVII:8 (August 1900), 678.
[39] *The Carpenter,* 23:4 (April 1903), 5; *Locomotive Firemen's Magazine,* 22:2 (February 1897), 125-126. For examples of other protests from Birmingham see *Railroad Trainmen's Journal,* 17:6 (June 1900), 499-510, and *Iron Molders' Journal,* 44:4 (April 1908), 287-288, 577-578.
[40] *Locomotive Firemen's Magazine,* 30:3 (March 1901), 440-441.
[41] *The Carpenter,* 23:1 (January 1903), 3.

portant than racial differences." Even when whites and blacks organized
in an integrated union, its editor insisted that "it is a response to conditions to which there is no other solution," and urged white workers
to "accept the inevitable with ready grace and strive to better the conditions of the Negro by every means, knowing that in doing this is the
only way to better [your] own condition."[42] Although some of Birmingham's white bricklayers had resisted the employment of a Negro union
member in 1899, a year later the local secretary of the International
Union of Bricklayers and Masons wrote the editor of his journal that
the arrival of their organizer would "wake up the colored man and
show him that he must join the I.U.—and when we get them [sic] in
this will be one of the best union towns in the United States."[43] In
response to assertions that black laborers would not remain loyal to the
union even if admitted, a white railroad fireman on the L&N replied
that "my experience with the Negroes shows me that they are easily
organized, and when organized they will stick to their lodges as long as
the average member of any other order."[44] A white painter concurred:
"Anyone who will study the character of the Negro," he wrote, "will
agree that he will stick to his union."[45] Although Richard Davis was discouraged by racial prejudice in the Birmingham district, he nevertheless
found "a number of good men both white and colored" among miners
he met who deplored the prejudice.[46] One miner, writing to the *Labor
Advocate* to support its position on organization of black workers, appealed to district unions not to leave black laborers to "the tender
mercies of the sweatshops," and insisted that "the only question for
consideration is, Will Organized Labor admit the black man, not only
thereby benefiting him, but adding strength to organization?"[47]

In addition to the question of whether labor unions would admit
Negroes, there was also the question of whether Negroes would join
these organizations. Despite the demands of prominent Negroes that
black workers remain diligent, dependent, and docile, other, less well-
known black men successfully encouraged them to organize. References to organizational meetings in Negro churches indicated that at

[42] *Labor Advocate*, April 2, 1898, April 27, 1901.
[43] John Ellison to Editor, *Bricklayer and Mason*, III:3 (June 1900) 10.
[44] Pat Filburn to Editor, *Locomotive Firemen's Magazine*, 31:1 (January 1901), 112.
[45] Birmingham painter to Editor, Brotherhood of Painters, Decorators, and Paperhangers
    Journal, March 1903, quoted in *The Carpenter*, 23:4 (April 1903), 7.
[46] Richard Davis to Editor, *UMW Journal*, January 6, 1898.
[47] W. T. Westbrook to Editor, *Labor Advocate*, June 30, 1900.

least some of the influential churchmen disagreed with one of their number who referred to labor organizers as "false prophets."[48] Richard Davis reported that he met one Negro minister in Birmingham, W. M. Storrs, who "had the manhood to attend a meeting . . . and speak a kind word for organized labor."[49] A letter from a white miner praised the Negro Odd Fellows and Reverend J. M. Morton in his camp for supporting the union.[50]

More active than churchmen in aiding organizing efforts were black workers who became union officials.[51] Some served as delegates to state and national labor conventions where they regularly sponsored resolutions advocating more black organizers for the South in general and Birmingham in particular.[52] Others became salaried organizers. In a society often hostile to black militancy their organizing activities occasionally subjected them to violence from racially hostile whites. Silas Brooks, vice-president of the Alabama United Mine Workers' (U.M.W.) district organization from 1898 to 1900, was stoned and beaten in one town while organizing miners in 1900, for example. A white mob led by a mining company official attacked both B. L. Greer, a successor of Brooks as vice-president, and a white organizer in 1903, "heaped various indignities upon them, some of which were too repulsive to print," and chased them out of Walker County. A year later, a white mob at a remote mining camp again attacked Greer when he arrived to organize the miners. These experiences did not seem to dampen the enthusiasm of Brooks or Greer for the union. Only a week after losing the district election for vice-president in 1900, Brooks urged black unionists to show no animosity towards their "white brethern," and to beware of any "outside influences" trying to separate them. In subsequent years, he remained an important organizer in the union and in the labor movement in Alabama. First elected vice-president of U.M.W. District 20 in 1902, Greer served until 1908, frequently visiting mining camps in Walker County to organize black and white miners. When he retired

---

[48] Birmingham *Free Speech*, April 25, 1903, June 20, 1903; *Labor Advocate* April 13, 1901.
[49] Richard Davis to Editor, *UMW Journal*, January 6, 1898.
[50] Peter Tidwell to Editor, *Labor Advocate*, March 5, 1898.
[51] Little is known about Birmingham Negroes who encouraged black workers to join unions—or about the men who joined. The particular experiences which drew them to the labor movement are unknown. Their relations with other Negroes and whites during Reconstruction, Populism or the coal miners' upheavals of the 1880s and 1890s, their experience with slavery, their length of residence in the district, their employment pattern, their family status, their age, are all unknown but important facts which could illuminate much of Alabama's labor history during this period.
[52] *Labor Advocate*, April 20, 1901, May 7, 1904, May 6, 1905; See note 33.

to a government job as mail carrier, the *Labor Advocate* praised him as "one of the best known colored men in the district."[53] Greer and other black labor leaders undoubtedly did much to counter the anti-union sentiments of prominent Negroes, and probably were more influential among the black masses than highly publicized figures like Booker T. Washington and Reverend William McGill.[54]

Black workers in the Birmingham district were organized most successfully by the U.M.W. Victory in the midwestern coal fields in 1897 strengthened the U.M.W. and enabled it to turn its attention to the organization of Alabama and West Virginia mines whose growing competition threatened the gains won in midwestern states. The Mine Workers' commitment to the organization of black miners, carried over from Knights of Labor locals and developed in the midwest during the early 1890s, did not lessen in Alabama. The need to prevent Birmingham Negroes from serving as strikebreakers in Illinois, Ohio, Kansas, and Colorado mines made their organization a practical necessity.[55] Perhaps most important to the U.M.W.'s success in organizing Alabama's black miners, however, was its structure as an industrial union. Most of the 6,000 Negroes who worked in the coal mines at the beginning of the twentieth century were employed by sub-contractors or as laborers by white and occasionally black miners.[56] This subcontracting

[53] Birmingham *News*, December 8, 10, 13, 1900; *Labor Advocate*, August 15, September 19, 26, October 3, 1903, June 2, 1908; *Age-Herald*, August 12, 1903. Six men were arrested for the assault on Greer and the white organizer, Joseph Hallier, in 1903. The U. S. Commissioner dismissed the charges when he ruled that Hallier was a citizen of Wales and thus could not sue in federal courts for deprivation of his civil rights, and that "lack of evidence" precluded a case against these six men for attacking Greer. The UMW appealed the decisions to the Federal District Court where Judge Thomas G. Jones, former governor and railroad attorney, sustained the dismissal on the grounds that conspiracy to interfere with an attempt to establish a labor organization was not infringing any right guaranteed by the Constitution and was thus not protected by law. Jasper *Mountain Eagle*, May 11, 1904.

[54] For evidence of a different reaction among Birmingham Negroes which also indicates a gap between Booker Washington and the black masses see Edwin S. Redkey, "Black Exodus: African Emigration Movements Among American Negroes, 1890-1910" (New Haven, 1969), *passim*.

[55] Gutman, "The Negro and the United Mine Workers," 46-110.

[56] U. S. Census, *Twelfth Census, 1900: Occupations, Part* I, reported 9,735 blacks among 17,898 miners in Alabama. *Annual Report of State Board of Alabama Inspector of Mines, 1900* (Montgomery, 1900), lists 12,881 *coal* miners. Contemporaries estimated that of the 5,000 iron ore miners, at least 80% were black, which means that approximately 5,800 Negroes, or 40%, of the state's coal miners were Negro. See J. H. McDonough memorandum, February 11, 1908, in Booker T. Washington Papers, Principal's Office Correspondence, 1908, Library of Congress, Washington, D. C. Report of an Alabama House of Representatives Mining Investigating Committee, in *Birmingham State-Herald*, January 26, 1897, describes most of the mining camps in the district in January 1897, and its estimates of black miners in each camp indicate about 35% at that time.

system divided miners and mine laborers along occupational as well as racial lines, and many miners who employed laborers saw little benefit to be derived from organization. Since not only miners but laborers and other workmen employed at the mines could belong to the U.M.W., however, the union could overcome the occupational and racial divisions which separated most of Alabama's black mine workers from white miners by bringing all of them into the union.[57]

Alabama miners were receptive to an interracial union. The Knights of Labor locals of the 1880s and the statewide miners' organization of the early 1890s had collapsed by the end of the nineteenth century, but local miners' organizations in several camps still existed, many of them with black officers and members.[58] After the state's miners voted to affiliate with the national United Mine Workers' organization in November 1897, these locals became the nucleus of U.M.W. organizing activity in the state. U.M.W. organizers' reports in 1898 and 1899 testified to "great enthusiasm for union among the colored brethern."[59] The district president rejoiced that black miners were "fighting to join" the union when eighty-five percent of 280 black miners at an isolated previously unorganized camp in Tuscaloosa County enlisted after his first visit.[60] By the beginning of the twentieth century, Negro membership in the Alabama U.M.W. was widespread. Although precise membership statistics by race are non-existent, there is no reason to doubt. the claims of contemporaries that in 1900 probably thirty-five to forty percent of the 6,500 members of District 20 were black and, by 1904, that more than one-half of the 13,000 U.M.W. members in the state were black miners.[61]

---

[57] Richard L. Davis to Editor, *UMW Journal*, February 10, 1898; *Birmingham State-Herald*, April 13, 1897; *Labor Advocate*, April 13, 1901, October 14, 1905. In addition to subcontracting, Alabama's infamous convict lease system complicated organizational efforts. By 1900 coal operators leased more than 1,500 state and county convicts per year to work in the mines. These convict miners, about fifty per cent of whom remained in the district after their release, were an important source of labor during, and after, their sentences. Alabama State Board of Convict Inspectors, *Biennial Report, 1900, 1902* (Montgomery, 1900, 1902); Shelby Harrison, "A Cash Nexus for Crime," in *Survey*, XXVII (4 January 6, 1912), 1541-1556.

[58] *Labor Advocate*, July 31, October 2, 1897, February 5, 1898.

[59] *Labor Advocate*, February 5, October 29, 1898, April 29, July 12, 26, 1899.

[60] *Labor Advocate* April 1, 1899.

[61] Total membership statistics for UMW District 20 for 1898-1907 published in *Labor Advocate*, June 14, 1907. Forty percent of the delegates to the 1900 District Convention were identified as Negro, from *Labor Advocate*, June 27, 1900. Unfortunately, no indication of the delegates' race appears in subsequent lists of delegates published in the *Labor Advocate*. William Fairley, UMW Executive Board Member,

An active administrative role in the state's U.M.W. organization over-
came initial Negro distrust of the miners' union. In every U.M.W. local
in Alabama with black members, whether all-black or integrated—such
as the local at Pratt City, the largest U.M.W. local in the country by the
early twentieth century—black miners served as officers: as presidents
and vice-presidents, as members of executive boards and grievance committees, as checkweighmen, and as delegates to the district and national
conventions. Some camps whose living conditions were almost completely segregated met at integrated union halls, heard reports from
black officers, and elected black men as local committeemen and as convention delegates. Even at camps with racially separate locals, black and
white representatives served on grievance committees and as checkweighmen together.[62] At district conventions as well as local meetings
black officers spoke from the same platforms as whites, delivered committee reports and, as the proceedings make clear, even chaired the meeting at district conventions. To guarantee continued black representation
in leadership posts, certain positions were allocated for black members.
These included the vice-presidency of the district organization and of
integrated locals, three of the eight positions on the district executive
board, and places on every union committee, whether functional or ceremonial. The satisfaction of black miners with this arrangement was
shown when some white miners introduced a plan, at the 1902 district
convention, to choose district officials by popular vote instead of having
convention delegates elect them. The black delegates, according to the
Birmingham News, "seem to think that if the officers were selected by
popular vote they would not have as many officers as they now have."
With the aid of the leadership they helped defeat this proposal.[63]

Black delegates at district conventions were not merely passive sub-
ordinates of white members and leaders, but actively participated in
committee discussions and floor debates. They often differed with white
miners—not only about such matters as whether to appropriate funds
to support a Birmingham exhibit at the St. Louis World's Fair in 1904,

---

and former president of District 20, testified before the 1903 Coal Arbitration Commission, that one-half the district's members were black. *1903 Coal Arbitration Commission Proceedings,* 239.
[62] *Labor Advocate,* December 17, 1898, July 15, 1899, June 23, 1900, July 2, 1901, June
28, 1902, June 13, 1904.
[63] Birmingham *News,* December 11, 1902. See also *News,* December 15-20, 1903; *Labor
Advocate,* May 21, 1898, February 11, 1899, June 23, 1900, March 6, 1901, December
19, 1903, June 17, 1905.

but also on the important issue of wage demands.[64] Even the presence of national president John Mitchell at an early District 20 convention in 1900 did not stifle Negro initiative. Although Mitchell, and the district president, supported a request from the coal operators that they be heard before the convention conducted any business, two black delegates were among those who objected, and the convention, forty percent of which was Negro, defeated the resolution to admit the operators. Mitchell also supported the request of the Birmingham Trades Council that the miners endorse a resolution stating that U.M.W. members would give their business only to union workmen. When Negro vice-president Silas Brooks objected to the resolution and made a "strong speech" declaring that the mine workers should not endorse it since the Trades Council and some of its affiliates discriminated against Negroes, Mitchell protested that as a member of the A.F.L. executive board he could assure black delegates that no A.F.L. affiliate barred Negroes. The black miners refused to be deceived and got the convention to table the resolution.[65]

Information about the organizational activities of other trade unions in Birmingham during this period is scarce, but material available indicates that the United Mine Workers was not alone in organizing urban black workers. In 1901 Birmingham's Negro barbers secured a charter from the national union with the approval of the city's white barbers.[66] The plasterers' union inaugurated black men into an integrated local which lasted throughout the decade.[67] Birmingham's building laborers, first organized in 1899 as an A.F.L. local, affiliated with the International Hod Carriers and Building Laborers' Union in 1903. With the support of other building trades organizations in the city, by 1905 it commanded $2 per-eight-hour day for its sixty members with time-and-one-half for overtime and double-time for Sunday work.[68] The Bricklayers and Masons' union, with black members in other locals in both the North and South, encouraged the Birmingham chapter to admit black bricklayers, and in 1904 a Negro organizer from Atlanta visited

---

[64] *Labor Advocate*, June 18, 1903, June 18, 25, 1904.
[65] *Labor Advocate*, June 23, 30, 1900; Birmingham *News*, June 22, 25, 1900, July 3, 1901.
[66] *American Federationist*, VIII:9 (September 1901), 378.
[67] "A White Friend of the Workingman," to Editor, *Birmingham Journal*, June 22, 1911; Du Bois, *op. cit.*, 162.
[68] *American Federationist*, VI:7 (September 1899), 171; International Hod Carriers and Building Laborers' Union of America, 2nd Annual Convention, *Report of Proceedings, (1904 Sayre, Penn.,* 1904), 33; *Age-Herald*, December 27, 1905.

TABLE II

Employment in Selected Occupations in Birmingham,
by Race, 1900[69]

Occupation	Total Workers	Black Workers	Per Cent Black	Per Cent Black to All Black Listed
BUILDING TRADES				
Plasterer	33	25	75.8%	.7%
Brickmason	130	36	27.7	.9
Carpenter	585	94	16.8	2.6
Plumber	32	5	15.6	.1
Painter	94	6	6.4	.1
Electrician	33	....	....	....
MECHANICS				
Blacksmith	122	27	22.2%	.6%
Printer	56	4	7.1	.1
Boilermaker	81	4	4.9	.1
Molder	142	2	1.4	.1
Sta. Engineer	82	1	1.2	....
Tinner	34	....	....	....
Puddler	89	....	....	....
Heater & Roller	28	....	....	....
Machinist	379	....	....	....
Harnessmaker	13	....	....	....
Carriagemaker	7	....	....	....
RAILROAD EMPLOYEES				
Brakeman	124	87	70.5%	2.3%
Locomotive Fireman	154	87	56.5	2.3
Switchman	51	16	31.4	.4
Railroad Repair Shop	179	7	3.9	.2
Flagman	93	1	1.1	....
Conductor	146	....	....	....
Locomotive Engineer	236	....	....	....
Streetcar Driver	70	....	....	....
SERVICE				
Barber	169	105	61.1%	2.9%
Shoemaker	99	49	49.0	1.5
Tailor	44	9	20.5	.3
FACTORY OPERATIVES				
Bottling and Brewing	43	4	9.3%	.1%
Avondale Cotton Mill	154	3	1.9	.1
Other	233	3	1.3	.1
OTHER: UNSKILLED				
Drayman and Teamster	355	271	80.9%	7.3%
Laborer—not spec.	3472	2844	81.9	77.1
TOTAL—INDUSTRIAL	7412	3691	49.8%	100%

[69] Compiled from *Birmingham City Directory, 1901*. Although city directories are uneven, and undoubtedly failed to count large number of people, those ignored are likely to be heavily weighted towards unskilled black laborers. Consequently, the proportion of black laborers in the industrial labor force is probably even higher. If the "service" category is eliminated, moreover, the proportion of black laborers to all black "industrial" workers would be almost 90%.

The occupations used are the same as those used in the city directory. Laborers are generally not otherwise specified, although sometimes an employer is listed. The seemingly low numbers of iron and steel workers is explained by the fact that many

the city to work among the city's black brickmasons.[70] After Birmingham's white carpenters ignored a request from the city's black carpenters for union membership, the United Brotherhood of Carpenters and Joiners appointed a Birmingham Negro organizer in 1903. When the Birmingham local objected, the editor of *The Carpenter* informed it that "as far as our Brotherhood is concerned the drawing of the color line should be stopped at once and for all time." Additional pressure must have been exerted, for the following year a Negro carpenters' local existed in Birmingham, its members working at union scale, participating in the meetings of the powerful Carpenters' District Council, and marching under the union banner in the annual Labor Day parade.[71] These craft locals, which were generally segregated, covered few black workers, and probably left them still powerless to protect their jobs or improve their working conditions. Despite these limitations, the locals represented at least some effort by skilled craft unions to reconcile the egalitarian principles of the labor movement and the need to control the job competition of Southern black workmen with the mounting climate of racial hatred and with their own exclusionist tendencies.

Bringing Birmingham's black workers into the labor movement depended not so much on organization of the trades as on organization of the unskilled. As indicated in Table 2, the city's black industrial wage-earners worked predominantly as common laborers by 1900. Black workers employed at coke ovens, blast furnaces, iron foundries, steel mills, and railroad shops in Birmingham and in other industrial communities in the district were almost all common laborers. But the craft union structure of the American labor movement at the beginning of the twentieth century impeded organization of unskilled workers. Committed to preserving union autonomy and protecting the interests of the skilled minority, few craft unions attempted to organize semi-skilled or unskilled workers—of any race or nationality.[72] The American Federation of Labor tried to take up the slack by organizing unskilled

---

of the furnaces and steel plants were located outside the city limits. A discussion of the changing numbers of workers in various occupations and the changing racial composition of these occupations from 1880 to 1914 is part of a work now in progress on "The Development of an Industrial Labor Force in Birmingham, Alabama."

[70] Du Bois, *op. cit.,* 162; *83th Annual Report . . . of Bricklayers and Masons' International Union, 1903* (North Adams, Mass., 1903), 116; Whether black bricklayers were inducted into a local in Birmingham is not clear. See *Bricklayer and Mason,* X:1 (February 1907), 3.

[71] *The Carpenter,* 23:1 (January 1903), 3; 23:4 (April 1903), 6-7; *Labor Advocate,* May 21, 1904, September 9, 1905.

[72] Foner, *op. cit.,* III, 174-218.

laborers into Federal Labor Unions directly affiliated with the A.F.L., but these locals were never of any importance and remained "the neglected stepchildren of the American labor movement."[73] Without a national union to bargain for them, without funds to sustain them when on strike, and subject to raids by craft unions, Federal Labor Unions could not protect their members' interests. Yet for a brief period at the beginning of the twentieth century, in Birmingham as in other cities of the country, these unions brought unskilled workers into the American labor movement.

Between 1899 and 1904, when financial stringency forced the A.F.L. to curtail its organizing efforts throughout the country, the Federation devoted as much attention to organizing Birmingham's black unskilled laborers as it did to organizing the city's skilled workmen. The Federation's Southern organizer visited Birmingham in May 1899, and most of his effort was directed toward black laborers. "Some objection has been raised," the Birmingham *Age Herald* noted, "but the leaders of organized labor recognize that negro labor, which works side by side with white labor, will necessarily hold the latter back, unless they—the blacks—are themselves organized."[74] Before leaving Birmingham the organizer had founded locals of coke workers, ore miners, furnace laborers, and draymen.[75] During the next several years Gompers urged A.F.L. organizers in Birmingham to "make friends of the colored man," and appointed several black men as special organizers.[76] Despite intensified racial antagonism in Alabama, by 1904, as listed in Table 3, thirteen more locals of unskilled black laborers had been organized in the district. Except for periods in which the unions were seeking recognition, membership in these locals was generally small. Moreover, although some Federal locals showed signs of stability, few lasted more than two years, and by 1904 all but the iron ore miners, iron pipe workers, and building laborers had collapsed. Nevertheless, during these years more than 2,000 unskilled black workers joined various F.L.U. locals. Added to the 6,000 black miners in the U.M.W. and to an unidentified number of black workers in craft union locals, this organization of the unskilled meant that at least 8,000 black workers in the Birmingham district belonged to labor organizations during the first

---

[73] Quoted in *ibid.*, 200.
[74] *Age-Herald*, May 24, 1899.
[75] *Age-Herald*, May 15, 1899; *American Federationist*, VI:3, 4, 7, 10 (May, June, September, December 1899), 59, 89, 171, 253-254; *Labor Advocate*, August 5, 12, 1899.
[76] Gompers to H. N. Randle [sic], March 19, 1903, Gompers Letterbooks.

years of the twentieth century. "A lot of colored men here in our jurisdiction would like to become [sic] into the A.F. of L.," Negro organizer
William Downey observed in 1904. "They are coming to the light of
Organization fast and see what an elevation it is to them." Henry Randall, the Federation's organizer, asserted confidently that same year
that, given more assistance by the A.F.L., he could organize all 4,000

TABLE III

Black AFL Locals in Birmingham, Alabama, District,
1899-1904[77]

Union	Year Org.	Maximum Number Members Identified
Furnacemen No. 7564, Bessemer	1899	647 (1900)
Coke Workers No. 7576, Bessemer	1899	118 (1900)
Coke Workers No. 7577, Johns	1899	120 (1900)
Iron Pipe Workers No. 7581, Bessemer	1899	100 (1905)
Team Drivers No. 167, Birmingham	1899	c.200 (1900)
Laborers No. 7575(?), Bessemer	1899	66 (1900)
Iron Ore Miners No. 19, Birmingham	1899, 1903	700 (1904)
(later locals No. 10, No. 13 Western Fed. of Miners, May 1904)		
Building Laborers No. 7174	1899	50 (1904)
(later No. 72, I.H.C.B.L.U., 1904)		
Stone Cutters, Birmingham	1899	. . . .
Iron Pipe Workers, Blocton	1899	. . . .
Furnacemen's No. 8359, Oxmoor	1900	40 (1900)
Furnace Workers No. 8051, Woodward	1900	. . . .
Core Makers, Birmingham	1900	. . . .
Coke Workers, Birmingham	1901	. . . .
Coke Workers No. 9648, Thomas	1902	. . . .
Rolling Mill Helpers No. 10592, Birmingham	1902	144 (1903)
		c.2185
Bessemer Central Labor Council	1900	1080 (1900)
Birmingham Central Labor Council	1903	(20 locals—1903)

[77] All of the locals listed, except the Team Drivers and Core Makers, were taken from the
monthly lists of "Charters Issued" in the *American Federationist*, 1899-1904. The
Team Drivers and Core Makers—as well as most other locals—were identified from
Birmingham or Bessemer newspapers. Membership figures for most locals were difficult to obtain. Where a local's Federal Labor Union number was available the A.F.L.'s
monthly financial statements, published in the *American Federationist*, could usually
be used to compute membership by dividing the total monthly tax collected from the
local by the A.F.L.'s monthly per capita tax. Unfortunately, dues were not always
collected every month, and statements of per capita tax collected were often unclear
about what time period the payment represented. The other major source of membership information was newspaper articles. Although these usually estimated union
membership, where possible to check their figures with computations from the
American Federationist they turned out to be substantially accurate. The estimated
membership for Team Drivers #167 is based upon reports of a Colored Drayman's
Association in the Birmingham *News*, January 5, 6, 1900, to which "almost every
colored man driving a dray" allegedly belonged. The membership figures presented
in Table 3 which are derived solely from newspaper reports are only the number of
workers reported as union members and are not the number of workers participating
in a strike, which was usually a much higher figure.

black iron ore miners and thousands of other black common laborers in the Birmingham district. And the head of the district's Negro labor council even suggested to Gompers that the cooks and washerwomen in the area could be unionized.[78]

Birmingham industrialists and other spokesmen of the New South frequently advertised the docility and tractability of their black labor, but a series of strikes by newly-organized black laborers in 1899 and 1900 demonstrated that these unskilled workers, like their counterparts in the mines, were prepared to resist the "place" assigned to them by their employers. Coke workers' strikes against the Tennessee Coal and Iron Company in 1899 erupted into violence. When a group of deputies attempted to disperse striking workers, they found the strikers "willing to resort to bloodshed before allowing the white officers of the law to arrest them." Hidden behind coke ovens, 250 strikers ambushed the deputies and killed two of them before being routed. Only the forced departure of "several carloads" of black workers returned the situation to normal.[79] The company's treasurer complained that coke worker strikes throughout the summer and fall continued to "make life a burden." When the company tried to fire the leaders of a Bessemer local, the newly-organized workers struck for their reinstatement, "even though their wages were advanced a week before" and despite an agreed-upon one-year moratorium on strikes, the T.C.I. treasurer noted incredulously. The company's refusal to reinstate the discharged leaders led the strikers to try to burn the company's quarters.[80] When Bessemer's cast iron pipe firm refused to recognize the newly-chartered A.F.L. local in 1899 and fired the committeemen who appealed for recognition, 300 pipe workers quit. They convinced 200 black strikebreakers brought in to replace them to leave their jobs and forced the company to import non-union white men, which a city newspaper reported they "had no trouble getting at $1.75 per day." But newspapers, in the following months, still reported incidents of strikers firing on company workmen.[81] Seven months later, 647 blast furnace workers at the T.C.I. plant in

---

[78] W. H. Downey to Gompers, quoted in Gompers to H. N. Randall, February 1, 1904, Gompers Letterbooks; Speech of Henry Randall in *Age-Herald,* May 7, 1904; Gompers to J. E. Smith, August 11, 1904, Gompers Letterbooks.
[79] *Birmingham State-Herald,* March 28, 29, 1899.
[80] James Bowron Diaries, October 3, 1899, and James Bowron, "Autobiography," I, 407-408, 477, University of Alabama Library, University, Alabama.
[81] *Bessemer Weekly,* October 28, November 18, 25, December 16, 1899; *Labor Advocate,* November 25, December 2, 1899; *American Federationist,* VI:10 (October 1899), 261.

Bessemer, all members of a recently-organized A.F.L. local, struck for a wage increase, semi-monthly pay days, the right to choose their own doctor, and recognition of their union. They persuaded hundreds of imported strikebreakers to return home and kept the furnaces closed for four months. The strike was finally settled after Samuel Gompers responded to an appeal from the Birmingham Trades Council and threatened the company that he would urge workmen throughout the country to boycott Bessemer unless T.C.I.'s manager met with a committee of the strikers to settle their grievances.[82]

The most disruptive strike during these two years occurred at the iron ore mines of Red Mountain on the Birmingham city limits. Few labor situations in Alabama rivalled that at these mines for sheer injustice. The ore was dug by subcontractors who hired laborers at 65¢ per day. Commissary prices were reputed to be the highest in the district, and housing conditions the worst. When hired, the men were compelled to agree to purchase all their supplies at the companies' commissaries and if, at the end of the month, their total purchases had lagged, their pay was docked. Whether or not they lived at the camps, at least 50¢ per month was deducted from each man's wages for rent. By the beginning of the twentieth century over eighty percent of the workers around the mines, and almost all of the laborers in the mines, were Negro. In April 1899, 350 ore miners struck one of the mines for several weeks. In May the A.F.L. organizer inducted sixty miners from the all-black camp at Ishkooda into a newly-chartered local. Two months later, when a union committee demanded a 12½¢ per-day wage increase, the Robinson Mining Company, subcontractors from T.C.I., fired them. Seventy-five miners quit immediately, and within the next few days all 1,000 black miners in the camp struck. Although Reverend McGill's *Hot Shots* praised the Robinson Mining Company "for standing for the right," and insisted that the "best elements" in the camp had returned to the job, only fifty-three of the strikers were reported at work six weeks after the strike began, and scattered incidents of violence against strikebreakers and guards erupted throughout the summer. Despite Gompers' appeals, company officials refused to meet the strikers' demands or to recognize the union. Since many

[82] *Bessemer Weekly*, June 16-30, 1900; *Bessemer Workman*, June 20, 1900; *Bessemer Herald-Journal*, September 18, 1900; Birmingham *News*, June 15-20, 29, July 16, September 18, 1900; Gompers to John Dowling, October 20, 1900, Gompers to J. C. Wilson, October 20, 1900, Gompers Letterbooks.

strikers refused to return to work, production lagged until the Tennessee Company, itself trying to obtain a regular output, took over the operation in 1901. Although improving living and working conditions, the company did not destroy union sentiment. Three years later more than 700 black iron ore miners joined locals affiliated with the Western Federation of Miners (W.F.M.), and although these lapsed when the Ishkooda camp was closed in 1905, when T.C.I. reopened the camp in 1907, Negro organizer William Downey claimed that if the A.F.L. would support an organizing campaign he could bring 1,200 to 1,500 ore miners in this camp and thousands in other camps into unions.[83]

These militant black laborers, and most other organized black workers in the district, were in segregated locals, but they were not isolated from the labor movement in Birmingham and in Alabama. As previously indicated, black miners in the U.M.W. participated actively in union affairs and district conventions. The Birmingham Trades Council inducted black delegates from the U.M.W. in 1900 and in the following three years also accepted representatives from the city's Negro barbers' local, the Negro carpenters, and from at least one of the Negro coke workers' locals.[84] The Trades Council remained integrated until 1903, even though the American Federation of Labor permitted the formation of segregated central labor organizations in 1900. In 1903, the Bessemer Negro Central Labor Council merged with Birmingham's black locals to form a Colored Central Labor Council with twenty affiliated unions. Although no longer represented in the Trades Council the black labor organizations continued to participate in the city's annual Labor Day parades, the chief activity of the Trades Council. These annual affairs were an important ceremony in which the district's union workers demonstrated their numbers and solidarity. The ceremonial nature of these occurrences should not obscure both the actual and symbolic importance of participation by black union members. Representatives of black skilled and unskilled unions marched under their union banners

---

[83] *Labor Advocate*, February 4, May 27, June 24, July 1-28, 1899; *Alabama Miner* (Jasper), July 22, 1899; *Oakman News*, July 21, 1899; *Bessemer Weekly*, April 15, June 17, 1899; *Hot Shots*, August 17, 1899; Birmingham *News*, January 19, 1900, April 11, 1899; Gompers to John Robinson, June 30, 1900, Gompers to Charles Bryant, June 30, 1900, Gompers to W. H. Downey, February 25, 1907, Gompers Letterbooks; *American Federationist*, X:2, 3, 9 (February, March, September 1903), 106, 185, 953, XIV:8, 10 (August, October 1907), 566, 796; Western Federation of Miners, *Miners' Magazine*, VI:57 (July 28, 1904), 15, first lists two Alabama locals of iron ore miners with their officers, and continued to list them through 1906, although by the end of 1905 they had probably lapsed.

[84] Birmingham *News*, August 13, 1900; *Labor Advocate*, March 3, 1901, September 5, 1903.

in every parade between 1900 and 1905 presenting, the *Labor Advocate* once observed, "a most credible appearance and preserving perfect order."[85]

Alliance between Alabama's black and white wage-earners during these years went well beyond joint participation in Labor Day parades. The major vehicle for racial cooperation was the Alabama State Federation of Labor. Formed in 1900, it sought to unite unions and central labor councils throughout the state in one powerful organization which could present a united front in labor's demands for favorable political action. It also encouraged further organization of the state's industrial workers, and attempted to rally support for strikes and boycotts. At its peak membership in 1904, the Federation claimed 235 local affiliates and nine central labor bodies, with a paid up membeership of 33,000 workers. During its first five years the Federation was dominated by locals from the United Mine Workers. William Kirkpatrick, a former U.M.W. district president, was the State's Federation's president three of these years and several other officers were also U.M.W. members. The Mine Workers' racial policies thus became the racial policies of the Alabama Federation of Labor. At the first convention, Silas Brooks, then vice-president of District 20, warned delegates who might be inclined to ignore black workers that if the Alabama labor movement excluded Negroes, they would side with their employers when the state's white workers struck. Just one month before Alabama's constitutional convention met to disfranchise the state's black voters, the labor convention demonstrated its racial attitude by selecting Brooks 1st vice-president and J. H. Bean, a Selma Negro carpenter, 2nd vice-president. "The only thing that remains," the *Labor Advocate* triumphantly proclaimed, "is for the colored race to wake up to the benefits of unionism and embrace the opportunity offered."[86]

The Alabama Federation of Labor, like the state's United Mine Workers, included black men in leadership positions during the first five years of the twentieth century. Among the five vice-presidents elected annually two or three each year were Negro. Every convention committee included black members. Despite disfranchisment, even the

---

[85] *Labor Advocate,* September 10, 1904; Birmingham *News,* September 5, 1904; *Age-Herald,* September 6, 8, 1903; *Labor Advocate,* September 1, 1900, August 30, 1902, September 5, 1903, August 20, September 10, 1904, September 16, 1905.

[86] *Labor Advocate,* April 27, 1901. See also April 20, 1901, May 7, 1904, April 15, May 16, 1905; Birmingham *News,* April 18, 1901.

political arm of the State Federation, the United Labor League, had black vice-presidents in 1903 and 1904. In 1906, five years after the state's Negroes were disfranchised, the League still elected two Negroes to a newly-formed committee designed to get out the vote for candidates favorable to labor.[87] Committed to the organization of the state's black workers, the Federation several times appealed to the A.F.L. to send salaried organizers to Alabama who would "devote their entire time and ability" to organizing black laborers. As David Williams, the Federation's secretary and former vice-president of the Birmingham local of the Amalgamated Association of Iron, Steel and Tin Workers, observed, Alabama's wage-earners must "lay aside all malice and prejudice against color, creed, or nationality, and as we are all wage-earners under the same banner of trades unionism, let us all work with one end in view."[88]

Although the admission of black workers to labor unions and the militancy of many of these black unionists conflicted with increasingly strident demands in the state for Negro subordination, black workers and their unions received aid and encouragement not only from white union members, but occasionally from other people in the white community. When, for example, Bessemer's blast furnace workers struck in 1900, the *Bessemer Weekly,* although feeling the strike untimely in the face of returning prosperity, conceded the legitimacy of the strikers' demands and urged the company to comply with them. Bessemer's Manufacturers and Merchants Association, faced with continuing shutdown of the city's blast furnaces, sent its executive committee to the company superintendant to ask him to settle the strike by recognizing the strikers' union. When he refused to compromise, the association called on the head of the Birmingham Trades Council to mediate. Although the furnaces remained closed for four months because of this walkout, and incidents of violence sometimes broke out, the city's newspapers and the Manufacturers and Merchants Association denounced company officials, not the strikers, for their intransigence.[89] During the iron ore miners' strike in 1899, Bessemer merchants, angered at the commissary policy which deprived them of a lucrative trade, supplied the strikers for several weeks. The *Bessemer Weekly,* "though generally not believing

[87] *Labor Advocate,* September 8, 1900, April 28, 1901, April 26, 1902, May 9, 1903, May 7, 1904, May 6, 1905, January 13, 1905; Birmingham *News,* April 27, 1906.
[88] *Labor Advocate,* May 9, 1903; April 25, May 2, 1903, May 6, 1905.
[89] *Bessemer Weekly,* June 16, 23, 30, 1900; Bessemer *Herald-Journal,* September 18, 1900.

in strikes," condemned the company for the miserable conditions in its camps and endorsed the strikers' demands. A petition from Bessemer and Birmingham merchants urged the Robinson Mining Company to give the strikers higher wages, regular payments, and "cash, not rations like slaves." A gun-battle between strikers and guards erupted at the end of July, when strikers fired into a boarding house containing strike-breakers, killing two of them. A coroner's jury, after sitting for three weeks and hearing 135 witnesses, implicated twenty-five men in the assassinations, but an all-white grand jury refused to indict most of them. Only one of the black strikers ever came to trial, and although the state claimed to have "an excellent case," an all-white Bessemer jury acquitted him.[90]

During this time of increased racial conflict in Alabama, black membership in the United Mine Workers and in locals affiliated with the A.F.L. and the State Federation of Labor of course met with opposition. When the state's labor leaders stood firm, however, they discovered that despite the mounting tide of segregation they could still gain acceptance for interracial labor organizations. At Birmingham's 1901 U.M.W. district convention, for example, owners of the hall used for meetings objected to the presence of black delegates and ousted the convention. William Kirkpatrick, U.M.W. district president, informed the city merchants who owned the hall that "The Negro could not be eliminated. He is a member of our organization and when we are told that we can not use the hall because of this fact then we are insulted as an organization." Convention delegates denounced Birmingham merchants, voted to hold their next meeting in Bessemer, and recommended to their locals that all trade be withdrawn from the city until they received an apology. Under the threat of losing considerable business from the district's miners, Birmingham's merchants apologized for the "oversight and misunderstanding." Such discourtesies, they promised, would not be repeated in future years.[91]

A similar incident occurred the following year at the State Federation of Labor convention in Selma. City officials refused to supply a decent hall for the convention because of the presence of black delegates. But Federation officials resisted this effort to force them to draw the color

[90] *Bessemer Weekly,* June 17, 1899, Birmingham *Arbitrator,* August 2, 1899, January 18, 1900; *Labor Advocate,* July 21, 1899; Birmingham *News,* January 19, 1900.
[91] Birmingham *News,* July 3, 1901.

line. "Rather than see one accredited delegate, black or white, thrown out of this convention," a member of Birmingham's typographical union asserted, "I would go to the woods and hold this meeting." This return to nature was not necessary, however, for both the city's streetcar company and the United Confederate Veterans offered the use of their halls after the convention threatened to leave the city.[92] The following year, at the annual convention held in Bessemer, the interracial State Federation was more favorably received by the city. At a smoker given by "Bessemer citizens," the Federation's black vice-president joined the mayor and the white president of the Federation on the platform to address the guests. At the end of the convention, several black delegates arose to thank Bessemer's citizens for their hospitality and courtesies.[93]

Alabama's labor leaders, led by the U.M.W., also resisted opposition from white workingmen to the organization of black workers and their incorporation into the state's labor movement. In 1900 the U.M.W. used the Birmingham Trades Council's request for a boycott of non-union work by the district's miners to secure an investigation of the discriminatory practices of the Trades Council and some of its affiliates. After a "lively discussion," during which several Trades Council members walked out, representatives of the U.M.W. convinced the Council to rescind its prohibition against Negroes, and to enroll delegates from black locals.[94] Some white delegates to early State Federation conventions also objected to the Federation's racial policies. After the Selma convention in 1902 they urged their locals to withdraw from the organization unless it expelled its black members. Within a few months after the convention only sixteen locals, most of them miners' organizations, remained in the Federation. The officials, however, refused to relent in their policy of admitting black workers. "A great many unions throughout the state did not seem to understand the question and desired the separation of the races," Federation president Kirkpatrick recalled in 1905. As he had done with the Birmingham Trades Council in 1900, Kirkpatrick pointed out to these locals that "the American Federation of Labor did not discriminate between creed, color or nationality," and insisted that "it was just as necessary to organize the colored workers as it was to organize the whites."[95] Whether these arguments were compelling or not, the Federation persuaded most of the secessionists to return by

[92] *Labor Advocate,* April 26, 1902, quoted in Francis Sheldon Hackney, "From Populism to Progressivism in Alabama, 1890-1910" (Yale University Ph.D. dissertation, 1966), 221.

[93] *Labor Advocate,* May 2, 9, 1903.

[94] Birmingham *News,* August 13, 1900. See *Supra,* 69, above.

[95] *Labor Advocate,* April 15, 1905.

the following year. Delegates from ninety-nine locals, thirty more than the previous year, attended this 1903 convention. Included among them, and participating actively in the convention proceedings, were black delegates from unions of ore miners, coal miners, coke workers, furnacemen, rolling mill helpers, hod carriers, and carpenters in Birmingham, as well as from locals in Mobile, Montgomery, Selma, Anniston and other cities in the state.[96]

Unionization of Alabama's black workers from 1897 through 1904 occurred during a period of economic prosperity and relative harmony in labor-management relations in the Birmingham district. Growing strength and success of the labor movement in the state, coupled with an economic recession in the district in 1903 and 1904, led to more vigorous employer assaults on labor organizations which severely tested the interracial alliance and helped destroy unionism in Birmingham. In 1904 the district's furnace companies, which operated about sixty percent of Alabama's coal mines, refused to renew their contracts with the U.M.W. and annnouced their intention to operate their mines on an open shop basis. Over 9,000 miners, probably half of them black, struck. Led by the Tennessee Coal and Iron Company, the companies resorted to their usual policies of importing Negro strikebreakers, sending out large forces of deputies to intimidate miners, and trying to split the white and black miners by offering Negroes the best places in the mines if they would return to work. The president of the Tennessee Company predicted that over eighty percent of the black miners would be back at work in less than a month. A black miner, however, promised that "there is no idea entertained by the colored members [of] . . . deserting the union," and four months after the walkout began less than fifty of 2,000 black strikers in the Pratt City mines, for example, had returned to work.[97] When, two years later the strike was finally called off, only 300 of the 9,000 strikers had gone back to work at the mines which had been struck. Striking Negro miners convinced many imported black strikebreakers to desert the coal companies, and the U.M.W. contributed over $1 million to support strikers and their families, both white and black. Continued coal output in convict mines, and the importation of Southern European immigrants from Pennsylvania and West Virginia mines and from the immigration station at

[96] *Labor Advocate,* April 25, May 2, 1903.
[97] *Labor Advocate,* October 1, 1904. The strike can be followed in the *Labor Advocate,* Birmingham *News,* and *Age-Herald* from June through November 1904, when news began to taper off as the companies succeeded in reopening enough mines to obtain about thirty percent of normal output.

Ellis Island, enabled the coal operators to maintain high enough production levels to outlast the union. Despite racial solidarity among
striking Alabama miners, sixteen months after the strike began the
U.M.W. had to admit defeat and call it off.[98]

Struggle with the coal operators was renewed in 1908 when these
immigrants joined with other white and black miners to resist wage
cuts and to attempt to re-establish the union. Aided by the governor
and the state militia, the operators responded by seeking to destroy the
remains of the mine workers' organization. Vigilante committees, made
up of leading citizens of Birmingham antagonistic to the union, har-
rassed and intimidated both black and white strikers, insisting that they
would not "tolerate the organization and striking of Negroes along with
white men." Train loads of imported strikebreakers were kept under
armed guard to prevent any intimidation by or contact with the strikers.
State militia broke up the interracial tent camp which housed striking
miners. In the face of the opposition of the state government and the
destruction of the miners' tent camp, the U.M.W. soon called off the
strike. The coal companies refused to rehire most of the white miners,
who were thus forced to leave the state. Led by T.C.I., Alabama's coal
companies initiated welfare programs to secure the loyalty of their
black employees and to upgrade their efficiency. By the end of 1908
U.M.W. membership in Alabama had dropped from 18,000 in the
midst of the strike to 700.[99] Only destruction of the union itself, however, ended black membership in the U.M.W. For a decade black
miners had remained loyal to the interracial union and, despite the
state's racial climate, cooperated with the white member. The U.M.W.,
a Negro school principal, himself a member of the union, lamented
shortly after the collapse of the 1908 strike, "has done more for the
colored man than all the secret orders combined."[100]

The racial principles of the Alabama Federation of Labor were also
tested in 1904. The previous year the Rolling Mill Helpers and Laborers' Union at the Republic Iron and Steel Mill in Birmingham had
sent a committee to the mill's general manager to appeal for union

---

[98] Birmingham *News*, August 24, 1904, April 11, 1906; United Mine Workers' Executive
    Board Minutes, August 24, 1904, August 1, 1906, in UMW National Executive Board
    Minutebooks, UMW National Headquarters, Washington, D. C.; *Immigrants in
    Industries: Bituminous Coal Mining*, IV, 142-161, 197-198, 215; Justin Fuller, "The
    History of the Tennessee Coal, Iron and Railroad Company" (University of North
    Carolina Ph.D. dissertation, 1966), 278.
[99] Spero and Harris, *op. cit.*, 358; Woodward, *Origins of the New South*, 363-364.
[100] B. H. Dillard to Editor, *Labor Advocate*, September 4, 1908.

recognition and a wage increase of ten cents per day. When the general manager fired the committee and threatened to fire every man who remained in the union, all 144 black members of the union struck, closing the mill for two weeks. Samuel Gompers, A.F.L. organizer Henry Randall, State Federation president Kirkpatrick, and J. E. Smith, head of Birmingham's Central Labor Council, all urged the strikers to stand firm. The Republic Iron Company offered the men a fifteen-cents per day wage increase, five cents more than they were asking, but the strikers refused to return to work without recognition of their union, even though Randall now advised them to accept the wage increase and forget about recognition. The company then brought in enough laborers to reopen the mill, and despite the objections of Gompers and Theodore Shaffer, national president of the Amalgamated Association, the skilled steel workers at the mill, members of the Amalgamated, returned to work with the strikebreakers. The walkout dragged on for fifteen months, at which time the black laborers finally returned to the mill and asked for their jobs back.[101]

The Amalgamated's action and the failure of the strike did not dampen the Alabama Federation of Labor's support for the organization of black workers. When Thomas Freeman, president of the Rolling Mill Helpers, complained to the Federation's convention in 1904 that the Amalgamated's return to work "with scabs and blacklegs to defeat the Helpers and Laborers . . . [was] not unionism," convention delegates agreed. Although the issue ostensibly revolved around a conflict between white and black workers, the predominantly white convention of Alabama workingmen sent resolutions to Gompers and to Shaffer denouncing the actions of white Amalgamated steel workers, and appealing to the labor leaders to use their "best efforts to organize the common laborers of the Birmingham district," and to take "immediate steps to bring about closer relationships between organized mechanics and organized laborers when they work in the same mill or place."[102]

Despite the appeal of the Alabama Federation, the Amalgamated Association refused to take any action about cooperating with black laborers in Birmingham steel mills. When the union's president, T. J. Shaffer, personally appealed to the 1905 Amalgamated convention to

[101] Most of the episode is taken from Samuel Gompers' letters. Gompers to H. N. Randall, July 11, 21, August 12, October 6, 1903, Gompers to Thomas Freeman, July 11, 21, 1903, Gompers to T. J. Shaffer, July 11, 1903, Gompers Letterbooks. See also *Labor Advocate*, July 4, 1903, May 7, November 19, 1904, May 6, 1905.
[102] *Labor Advocate*, May 7, 1904.

organize unskilled workers in the Republic steel mill in Birmingham, the convention ignored his request.[103] The Amalgamated's animosity towards black laborers in Birmingham, however, cannot be understood solely in terms of racial prejudice. In steel mills in other sections of the country the Association remained just as adamant about not cooperating with unskilled immigrants.[104] To most Amalgamated members, and to most craft unionists, the primary purpose of the labor movement was to provide job security for skilled workmen. Their unions' exclusionist racial policies were part of a larger program designed to protect them against competition from unskilled workers and to preserve the domination of skilled workers in the labor movement. The triumph of this position, not the racial hostility of Alabama's white workers or the apathy of the state's black workers, prevented successful organization of Birmingham's black workers at the beginning of the twentieth century.[105]

To wage-earners who belonged to the Alabama Federation of Labor and to the state's United Mine Workers, the labor movement was an instrument for the cooperation of all workers, skilled and unskilled, white and black. "I may dig coal on one entry and the black man on another some distance away, yet we work together," a white miner observed in 1900. "You may work in one shop and he in another, yet you work together; you may work in a rolling mill and he may fire the engine that runs on the rail you forged into shape, yet you work together."[106] During the early years of the twentieth century, this vision permeated Alabama's labor movement, encouraging organization of Birmingham's black workers, opposing the growth of exclusiveness in trades unions, and resisting the spread of racial conflict in Alabama.

Lack of support from the American Federation of Labor also contributed to the collapse of Negro union membership in Birmingham after 1904. As the Alabama Federation recognized, bringing Birmingham's black workers into labor unions depended upon the willingness of the American labor movement to commit organizers and money to this project. For five years, the A.F.L.—like the U.M.W.—had supported the organization of Alabama's black industrial laborers. In 1904, however, the Federation was in retreat from the organization of unskilled labor throughout the country. Committed to protection of its craft union

---

[103] *Amalgamated Journal,* May 11, 1905.
[104] David Brody, *Steelworkers in America: The Non-Union Era* (Cambridge, Mass., 1960), 120–146.
[105] Spero and Harris, *op. cit.,* 53–56.
[106] W. T. Westbrook to Editor, *Labor Advocate,* June 30, 1900.

members, its treasury depleted by a drop in membership and by the costs of defending itself against employer counteroffensives being mounted in every section of the nation, the A.F.L. could not expand its organizing efforts among Birmingham's black workers, as the Alabama Federation of Labor requested; rather, after 1904, it was forced to reduce them. Federal Labor Unions throughout the country collapsed, and in Birmingham the locals of black workers disappeared.[107]

Consequently, Birmingham's trade union strength rapidly declined after 1904. The United Mine Workers struggled unsuccessfully to defend itself against coal operators' efforts to destroy unionism in the Alabama coal fields, and other unions desperately attempted to protect their hard-won gains from employers who sought to crush unions. As unions lost ground, Alabama's interracial labor movement evaporated. The Alabama Federation of Labor turned its attention from the organization of black laborers to a political alliance with the Farmers' Union. Discrimination and racial hostility, no longer held in check by cross-pressures from the state's labor movement, came to the fore among white workers. Yet, for a brief period in the Birmingham district at the beginning of the twentieth century, the state's labor movement, struggling to overcome both craft union exclusiveness and growing racial conflict in Alabama, organized more than eight thousand black workers and challenged the industrialists' ability to use racial hostility to discipline the class antagonisms of the New South.

[107] Foner, *op. cit.,* III, 32-33; Wolman, *op. cit.,* 33-34; Gompers to H. N. Randall, June 19, 1904, Gompers to Andy Marx, June 13, 1907, Gompers Letterbooks.

4

Labor Conflict and Racial Violence: The Black Worker in Chicago, 1894-1919

WILLIAM M. TUTTLE, JR.

On a crowded South Side Chicago beach on the afternoon of Sunday, July 27, 1919, white and black swimmers clashed in savage combat. Sparked by this clash during which a Negro youth drowned, the interracial resentment that had been smoldering in Chicago for the past few years exploded in furious rioting. The violence raged uncontrolled for five days, as whites mauled Negroes and Negroes in turn assaulted white peddlers and merchants in the "black belt." Members of both races craved vengeance as stories of atrocities, both real and rumored, rapidly spread throughout the city. White gunmen in automobiles sped through the ghetto shooting indiscriminately as they passed, and black snipers fired back. Roaming mobs shot, beat, and stabbed their victims to death. The undermanned Chicago police force was an ineffectual deterrent to the waves of violence that soon overflowed the environs of the black belt and flooded the North and West Sides as well as the Loop, the city's downtown business district. Only six regiments of state militiamen and a cooling rain finally quenched the passions of the rioters, but by then thirty-eight lay dead, twenty-three Negroes and fifteen whites, and well over 500 others had sustained injuries.

There were several factors precipitating this riot. From July 1917 to the eruption of the disorders two years later, for example, no less than twenty-six bombs were hurled at isolated Negro residences in once all-white neighborhoods and at the offices of certain realtors who had sold to blacks. Well over half these bombings occurred during the six tense months leading up to the riot.[1] Politics, too, were important. Chicago's

---

[1] Interchurch World Movement, *The Inter-Racial Situation in Chicago*, Bulletin No. 1 (Chicago: n. pub., *ca.* 1920), *passim.*

William M. Tuttle, Jr., *is Assistant Professor of History at the University of Kansas.*

notoriously corrupt Republican mayor, William H. ("Big Bill") Thompson, was anathema to reformers and Democrats alike. Many of these Democrats, moreover, were blue-collar workers who lived in neighborhoods contiguous to the black belt and who felt threatened, politically and economically, by the "invading" Negroes. Yet Thompson was a favorite of the predominantly Republican black electorate, some of whose leaders had been rewarded with posts in his administration. The mayor was re-elected in April 1919, after a bitter campaign which had racial overtones, and the Democratic organ, the *Chicago Daily Journal,* boomed out at dusk on election day in bold front-page headlines: "NEGROES ELECT BIG BILL."[2] As racial friction mounted with the heat in the spring and summer of 1919, whites and blacks battled on the city's streetcars and in its parks and schools. Several Negroes were murdered in mob assaults, and both blacks and whites armed themselves for the riot that numerous Chicagoans feared would erupt at any moment.

This riot was also the result of longstanding discord between white and black job competitors in the Chicago labor market. Several contemporaries claimed that job competition was not only a cause but perhaps the most significant one.[3] Later students of the riot, however, while admitting that interracial labor friction might have precipitated some bloodshed, have listed it as merely a minor cause. The most exhaustive study, *The Negro in Chicago,* by the Chicago Commission on Race Relations, for example, concluded that it was relatively unimportant since "race friction" was "not pronounced in Chicago industries."[4] Recently Allan H. Spear in *Black Chicago* has similarly asserted that the riot "had little to do with labor conditions. . . ."[5]

Both the Chicago Commission and Spear support this contention by pointing out that during the riot there was an almost total absence of violence in the stockyards, which was by far the largest single area of employment for black Chicagoans. And, indeed, there was far less bloodshed there than knowledgeable observers had feared. But does this

[2] *Chicago Daily Journal,* April 1, 1919.
[3] See footnote 79.
[4] Chicago Commission on Race Relations, *The Negro in Chicago* (Chicago, 1922), 395, 399.
[5] Allan H. Spear, *Black Chicago: The Making of a Negro Ghetto, 1890-1920* (Chicago, 1967), 163. The other recent study of events leading up to the riot is Arthur I. Waskow, *From Race Riot to Sit-In, 1919 and the 1960s* (Garden City, N. Y., 1966). Waskow contends that friction in the labor market was significant and he quotes numerous contemporaries to that effect, but he makes no attempt himself to establish the relationship.

negative evidence prove anything other than that black workers did not dare return to the stockyards until after the militia had been ordered out of the armories to protect them? The absence of violence in the stockyards in the early days of the riot was, as Negro Alderman Louis B. Anderson explained, simply the result of fear of attack. "Colored men," Anderson said, "have refused to go to the stockyards to get paid even though their families were starving. . . ."[6] And what happened when Negroes returned to work? Even under military and police protection, on the first day back, one worker was savagely struck with a hammer wielded by a white man. A mob then chased the dazed Negro through the sheep pens and finally killed him with shovels and brooms. When police rescued a second black man after a severe beating, white workers retaliated, and a vicious battle against police and soldiers ensued. Several days later the packers notified non-union black workers that order had been restored to the yards, and that additional police and soldiers armed with rifles and machine guns would be there to insure their safe return to work. Organized labor disagreed, arguing that the situation was still volatile. The packers "thought that if they would be able to jamb [sic] the colored laborers," charged President John Fitzpatrick of the Chicago Federation of Labor, "that is, the great body of colored laborers, and the white union men in the stock yards . . . that there would be murder there, and that they would destroy our organization. There was no other purpose in it, absolutely no other purpose in it. . . ."[7]

Herbert Gutman has recently made a plea to labor historians "to explore in detail the confrontation of the black worker and industrial America in particular settings."[8] The history of the black worker in Chicago from the Pullman strike of 1894 to the race riot of 1919 provides such an opportunity—in large part because the race riot was in many ways the tragic culmination of this twenty-five years of conflict between blacks and whites in the labor market.

The seeds of discord between white and Negro job competitors in the Chicago labor market had been planted in the stockyards in 1894, when masses of packing and slaughterhouse workers had conducted a sympathetic strike with Eugene V. Debs' American Railway Union.

[6] *Chicago Tribune,* August 3, 1919.
[7] Cook County, Illinois, Office of the Coroner, *Transcript of Evidence Concerning the Race Riot, July and August, 1919* (mimeographed), in Graham Taylor Papers, Newberry Library.
[8] Sterling D. Spero and Abram L. Harris, *The Black Worker* (N. Y., 1968), xi.

Violence marked this strike; and, in the midst of it, Negro strike-breakers were hired for the first time in the history of the meat packing industry. Although the packers initially disclaimed any intention of adopting this practice, less than a week later Negro strikebreakers were working, eating, and sleeping in the stockyards, and their presence fired racial animosities. "Cases of attacks on colored men were numerous yesterday," the *Chicago Record* reported on July 19. "Swinging from the cross tree of a telegraph pole . . . near the entrance to the yards, the effigy of a negro roustabout was suspended. A black false face of hideous expression had been fixed upon the head of straw, and a placard pinnned upon the breast of the figure bore the skull and cross-bones with the word 'nigger-scab' above and below in bold letters. . . ."[9]

The strike ended in August, and the Negro strikebreakers were intimately associated with the defeat. The workers had been thoroughly vanquished. They seemed "unmanly and without self-respect," recalled Mary McDowell of the settlement house "back-of-the-yards." "A community cowed is a sad sight to one who has been used to freemen."[10]

Gradually, the workers built a new union—the Amalgamated Meat Cutters and Butcher Workmen (A.M.C.B.W.). Chicago was its target, for "if a start could be made in Chicago," the center of the industry, the A.M.C.B.W.'s president Michael Donnelly wrote Samuel Gompers, "our success nationally would be virtually established."[11] Success was slow in coming, but by 1902 Donnelly could proudly announce that twenty-one locals had been chartered in Chicago and that the union rolls had burgeoned to 4,000. Accompanying organizing successes were concrete gains in wages and hours.[12]

Yet these benefits went only to skilled workers, and at the turn of the century less and less skill was required in the meat packing industry because of the minute subdivision of labor. The "facts are these,"

[9] *Chicago Record*, July 17, 19, 27, August 3, 1894; *Chicago Tribune*, July 13, 15, 1894; *Chicago Times*, July 19, 1894; and other references cited in Alma Herbst, "The Negro in the Slaughtering and Meat Packing Industry in Chicago," unpublished Ph.D. dissertation, University of Chicago, 1930, 43-45; and Spero and Harris, *op. cit.*, 265.

[10] *Chicago Daily News*, July 29, 1904.

[11] Donnelly, Kansas City, to Gompers, Washington, D. C., December 29, 1896, AFL Papers, State Historical Society of Wisconsin; A.M.C.B.W. *Proceedings*, 1899, 14-18; 1902, 15; 1904, 14; 1906, 10; and AFL *Proceedings*, 1896, 93.

[12] See Mollie Daley to Mary McDowell, August 1, 1902; M. Donnelly to To Whom It May Concern, September 19, 1902, both in Mary McDowell Papers, Chicago Historical Society; A.M.C.B.W. *Official Journal*, II (December, 1901, February, August, 1902, October, 1903), 13; 18; 71, 72; 23; H. D. Call in *Chicago Record-Herald*, August 1, 1904; A.M.C.B.W. *Proceedings*, 1900, 5-6; 1902, 12, 16, 23; Mary McDowell, "The Story of a Women's Labor Union," *Commons*, VII (January, 1903), 1-3; and A.M.C.B.W. *Official Journal*, II (March, 1903), 1-12.

Homer D. Call, the A.M.C.B.W.'s secretary treasurer, explained to
Frank Morrison of the A.F.L., "twenty years ago the trade of the butchers was one of the best in the country." Then, after the consolidation of
smaller packing houses into a handful of "large packing houses . . . they
began a system to crowd out the expert butchers and replace them by
cheaper men in every way. . . ." The owners "divided the business up into gangs consisting of enough to dress the bullock, one man doing only
one thing . . . , which makes it possible for the proprietor to take a man
in off from the street . . . and to day [sic] the expert workers are, in
many cases crowded out and cheap Polackers and Hungarians put in
their places. . . ." The skilled worker realized that this specialization enabled unskilled workers with "muscle" to replace him; it appeared inevitable that unless a minimum wage were obtained for the unskilled,
cut-throat job competition would drive all wages down. The unskilled
were "the club held above our heads at all times," a skilled butcher complained. "If the packers refuse to agree to any minimum wage for the
unskilled," asked Call, "how long will it be before they attempt to reduce the wages of the skilled men?"[13] The skilled workers thus cham-
pioned the demand for a minimum wage of 20 cents an hour.

   This minimum was the union's objective, but it still faced an obstacle
that had perpetually plagued unionization of the stockyards—the vast
heterogeneity of races and nationalities that competed for jobs. No other
divisive force more ominously threatened the union's goal of solidarity.[14] Racial jealousies and antagonisms crumbled, however, as the
unskilled enthusiastically joined the union because of dissatisfaction
with the prevailing wage of 15 to 18½ cents an hour, and Negroes
joined as well as whites.[15] Many of the 500 black workers in the Chicago
yards had become members, U. S. Labor Commissioner Carroll D.
Wright reported to President Theodore Roosevelt.[16] The women's local

---

[13] Call, Syracuse, to Morrison, Washington, D. C., February 20, 1899, AFL Papers. See
also *Report of the Commissioner of Corporations on the Beef Industry* (Washington:
Government Printing Office, 1905), 17-19; W. Joseph Grand, *History of the Union
Stockyards* (Chicago: Thomas Knapp Co., 1896), 49-51; John R. Commons, *Trade
Unionism and Labor Problems* (Boston: Ginn & Co., 1905), 225; J. C. Kennedy,
Wages and Family Budgets in the Stock Yards District (Chicago: University of
Chicago Press, 1914), 7; William Hard, "The Stock Yards Strike," *Outlook*, LXXVII
(August 13, 1904), 887; *Chicago Record-Herald*, August 1, 1904; Mary McDowell,
"A Lost Strike, but not a Dead Cause," *Union Labor Advocate*, V (October, 1904),
12; "The Butcher Workman's Strike," *Railroad Trainmen's Journal*, XXI (October,
1904), 768-69.

[14] Call, Syracuse, to McDowell, Chicago, November 22, 1902, McDowell Papers.

[15] "The Great Strike," unpublished and undated manuscript in *ibid.*

[16] Wright to Roosevelt, September 8, 1904, in *Bulletin of Bureau of Labor*, X (January,

reportedly greeted its black applicants with "a hearty welcome," and Mary McDowell noted that "black men sat with their white comrades" at union meetings.[17] This fellowship extended beyond the confines of the meeting room. The A.M.C.B.W., for example, held a funeral for "Bro. Wm. Sims (colored) tail sawyer at Swift's east house," with sixty-eight whites and seven Negroes attending these last rites.[18]

Negotiations with the packers over the minimum wage were fruitless, breaking down in late June 1904, and when the packers announced a wage reduction, 23,000 packing house workers struck. Seven thousand mechanical tradesmen later joined the strike, which dragged on for ten weeks before the workers sporadically drifted back to work.[19] The A.M.C.B.W. had launched its strike in the face of a depression. Outside the stockyards each morning as many as 5,000 men stood lined up to replace the strikers.[20] The strike was further doomed because the strikers' resources were so paltry compared to the combined assets of the packers. Moreover, the heterogeous nationalities, races, and foreign languages, which had united confidently in 1903 and 1904, were in the final analysis divided and weak.[21]

Despite the hopelessness of the strike, the arch villains to emerge from the defeat were the packers and their black strikebreakers. One observer estimated that upwards of 10,000 Negroes served as strikebreakers, with almost 1,400 arriving in one trainload. To white workers their disturbing presence seemed to be ubiquitous. Five white women strikebreakers described the prevalence of Negroes in the yards. These women, who had been hired by a black man representing Armour, worked in the canning room, ate their meals in a massive improvised dining hall

1905), 2; and Commission on Industrial Relations, *Final Report and Testimony* (Washington: Government Printing Office, 1916), IV, 3471.

[17] Mary McDowell, "The First Women's Union," *Official Journal*, II (October, 1902), 28-29; Commission on Industrial Relations, *Final Report*, 3, 330; "The Great Strike"; and Graham Taylor's remarks in *Chicago Daily News*, July 30, 1904.

[18] *Official Journal*, II (May, 1903), 23-27. See also *Chicago Daily News*, July 29, 1904; A. Kaztauskis, "From Lithuania to the Chicago Stockyards," *Independent*, LVII (August, 1904), 241-48; and David Brody, *The Butcher Workmen: A Study of Unionization* (Cambridge, 1964), 41.

[19] A.M.C.B.W. *Proceedings*, 1904, 33, 92-93, 193; *ibid.*, 1906, 7-10; *Chicago Tribune*, July 13, 1904; *Chicago Record-Herald*, July 13-16, 24-26, 1904; *Official Journal*, V (July, 1904), 33; and Edna Louise Clark, "History of the Controversy between Labor and Capital in the Slaughtering and Meat Packing Industries in Chicago," unpublished M.A. thesis, University of Chicago, 1922, 116 ff.

[20] A.M.C.B.W. *Proceedings*, 1906, 12; and Ernest Poole, "The Meat Strike," *Independent*, LVII (July 28, 1904), 80.

[21] *Report of the Commissioner of Corporations on the Beef Industry*, 39-51; and Samuel Gompers to Thomas I. Kidd, July 26, 1904, Gompers Letterbooks (91), Library of Congress.

one floor below, and at night slept in the canning room which "had 40 cots arranged as close together as possible." They reported seeing many Negro strikebreakers, including thirteen- and fourteen-year-old boys.[22]

Since the violence of the 1894 strike had alienated public opinion, in 1904 the union posted notices on trees and fences which admonished the strikers "to molest no person or property, and abide strictly by the laws of this country." Non-violence was also the theme of union meetings. These exhortations notwithstanding, the strikers' animosities frequently boiled over. A mob of 500 mauled a black laborer and his 10-year-old son, and in another skirmish white strikers stabbed both eyes of a Negro strikebreaker. Other black people were hauled off streetcars. A full-scale riot threatened to erupt when 2,000 angry strikers hurled brickbats and other missiles at 200 Negro strikebreakers and their police escorts. Harry Rosenberg, a worker at Mary McDowell's settlement house, reported witnessing a mob of women and children chasing a Negro down the street, crying "kill the fink," and in late August union pickets fatally stabbed a Negro suspected of strikebreaking.[23]

Their fortunes waning in late August, union leaders desperately wired Booker T. Washington. "Hundreds of Negroes are acting as strikebreakers," they informed Washington, as they begged him to come to Chicago to lecture on the subject, "Should Negroes Become Strike Breakers?" Washington, however, declined the offer.[24]

The words "Negro" and "scab" were now synonymous in the minds of numerous white stockyards workers; and, lest they forget, anti-Negro labor officials and politicians were present to remind them. The strike, one union official wrote, was broken "by such horrid means that a revelation of them makes the soul sicken and the heart beat faint with

[22] R. R. Wright, Jr., "The Negro in Times of Industrial Unrest," *Charities,* XV (October 7, 1905), 70; *Chicago Tribune,* July 13, 24-26, 1904; *Chicago American,* August 26, 1904; William M. Tuttle, Jr., "Some Strikebreakers' Observations of Industrial Warfare," *Labor History,* VII (Spring, 1966), 193-196; Notarized statement of five women strikebreakers, August 18, 1904; "The Great Strike"; Harry O. Rosenberg, "The Packing Industry and the Stockyards," manuscript in McDowell Papers; Mary McDowell, "A Quarter of a Century in the Stock Yards District," Illinois State Historical Society, *Transactions* (1920), 81; and Eric W. Hardy, "The Relation of the Negro to Trade Unionism" (Unpublished M.A. thesis, University of Chicago, 1911), 35-36.

[23] Rosenberg, "The Packing Industry"; Poole, "The Meat Strike," 184; "The Stockyards Strike and Immigrant Workers," *Charities,* XIII (February 4, 1905), 413; *Chicago Tribune,* July 16, 1904; and *Chicago Record-Herald,* July 22, 24, 27, August 1, 18, 21, 23, 25, 1904.

[24] *Chicago Record-Herald,* August 24, 1904; *Chicago Tribune,* August 24, 26, 1904; *New York Tribune,* August 25, 27, 1904; cited in Spero and Harris, *op. cit.,* 267; and Wright, "Negro in Times of Industrial Unrest," 70-73.

an awful fear." It was broken by Negroes, most of them "huge strapping fellows, ignorant and vicious, whose predominating trait was animalism."[25] South Carolina's Senator Ben Tillman traveled to Chicago a month after the end of the strike. "It was the niggers that whipped you in line," he told a group from the stockyards district. "They were the club with which your brains were beaten out."[26]

It was not mere words, however, but another strike, the bloody teamsters' strike of 1905, that made the image of Negroes as a "scab race" even more indelible. Just days after the teamsters struck in April, trainloads of Negroes began streaming into Chicago. Shootings, knifings, and stonings soon paralyzed the city's commerce. Showers of bricks and stones greeted the black drivers as they attempted to deliver milk, coal, and other merchandise; and the injuries inflicted were recorded in the box scores of "strike victims" that Chicago's newspapers printed as front-page news. Pummeled with brass knuckles, "right ear almost torn off"; "injured by bricks, severely bruised and cut, struck on head and left leg with clubs during riot at Rush and Michigan"; struck on the head by a brick "said to have been thrown from the tenth floor"; beaten into unconsciousness, "three shovels broken over his head"—these were but a few of the injuries.[27]

Fearing that such acts of violence would erupt into full-scale rioting, the city council enacted an order requesting the corporation counsel to file an opinion "as to whether the importation of hundreds of Negro workers is not a menace to the community and should not be restricted." The employers' association responded by consenting not to import any more Negroes, though it refused to discharge any of its black drivers.[28]

Not only was the employers' gesture futile, but its very futility indicated that new elements had entered into the relationship between labor conflict and racial violence in Chicago. In this dispute, unlike the stockyards strike of eight months before, the hostility of striking whites toward strikebreaking Negroes had been generalized into hatred for the black race as a whole; any Negro was a potential target. Now, no longer were mob assaults limited to just one district; presaging the 1919 riot, racial violence had spread throughout the city but it was especially prevalent in the blue-collar neighborhood to the west of the black belt.

[25] John Roach, "Packingtown Conditions," *American Federationist*, XIII (August, 1906), 534.

[26] Chicago *Broad Ax*, October 15, 1904; quoted in Spear, *op. cit.*, 39.

[27] *Chicago Tribune*, May 2-4, 1905; and Wright, "Negro in Times of Industrial Unrest," 73.

[28] Spear, *op. cit.*, 39-40; and *Chicago Tribune*, May 2-6, 10, 12, 1905.

"You have the Negroes in here to fight us," the teamsters' president told the employers' association, "and we answer that we have the right to attack them wherever found." Moreover, as Graham Taylor of the Chicago Commons settlement house observed, the "great intensity of class consciousness" in the teamsters' strike forged a firm bond between strikers and their families, neighbors, other wage-earners, and even the little children who supported them by hurling rocks at the strike-breakers. The focus of their violence was facilitated by the distinguishing physical characteristic of the Negroes—the black skin that represented so many varieties of evil and danger to them. Finally, the besieged Negroes were determined to defend themselves, unlike 1904 when, unarmed, they had generally fled.[29]

Some of the non-strikebreaking black victims were mistaken for non-union drivers. One of these was a dishwasher, who was kicked and beaten and his head smashed through a car window; when policemen came to his aid, the crowd began to yell: "That's what they will all get." Another was a porter who was attacked by a crowd that ran after him screaming that he was a scab; beaten into unconsciousness, the porter died several days later of a fractured skull. The only offense committed by other Negroes, however, was that their color was "black and displeasing." A Negro medical student, for example, was pummeled to the ground. Even a black union member was pelted with rocks; when he called out to his attackers that his employer was not involved in the strike, one of them replied that being a "nigger" he deserved a beating anyhow.[30]

Perhaps there was no better example of white solidarity during these turbulent weeks than the sympathy strike conducted by hundreds of grade-school students. Protesting the delivery of coal at school buildings by black strikebreakers employed by the Peabody Coal Company, the students not only hurled missiles at the drivers but organized a "skilled pupils' " union with a kindergarten local affiliated. "We are on strike. Hurrah for the unions," read the paper badges of the students who threw bricks, stones, and pieces of wood at those classmates refusing to join the picket line. Many parents supported the strike, some asserting that they would never permit their children to return so long as scabs continued to deliver coal. They also sanctioned violence. One

[29] *Ibid.;* and Graham Taylor, *Chicago Commons through Forty Years* (Chicago, 1936), 118.
[30] *Chicago Tribune,* May 4, 9, 12, 14, 1905.

father, for example, told a judge that his son was "amply justified" in flinging coal at Negro drivers because these men were "black" and "nonunion." Even teachers encouraged the strikers. "I will invite the pupils to strike," one principal allegedly said, "if the dirty 'niggers' deliver coal at this school."[31]

Negroes appeared resolved to defend themselves. When a white man made a crude remark about a black strikebreaker who was standing at the rear of a custom house, the Negro leaped down from the platform and leveled a revolver at the white. "Why, I was only joking," the white man quickly said. "You're just white trash and I ought to shoot you anyhow," replied the Negro.[32]

It was this resolve that helped to precipitate unrestrained violence in mid-May. An 11-year-old boy died on May 16, after two Negro strikebreakers, leaving work at the Peabody Coal Company, had fired into a group of jeering children. Hysteria swept the neighborhood as enraged mobs hunted for Negroes. White anger swelled menacingly, so that black people feared to appear in the streets. Then, on the evening of May 20, rioting surged out of control. Parading down the streets and proclaiming their intention of "driving the blacks off the face of the earth," whites met armed resistance. Surrounded by attackers, another strikebreaker from Peabody fired and fatally wounded a white man. The next day, as the rioting spread to other districts, police were unable to prevent the outbreaks and disturbances that grew bloodier as night approached. That evening a Negro was murdered by a white bartender in a saloon brawl, and other black men were dragged off streetcars. In the black belt, where Negroes marched the streets crying for "justice" and "down with the white trash," white men were chased and beaten. When the violence subsided on May 22, two people were dead and a dozen severely injured. It had been, as Allan Spear has written, "the bloodiest racial conflict in the city before the riot of 1919."[33] Labor conflict, it was readily apparent, could easily escalate into racial violence.

The image of black people as a scab race no doubt continued to fester in the minds of white workers, even though Negroes did not reinforce it again until 1916. Pullman car porters and other black men

[31] *Ibid.*, May 12-24, 1905.
[32] *Ibid.*, May 7, 9, 15, 1905.
[33] *Ibid.*, May 17, 19, 21-23, 1905; and Spear, *op. cit.*, 40.

and women replaced striking railroad car cleaners in the spring of that year. Fed in dining cars and sleeping in the Pullmans, the Negroes, according to the employer, were hired "not as strikebreakers, but with the understanding that their positions would be permanent," and they were "proving themselves much more efficient in every way than the cleaners who left. . . ." Most of these workers stayed on the job after breaking the strike.[34]

In 1916, too, as a result of increased meat production to feed Europe's armies and a sharp decline in immigration, the lines of men waiting outside the stockyards each morning evaporated. "In the past years," Mary McDowell wrote a friend, "we have seen three to five thousand men and women waiting every morning for work and have been told that while there was such a surplus of labor a raise in wages could not be given to the unskilled workers."[35] Surely, this must change.

Union leaders realized not only that the moment was propitious to organize all the stockyards workers, but that in this mass-production and minutely specialized industry some sort of industrial unionism would be required to do it. Under the leadership of John Fitzpatrick, president of the Chicago Federation of Labor (C.F.L.), and William Z. Foster, an organizer for the railway carmen's union, all the trade unions in the yards, with the exception of the A.M.C.B.W., united in July 1917 to form the Stockyards Labor Council (S.L.C.).

Next to persuading the nationals to lay aside jurisdictional jealousies for the benefit of central organization, the S.L.C.'s most formidable problem was that of unionizing Negro workers, of whom there were between 10,000 and 12,000 in the yards, or about one-quarter of the total laboring force.[36] The C.F.L. asked Samuel Gompers to provide a method by which the S.L.C. could grant membership to Negroes without violating the constitutions, rituals, and other color bars of the nationals. Gompers' solution was that the A.F.L. would award federal

---

[34] Mark L. Crawford, Commissioner of Conciliation, to Secretary of Labor, April 17, 1916; Clive Runnels to Crawford, April 14, 1916; John Fitzpatrick to William B. Wilson, March 30, 1916, all in Records of Federal Mediation and Conciliation Service, Suitland, Maryland (RG 280), 33/192; and *Negro in Chicago*, 430-32.

[35] McDowell, Chicago to Mechem, Chicago, [?], 1916, McDowell Papers.

[36] George E. Haynes, memorandum in re proportion of Negroes employed in meat packing in Chicago, January, 1916-February, 1919, to H. L. Kerwin, March 14, 1921, RG 280, 170/1365. See also [Fred L. Feick] to Louis F. Post, *ca.* December, 1917, RG 280, 33/864; Monroe Work (ed.,) *Negro Year Book, 1918-1919* (Tuskegee Institute, 1919), 13; Herbst, *op. cit.*, xiv-xv, 29, 61; Clark, *op. cit.*, 27-28; Department of Commerce, Bureau of the Census, *14th Census*, IX: *Manufactures, 1919* (Washington: Government Printing Office, 1923), 316, 312, 317, 322, 326, 346; and Brody, *op. cit.*, 85.

charters to all-Negro locals, if no serious objections were raised by the nationals. Despite the established unworkability of federal locals, and the cries of "Jim Crow" that they would arouse, the S.L.C. confidently embarked on its campaign to organize Negroes. To assist in the drive, the Illinois coal miners donated two black organizers, and others later joined the team.[37]

The yards, rather than the steel mills or other mass-production industries, were the focus of the unions' efforts to solicit Negro membership. Not only were the packers by far the major employers of Negro labor but, nearly as significant, success in organizing Negroes in the yards was generally considered a gauge of the unions' ability to organize them in any of Chicago's industries. Moreover, the slaughtering and meat-packing industry was the city's largest, employing over one-eighth of Chicago's wage-earners and ranking first in value added by manufacture and total value of its products.[38]

A mass organization drive began in September 1917, with parades, smokers, hall and street meetings, and the distribution of 50,000 pieces of literature in various languages. "Brother's [*sic*] in all the Packing Houses. . . . BE MEN—JOIN THE UNION" read the handbills summoning black workers to a union meeting. The strike failures of 1894 and 1904 haunted union members, and it was rumored that the packers wanted a strike and had imported an enormous labor reserve of Negroes to break it and crush unionization. And, indeed, it seemed to be a fact, though a much disputed one, that employers were importing black laborers from the rural South.[39]

On March 30, 1918, however, through the intervention of the federal government, Judge Samuel Alschuler, who had been appointed U. S. Administrator for Adjustment of Labor Differences in Certain Packing

[37] William Z. Foster "How Life Has Been Brought into the Stockyards," *Life and Labor*, VIII (April, 1918), 64; Brody, *op. cit.*, 85-87; William Z. Foster, *The Great Steel Strike and Its Lessons* (N. Y., 1920), 211-12; Gompers to Fitzpatrick, August 22, 1917, Gompers Letterbooks (237); Spero and Harris, *op. cit.*, 270.

[38] See references to the 1920 census cited in footnote 36. For the fact that the unions in steel did not make a concerted effort to organize black workers, see Spero and Harris, *op. cit.*, 260.

[39] Investigation by R. T. Sims to E. N. Nockels, January 19, 1917, enclosed in Frank Morrison to W. B. Wilson, February 22, 1917, in U. S. Department of Labor Records, National Archives (RG 174), 205, 13/65; handbill in RG 280, 33/864; Illinois Federation of Labor *Weekly News Letter*, September 28, 1918; *Butcher Workman*, III (November, 1917), 2; Fitzpatrick, as quoted in Herbst, *op. cit.*, 74; and the colloquy in U. S. Senate, 65th Cong., 3rd Sess., Committee on Agriculture and Forestry, *Government Control of the Meat-Packing Industry* (Washington: Government Printing Office, 1919), 1498-1503.

House Industries, awarded the eight-hour day and other benefits to workers in the yards. Such gains, the workers felt, were a tremendous union victory. Fitzpatrick jubilantly proclaimed to an excited crowd of thousands assembled in a Chicago public park: 'It's a new day, and out in God's sunshine, you men and you women, black and white, have not only an eight-hour day but you are on an equality.'[40] Union membership soared in the weeks following these awards.

"I suppose you have heard from official sources that the Stockyards will soon be a hundred percent organized," Ida Glatt, an officer of the Women's Trade Union League, happily recounted to Agnes Nestor, former president of the League. "From intimate connection with the white and colored English-speaking women workers I can tell you first-hand that the women are just rolling into the organization." The unions' secretaries "do nothing but take in applications from morning to midnight." Negro men and women were also participating in the meetings of the S.L.C.[41]

Not everybody shared Miss Glatt's optimism. Irene Goins, a Negro who was actively organizing in the yards, expressed her disappointment: "My people . . . know so little about organized labor that they have had a great fear of it, and for that reason the work of organizing has proceeded more slowly than I anticipated." Another black organizer, John Riley, echoed her disappointment.[42]

The urgent need to organize black workers increased in the fall of 1918. The war was drawing to a close, and accompanying demobilization would be the termination not only of government contracts but of the federal wartime agencies which had supported union recognition, collective bargaining, and non-discrimination against union members. It was imperative for labor to meet with greater solidarity the em-

---

[40] File in RG 280, 33/864; 864-A; *Report of the President's Mediation Commission to the President of the United States* (Washington: Government Printing Office, 1918), 16; *Monthly Labor Review*, VI (May, 1918), 115-27; *Survey*, XL (April 13, 1918), 35-38; Illinois Federation of Labor *Weekly News Letter*, September 28, 1918; A.M.C.B.W. *Proceedings*, 1920, 84-85, 109-10, 211-12; *The New York Times*, December 26, 1917, January 21, 23, 25, 28, 1918; *Butcher Workman*, III (December, 1917), 1; *ibid.*, IV (January, 1918), 1, 2; *ibid.*, VII (March, 1921), 4; and *ibid.*, VIII (April, 1922), 1, 2; and Mary McDowell, "Easter Day after the Decision," *Survey*, XL (April 13, 1918), 38.

[41] Glatt, Chicago, to Nestor, in England, April 22, 1918, Agnes Nestor Papers, Chicago Historical Society; and John B. Lennon to H. L. Kerwin, April 24, 28, 1918, RG 280, 33/1211, 33/1233.

[42] Council of National Defense, Women's Committee, Conference of Departments of Women in Industry of the Middle-West State Divisions, *Report* (n.pl.pub.: n.pub., n.d.), 8; and *Butcher Workman*, IV (October, 1918), 5.

ployers' efforts to re-establish the pre-war pattern of industrial relations. Unorganized Negroes, union leaders feared, would be pawns of the employers in the future struggle. Southern Negroes continued to pour into the city; in recent years the Negro population in Chicago had more than doubled, increasing from 50,000 to over 100,000, while the Negro industrial force had risen from 27,000 to almost 70,000. In 1910, black men comprised just 6 percent of the laboring force in the yards; ten years later, they comprised 32 percent. The black laboring force of every packing house, reported Dr. George E. Haynes of the Labor Department's Division of Negro Economics, had increased rapidly from three to five times over the level of January 1916.[43]

In addition, the image of Negro strikebreakers had not dimmed during the war. Hotel keepers, for example, locked out waiters in April 1918, hiring Negroes in their place. "This is a deliberate attempt to start a race war," Fitzpatrick wrote Secretary of Labor William B. Wilson. Wilson's conciliator in Chicago agreed that the dispute was "full of danger because of the Race problem."[44] Negroes also broke strikes of egg candlers and garment workers.[45]

With the Armistice, as the forces of demobilization touched all levels of the economy, the battle lines between employers and workers hardened. But the peace was also portentous to black Chicagoans whose employment security was in large measure attributable to the government's demands for war products. That spring, the prospect of a peacetime labor market disturbed people who were usually the first to feel the effects of the immediate postwar unemployment. Negro women were the first to be discharged; Negro men and white women soon followed. At the stockyards' National Box Company, where half of the workers and almost all the unskilled workers were black, Negro women were discharged after a pay raise for women workers. "After they gave

---

[43] Estelle Hill Scott, *Occupational Changes Among Negroes in Chicago* (Chicago: WPA District 3, 1939), 175; *Chicago Daily Journal,* April 3, 1919; Department of Commerce, Bureau of the Census, *Women in Gainful Occupations, 1870 to 1920* (Washington: Government Printing Office, 1929), 11, 31; and Haynes' memorandum to Kerwin, March 14, 1921, RG 280, 170/1365.

[44] Fitzpatrick to Wilson, April 27, 1918, RG 280, 33/1280; John B. Lennon to H. L. Kerwin, April 24, 28, 1918, *ibid.,* 33/1211, 33/1233; Fitzpatrick and Nockels to W. B. Wilson, January 10, 1919, *ibid.,* 170/41; *New Majority,* January 11, 1919.

[45] Report on Egg Inspectors' Union, undated; Oscar F. Nelson to H. L. Kerwin, November 3, 1918, both in RG 280, 33/2602; file on garment workers in *ibid.,* 33/369; Commission on Industrial Relations, *Final Report,* 3246-47; *Negro in Chicago,* 414-15; Joel Seidman, *The Needle Trades* (N. Y., 1942), 38; and Department of Labor, *Report of the Secretary, 1919* (Washington: Government Printing Office, 1920), 50-51.

that," a black woman complained, "there came a whole lot of white ladies." This woman, who wanted to remain at National Box, was told she could stay if she were willing to do the gruelling work of loading trucks formerly done by men. "If you don't want to do that," her foremen told her, "you will have to go home, because they are going to have all whites."[46]

Upwards of 10,000 Negroes were unemployed in early May 1919. Employment in the stockyards had fallen from over 65,000 in January to 50,000. Returning soldiers aggravated this situation, and thousands of black troops were mustered out in or near Chicago, many of them southerners who had little desire to return home.[47] A. L. Jackson of the Wabash Avenue YMCA pleaded with the Chicago industrialists to hire these veterans; and in boosting their qualifications he even invoked the nativism so prevalent in 1919: "These boys are all good Americans. There are no slackers, no hyphens among them."[48] To alleviate this distress, the Chicago Urban League distributed portions of the labor surplus to Battle Creek, Flint, and Detroit, and to areas of Wisconsin and Illinois, but it could place only a few hundred compared to the many thousands of placements it had made during the war.[49] Even during the prosperous summer months of 1919, black Chicagoans doubtless realized that during a labor depression they were the most expendable, and many did not want to jeopardize their tenuous positions by unionizing.[50]

In early June the stockyards unions kicked off their most spirited organization drive since 1917. Following a parade and the distribution of campaign buttons on June 8, John Kikulski, an organizer of butchers and meat cutters, outlined the goals of "this great campaign," in which "Polish, Irish, Lithuanian, and in fact every race, color, creed, and nationality is to be included. . . ." "While there will be varied differences in our physical makeup and thoughts," he continued, "there is one thing which we all hold in common, and that is our right to a liv-

---

[46] Other women verified this report; see hearings on National Box, March 14, 1919, RG 280, 33/864-B, 62-63, 88-105, 108-17, 120, 125-33; and Forrester B. Washington, "Reconstruction and Colored Women," *Life and Labor*, VIII (January, 1919), 3-5.
[47] Dr. Haynes' activity reports for the Division of Negro Economics for the weeks ending March 22-May 31, 1919, in RG 174, 8/102-E,F; and *14th Census*, IX, 316.
[48] "Chicago's Negro Problem," City Club of Chicago *Bulletin*, XII (March 17, 1919), 76.
[49] Chicago Urban League, *Annual Report*, III, 3; and *ibid.*, IV, 10.
[50] For increased employment that summer, see Dr. Haynes' activity reports for July 1-31, 1919, in RG 174, 8/102-F; and in *ibid.*, Division of Negro Economics, U. S. Employment Service, "Clearance Bulletin," July 29, 1919.

ing wage, and our rights in the pursuit of happiness as American citizens. . . ." In other attempts to organize black workers, and to convince them that labor's cause was also theirs, the C.F.L. devoted portions of its newspaper, *The New Majority,* to the Negro. The organ of the A.M.C.B.W., the *Butcher Workman,* likewise published pointed appeals to black workers. An article authored by a Negro woman appeared in the May issue. Entitled "The Negro's Greatest Opportunity as I See It," it was both a slashing attack on race prejudice and an announcement that the A.M.C.B.W. had "broken down the bars and . . . and invited us in." "Therefore, the black man should take advantage of this great opportunity [membership in the A.M.C.B.W.], so that he may be the instrument through which discrimination may be driven out of this country—the home of the free and the home of the brave."[51]

White and Negro workers paraded through the black belt on Sunday, July 6, and congregated in a playground near the yards. Brass bands led the way, and the marchers waved miniature American flags and carried placards, on one of which was printed: "The bosses think because we are of different colors and different nationalities that we should fight each other. We're going to fool them and fight for a common cause—a square deal for all." Union leaders delivered speeches at the playground. The seven speakers, of whom three were Negroes, did not betray the advertised purpose of the meeting—to organize Negro workers. "It does me good . . . to see such a checkerboard crowd," said J. W. Johnstone of the S.L.C. in welcoming the workers. "You are standing shoulder to shoulder as men, regardless of whether your face is black or white." John Kikulski then addressed the Polish in their native language to explain the need for "cooperation between blacks and whites."[52]

Yet events just two days later belied the union leaders' rhetorical optimism. For on July 8, as a hot spell settled on the city, the most violent strike of the summer occurred. Two thousand employees of the Corn Products Refinery at Argo struck that morning, after the company's president had reneged on an agreement to hold a referendum on the closed shop. Anticipating trouble, the company had requisitioned

[51] *The New Majority,* April 26, June 14, 21, July 5, 19, 1919; Department of Labor, Division of Negro Economics, *The Negro at Work during the War and during Reconstruction* (Washington: Government Printing Office, 1921), 26-27; *Butcher Workman,* V (May, June, July, 1919), 4, 1, 1.
[52] *New Majority,* July 12, 1919; Chicago *Whip,* July 19, 1919; and *Butcher Workman,* V (July, 1919), 1, 3.

a shipment of rifles and reinforced its special police force. The next day, during a fracas at the plant's entrance, armed guards shot and killed two strikers and seriously wounded eighteen others, one of whom soon died. A howling, stone-throwing mob of strikers' wives and daughters added to the turbulence by chasing the mayor of Argo, who was also superintendent of the company's machine shops, two miles to Chicago's city limits for threatening local grocers and druggists with discontinuance of the refinery's accounts if they extended credit to the strikers. The day after the shootings, the strikers and several thousand other Russian, Lithuanian, and Polish workers, mainly from the stockyards district, marched in a guard of honor at the funeral of the murdered men. During the funeral the rumor was rife that the company had asked numerous Negroes to "come back Monday and bring all of your friends." Argo's citizens feared that the introduction of Negroes would ignite another round of bloodshed; and on Monday refinery officials deputized a number of black men whom they strung out in a line in front of the plant. Their presence particularly incensed the strikers, and disorder erupted during which three strikers were wounded. A mother of four was shot in the leg and then beaten down from a trolley wire, but not before she had disengaged it in order to allow strikers to hurl bottles and bricks at a stalled streetcar filled with strikebreakers. Altogether 600 Negroes were brought in as strikebreakers in this bloody dispute; doubtless, the immigrant strikers in Argo and around the stockyards did not forget the Negroes' role.[53]

A confrontation between labor and management in the yards was not long in coming. The first week of July witnessed the introduction of 300 mounted policemen to patrol the stockyards district, apparently to reverse the unions' organizing successes. As workers gathered around a union speaker, the police would ride into the crowd and disperse it. After protesting to the packers, 10,000 workers walked out on Friday, July 18. Although they returned to the stockyards Monday, it was evident that one of the most serious strikes in Chicago's history was imminent. That evening, union members voted to demand wage increases and other benefits, to submit these demands Saturday, July 26—just the day

---

[53] Oscar F. Nelson to H. L. Kerwin, August 4, 1919; Fitzpatrick to Woodrow Wilson, July 9, 1919; in RG 280, 170/606; *Chicago Daily News,* July 8-10, 14, 1919; *Chicago Herald-Examiner,* July 9, 1919; *Chicago Daily Journal,* July 10-11, 14, 1919; Department of Labor, *Report of the Secretary of Labor, 1920* (Washington: Government Printing Office, 1921), 117; William L. Evans, "The Negro in Chicago Industries," *Opportunity,* I (February, 1923), 15; *New Majority,* August 2, 1919.

before the outbreak of the race riot—and to allow the packers forty-eight hours either to accept them or prepare for a strike.[54] Ninety percent of the whites were unionized by that fateful weekend, while three-fourths of the Negroes, or 9,000 workers, were still outside the labor movement.[55] What had retarded unionization among black workers?

Negroes in labor histories too often appear as faceless figures either to be praised, pitied, or damned. It is evident that black workers had very real reasons for resisting unionization. Many unions, of course, barred black craftsmen in order to control their portions of the labor market. These Negroes thus had to seek out unskilled positions, and it would be unreasonable for them then to unionize with common laborers, especially if they accrued employment benefits as non-union men. Unfortunately for the stockyards organization drive, neither all the A.F.L. national unions nor their members followed the lead of the C.F.L. Negroes were induced to join the federal locals recommended by Gompers, although some over-zealous organizers enlisted black workers with the false promise that they would be transferred later to the locals of their respective crafts. A steamfitter expressed the dilemma of many of the Negro tradesmen in the yards: "I have worked as a steamfitter at the stockyards for fifteen years and tried to get into [all-white] Local 563 as have others of my race, but we have always been put off with some excuse until we gave up the attempt to get in." Other Negroes had become union members during labor disputes, only to be discharged after the strike was over. They felt betrayed, certain that unions were motivated not by a spirit of brotherhood but solely by self-interest.[56] The exclusionist policies of southern unions had likewise alienated Negroes from the labor movement, and some of the migrants to Chicago during the war had traveled there to escape the job control exercised by the unions.[57] Other migrants had peculiarly individual

[54] Alschuler Hearings, August 13, 1919, 23-29, in RG 280, 33/864; Fitzpatrick and J. W. Johnstone to W. B. Wilson, August 23, 1919; Wilson to Fitzpatrick and Johnstone, August 28, 1919, *ibid.*, 33/864-C; Herbst, *op. cit.*, Meat Packing," 70-73; *Chicago Daily News*, July 17, 21, 1919; *New Majority*, July 26, 1919; *Chicago Herald-Examiner*, July 21, 1919; *Chicago Tribune*, July 21, 1919; and *Chicago Whip*, July 25, 1919.

[55] *Chicago Daily Journal*, August 6, 1919; and Haynes, memorandum to H. L. Kerwin, March 14, 1921, RG 280, 170/1365.

[56] Letter to the editor in *New Majority*, February 15, 1919. See James Weldon Johnson, "Changing Status of Negro Labor," National Conference of Social Work, *Proceedings*, 1919, 383-88; and *Negro in Chicago*, 426-27, for 1903 waiters' strikes in which Negro union members felt betrayed.

[57] Emmett J. Scott (comp.), "Additional Letters of Negro Migrants of 1916-1918," *Journal of Negro History*, IV (October, 1919), 417.

motives for not unionizing; some Negroes' life insurance policies were even voided if they did.[58] Still others hesitated to join with whites who, during earlier labor depressions, had replaced them in domestic services, in the operation of barber shops, bootblack parlors, and contractual janitorial services, and in cooking, waiting tables, and dishwashing.[59]

Negroes who traveled from the South to work in Chicago's industries brought with them not only a rural psychology but, in many cases, a total ignorance of strikes and unions. Fully 90 percent of the northern-born black workers in the yards, for example, wore the union button, but few of the migrants did.[60] Other Negroes, however, were fully aware of how Negroes broke strikes, undermined wages, and reduced the white workers' bargaining power. Strikebreaking presented an opportunity to enter industries which formerly had been closed. Even if a Negro strikebreaker were employed at less than the union scale, he was generally paid more than he was accustomed to earning; and by refusing to go out on strike with whites, Negroes received promotions into more highly skilled fields which had not been previously open to them.

The readjustment from life on the farm to that of industrial wage-earner was so immense that Negro migrants often followed the advice of black leaders. Their advice was understandably more influential than that of white union members. A frequent source of counsel was the Urban League, the main employment agency in the black belt. The Urban League took a pragmatic view of unions, although the officers of the local branch were clearly cognizant of the danger of post-war labor conflict along racial lines. Robert E. Park, a white sociologist and president of the Chicago Urban League, feared that all the Negroes' perplexities after the Armistice would be "intimately bound up with the labor scene"; and, as early as November 1917, the League annnounced that it "would welcome any effort tending to an amicable settlement of this vital problem." It met with officers of the Chicago and Illinois Federations of Labor, and it advised the Women's Trade Union League during its campaign to organize Negro women in the yards, but these efforts accomplished little toward persuading unions to lower their color

[58] *Ibid.*, 433.
[59] See, for example, the statements of Fannie Barrier Williams, a socially conscious Negro, in the *New York Age*, June 15, September 28, 1905; quoted in Alfred H. Stone, *Studies in the American Race Problem* (N. Y., 1908), 157-58.
[60] Brody, *op. cit.*, 85; Spero and Harris, *op. cit.*, 271.

bars. The dilemma of the League, as of many Negro leaders, was that though it recognized the exigency of unionizing Negroes, it left little doubt that the first move had to be the unions' obliteration of all discriminatory membership policies. The League sought to plot a course between management and organized labor. For two reasons, however, it was more often on management's side: the unions did not lower their color bars, and Chicago's large industries could provide immediate opportunities for the migrants.[61]

The attitude of Chicago's most widely circulated Negro newspaper, the *Defender*, paralleled that of the Urban League. "We have arrayed ourselves on the side of capital to a great extent," the *Defender* proclaimed in an editorial in late April 1919, "yet capital has not played square with us; it has used us as strikebreakers, then when the calm came turned us adrift." If it were to the race's "economic, social and political interest to join with organized labor now, it should not make the least bit of difference what was their attitude toward us in the past, even if that past was as recent as yesterday. If they extend the olive branch in good faith accept it today." In July, however, after the A.F.L. convention had done nothing to remove the exclusion clauses of some A.F.L. unions or the segregation clauses of others, the *Defender* complained: "Unwillingly we assume the role of strikebreakers. The unions drive us to it."[62]

To most leaders in the black belt, exclusion and segregation were the roots of the problem. There was also a widespread attitude that employers were the Negroes' natural allies and that they, rather than unions, provided security and industrial opportunity. Negroes have found, Booker T. Washington wrote in 1913, that "the friendship and confidence of a good white man, who stands well in the community, are a valuable asset in time of trouble." For this reason, the Negro worker "does not always understand, and does not like, an organization [that is, a union] which seems to be founded on a sort of impersonal enmity to the man by whom he is employed. . . ."[63] Mary McDowell recalled an example of the personal relationship which

[61] Arvarh E. Strickland, *History of the Chicago Urban League* (Urbana, 1966), 48, 50-51, 56-63, 66-67, 72-74, 110; Chicago Urban League, *Annual Report*, I, 10; II, 6; and III, 2; E. K. Jones, "The Negro in Industry," National Conference of Social Work, *Proceedings*, 1919, 438-41; and *Chicago Whip*, July 19, 1919.

[62] *Chicago Defender*, April 26, July 5, 1919; see also the issues for September 30, 1916, February 9, May 4, 1918. The *Chicago Whip* supported unionization.

[63] Washington, "The Negro and the Labor Unions," *Atlantic Monthly*, CXI (June, 1913), 756-57.

Negroes often believed existed between employer and employee. During the campaign to organize the stockyards, an organizer approached a newly-arrived Negro and explained to him the advantages of union membership. "It all sounds pretty good to me," the Negro replied, "but what does Mr. Armour think about it?"[64]

Union leaders accused the packers of subsidizing black clergymen and other professional people, YMCAs, and welfare clubs to spread anti-union propaganda.[65] Certain clergymen, among them unprincipled labor recruiters, did urge their parishioners to spurn union advances. Others, however, endorsed the endeavors of unions that were organizing without regard to race, arguing that union membership would help to minimize racial conflict; and among these were two of the city's most eminent ministers, L. K. Williams of the Olivet Baptist Church and John F. Thomas of Ebeneezer Baptist. In addition, black clerical associations, such as the Colored Baptist Ministers' Alliance and the AME Sunday School Convention, invited union organizers to use their groups as forums for outlining labor's views.[66]

The YMCA, where at least two packers, Wilson and Armour, financed "efficiency clubs," was anti-union. Armour also gave an annual membership to the YMCA to each black worker after his first year of employment. Negroes at the club meetings, J. W. Johnstone charged, were "lectured and taught that the thing they have to do is to keep out of organized labor."[67]

But were ministers and the YMCA witting instruments of the packers? Dr. George E. Haynes thought not. It was obvious, he reported after investigating the origins of the race riot, that certain black leaders were adamantly opposed to workers unionizing, "but there was no evidence that could be obtained that they were influenced to these opinions or used as tools of the employers."[68]

---

[64] Spero and Harris, *op. cit.*, 130.

[65] Alschuler Hearings, August 13, 1919, 96, in RG 280, 33/864; Dr. Haynes' memorandum to H. L. Kerwin, March 14, 1921, RG 280, 170/1365; *Negro in Chicago*, 427-29; Foster, *op. cit.*, 211-12; *Chicago Tribune*, August 1, 1919; *New Majority*, January 11, August 9, 1919; Department of Labor, Division of Negro Economics, *Negro Migration in 1916-17* (Washington: Government Printing Office, 1919), 117-130.

[66] *Chicago Whip*, July 25, 1919; *Negro in Chicago*, 415, 422; Carl Sandburg, *The Chicago Race Riots* (N. Y., 1919), 48; Miles Mark Fisher, *The Master's Slave: Elijah John Fisher, a Biography* (Philadelphia, 1922), 189.

[67] Alschuler Hearings, June 21, 1919, 267-77; June 23, 1919, 508-10, 545, in RG 280, 33/864; *Negro in Chicago*, 427; Kate J. Adams, *Humanizing a Great Industry* (Chicago, *ca.* 1919), 21.

[68] Haynes' memorandum to H. L. Kerwin, March 14, 1921, RG 280, 170/1365.

It is not so difficult to determine the motives of Richard E. Parker, a notorious anti-union propagandist. Parker admitted that in 1916 he had distributed 20,000 handbills to "All Colored Working Men in the Stockyards," warning them not to "Join Any White Man's Union." He claimed that he had paid for these himself because of his "personal interest" in his race; but he also acknowledged that he had gone to the South in 1916 while working for several packing and steel companies, and had "imported more Negroes than any man in Chicago." Parker edited a newspaper in which he advised black workers not to join the established unions but to join the American Unity Labor Union, which he had founded and of which he was business agent. A card from his union, he boasted, would secure employment for Negroes in the building trades, steel mills, and stockyards. Parker was a demagogue and he was doubtless on the payroll of employers, but he might also have been working in the race's interest, as he perceived it. Because "the Negro happened to be born black," he wrote, "the Unions have labelled him inferior." As a result, they barred him not only from membership but also from apprenticeships and the chance to secure work in skilled jobs. "For this reason we formed the American Unity Labor Union," for we could expect "fairness from no local."[69]

Above all, it was conflict between the white rank and file and their black counterparts that retarded unionization. Labor historians have wasted much energy debating the A.F.L.'s attitudes toward black workers, when the truly bitter, and functional, racial animosities were not at the national but at the shop level. Unions have too often directed their recriminations at anti-union Negroes, rather than conceding their own inability to control the racial hatreds of white members. Evidence of racial conflict at the shop level is scarce and difficult to find, but it is extant; and in few places was such conflict more pervasive than in the stockyards in 1919, where just a month before the race riot there was a series of spontaneous walkouts, all racially inspired.

"Well, are you going to join or not," the smokehouse floor steward impatiently asked the black worker. "No, I would rather quit than join the union." "If you don't join tomorrow, these men won't work with

---

[69] R. E. Parker to President Harding, March 11, 1921, in *ibid.;* Parker to Harding, March 14, 1921; and to Secretary of Labor Davis, March 14, 1921, RG 174, 8/102-F; *Pittsburgh Courier,* March 22, 1917, copy in NAACP Papers, Library of Congress, C-438; *Chicago Tribune,* March 13, 1921; *Negro in Chicago,* 422-23; Spero and Harris, *op. cit.,* 272-73.

you." "Fuck you." "God Damn you." Then the black man drew a knife
from the pocket of his overalls. "He was big enough to eat me . . . ,"
the floor steward recalled, so "I called for help." The union men,
"practically all of them are in the union except . . . these three colored
fellows," came to his assistance. It was after this encounter that the
white men in the smokehouse walked out, declaring that they could no
longer work with non-union blacks. Similar confrontations were occur-
ring simultaneously in various shops at the yards. Leaving dead hogs
hanging on the conveyor belt or after only partially dressing the beef,
hundreds of workers informed their foremen that black men on the
floor were non-union, and that they would not return until these men
were discharged or made to join the union.[70]

"We are paying the union and wearing the buttons," one member
complained, "and they are getting just as much." Other members
echoed this resentment. "Fuck the Union," a black worker had reportedly told one of them. "I am making as much money as you are.
What is the use of joining the Union?" Another grievance was that
Negroes allegedly received preferential treatment, such as not being
docked for reporting late or punished for stealing meat.[71]

Negro as well as white members accused certain black men who used
abusive language and incited violence of being anti-union agitators.
The only task of "Heavy" Williams, they said, was to bring new workers
from the company employment office to the cattle-killing floor, and "he
brings up all non-union men and keeps the non-union men from joining
the union." " 'Let me tell you,' " he would instruct the new men,
" 'when they get after you about this union, don't you join it. . . . You
stay out. If you don't you won't be here long.' " Williams also fought
with whites, among them "Tubs," whom he threatened to "split open"
with a meat cleaver. Williams had been a union member; so had Joseph
Hodge, until a black friend of his had been hit over the head with a
blunt instrument. Hodge continually cast such vicious and obscene slurs
at the union that whites warned that he would "agitate a race riot or
perhaps . . . get killed." Another anti-union Negro stabbed a white
man on the killing floor after damning the union and branding black
union men "a lot of bastards," "a lot of white folks' niggers."[72]

---

[70] Alschuler Hearings, June 20, 1919, 1-83, 110-11; June 21, 303-45, 382-86; June 23,
    511-13, 546-47, 550, in RG 280, 33/864.
[71] *Ibid.*, June 20, 114, 176-77, 180; June 21, 307, 389.
[72] *Ibid.*, June 20, 148-82; June 21, 220-40, 258-99; June 23, 426.

Negroes frequently replaced striking whites in the stockyards that summer. In the hair house, for example, the all-white union of spinners struck, and Negroes from various other departments were recruited to fill their jobs. Few whites in the yards could have been unaware of the strike; for, as one man reported, "at the noon hour these colored men are looking out of windows and doors, and these [white] men come out for lunch, and . . . it creates a dis-harmony and hard feelings among the races. . . ."[73] It was also a fact, however, that sometimes Negroes who joined unions were also discharged.[74]

Organizers and black workers had difficulty communicating with each other, and this was a major cause not only of friction but also of the unwillingness of Negroes to unionize. Numerous floor stewards and union committeemen spoke English poorly, if at all. How, a non-English-speaking Polish steward was asked by an interpreter, did he expect to explain the benefits of unions to black workers. He did not even try, he said, but there was a Negro committeeman who "talks the best way he can." Well, then, did he instruct the Negro committeeman? "I don't tell him nothing," he replied. "They have got to get it for themselves."[75]

A Negro who did not "get it," however, would have "it made hot for him," with his "face pushed in" or bricks hurled at him. Frustration as well as racial bitterness provoked these acts of violence. "When I was coming in [to work]," recounted a Negro, "6 or 7 or 8 Polocks grabbed a colored fellow out there, and carried him on the [union] wagon, and said 'you son-of-a-bitch, you will join the union,' and made him go up, and one had him by this arm, and the other by this arm, and one fellow had him by the neck. . . ."[76]

Black resistance—and, with it, interracial abuse and violence—only mounted in the weeks before the riot. "Fuck the union, fuck you in the [union] button," raged a black worker. Knives and revolvers proliferated on both sides. 'If I catch you outside I will shoot you," a Negro warned an insulting committeeman. Yet the unions became even more aggressive. "Where is your button?" demanded an organizer. "I ain't got none on," was the angry reply, "but [if I did] I would put it on the end of my prick.'"[77]

[73] *Ibid.,* June 20, 182-86.
[74] *Ibid.,* June 23, 525-30.
[75] *Ibid.,* June 20, 103-4.
[76] *Ibid.,* June 21, 241, 320-22; June 23, 476-78.
[77] *Ibid.,* June 21, 220, 249-58, 345; June 23, 392-93, 493-505, 511-13, 534-36.

Union leaders claimed that there was no racism involved in this bitterness—that it was simply a labor matter. But it was obviously much more than that by late July 1919; the two were inseparably fused. The Irish, Polish, Lithuanian, and other workers who clashed with Negroes in other spheres of human relations had their racial antagonisms reinforced if not initiated at the stockyards and in other industries. Labor in Chicago, moreover, was possessed of an intense class consciousness; anyone who was not with it was against it—and the black workers were notoriously not with it. The hostility was so intense that, as in 1905, hatred of Negro "scabs" could be generalized into hatred of an entire race.[78] The factors retarding unionization—Negro distrust of unions and white workers, the economic advantages to be accrued as non-union workers, the manipulation of black workers by management, and, above all, the hatred of black workers by whites arising from racial antipathy and conditioned by strikebreaking and by other anti-union acts—left a legacy of twenty-five years of violence and helped produce a bloody race riot in 1919.[79]

---

[78] *Ibid.,* June 20, 83-92, 92-94, 131. Ray Stannard Baker called Chicago in 1919 the most class-conscious city in the nation, and that year it was second only to New York in numbers of strikes and workers affected by industrial unrest: Baker, *The New Industrial Unrest* (Garden City, N. Y., 1920), 112; and Edson L. Whitney (comp.), "Strikes and Lockouts in the United States, 1916, 1917, 1918, and 1919," *Monthly Labor Review,* X (June, 1920), 1509.

[79] Certain contemporary observers of the racial violence in 1919, among them Mary White Ovington, A. Philip Randolph and Chandler Owen of *The Messenger,* Graham Taylor, Walter White, Dr. Roscoe C. Giles, Dr. George E. Haynes, and James Weldon Johnson, felt that labor conflict was not only a major cause of the Chicago riot but perhaps the major cause: see Miss Ovington to J. R. Shilladay, August 11, 1919, and to Bolton Smith, August 15, 1919, in the N.A.A.C.P. Papers, in the possession of Kenneth Brown, Regional Youth Director of the N.A.A.C.P., Washington, D. C.; in *ibid.,* White's "Notes on Chicago . . . ," September 17, 1919; *Brooklyn Daily Eagle,* August 25, 1919; *Brooklyn Standard Union,* August 25, 1919; *Boston Herald,* November 10, 1919; *Buffalo Express,* August 25, 1919; Report from Director, Division of Negro Economics, to Secretary of Labor, September 12, 1919, in RG 174, 8/102-E; *The Messenger,* II (September, 1919), 11-21.

5

The Wilson Administration and the Wartime Mobilization of Black Americans, 1917-1918

JANE LANG SCHEIBER and HARRY N. SCHEIBER

The national reform laws that were enacted during the first Wilson Administration, from 1913 to 1917, were the achievements of a lily-white progressivism. For the black man, the years of the New Freedom were barren of achievement or even hope. A few measures, such as the LaFollette Seaman's Act and the move toward child-labor controls, peripherally touched Black America. But black voters had deserted their traditional Republican allegiance and supported Woodrow Wilson in the 1912 election because he had promised them far more. Wilson said in the 1912 campaign: "Should I become President of the United States they may count on me for absolute fair dealing and for everything by which I could assist in advancing the interests of their race in the United States."[1] Booker T. Washington had declared his faith that "Mr. Wilson is in favor of the things which tend toward the uplift, and improvement, and advancement of my people." *The Crisis,* journal of the National Association for the Advancement of Colored People, welcomed the evidence of "at least 100,000 black votes" for Wilson in 1912, because he had declared "his willingness to deal fairly with the Negroes"; and even such militant leaders as William Monroe Trotter,

---

[1] Quoted in Kathleen Long Wolgemuth, "Woodrow Wilson's Appointment Policy and the Negro," *Journal of Southern History,* XXIV, No. 4 (November 1958), 457. See also Arthur S. Link, *Wilson: The Road to the White House* (Princeton, 1947), 501ff.; Henry Blumenthal, "Woodrow Wilson and the Race Question," *Journal of Negro History,* XLVIII (January 1963), 4-5; and Link, "The Negro as a Factor in the Campaign of 1912," *ibid.,* XXXII (Jan. 1947), 81-99.

JANE LANG SCHEIBER *is a former Woodrow Wilson Fellow in History at Cornell University and has served as a research associate in the Public Affairs Center of Dartmouth College.* HARRY N. SCHEIBER *is a Professor of History at Dartmouth College.*

editor of the Boston *Guardian,* and William E. B. Du Bois had thrown their energetic support behind Wilson during the campaign.[2]

By the end of Wilson's first administration, however, the premises on which black people had predicated their support in 1912 had been thoroughly shattered. As indicated in the careful historical studies by Kathleen Long Wolgemuth, Constance M. Green, Arthur S. Link, and others, the President's policies proved detrimental to black men's interests in nearly every respect. Even the tokenism which had been so diligently pursued by the Republicans (and indeed by Grover Cleveland in the only other Democratic presidencies since the Civil War) was now abandoned in the matter of patronage appointments. Positions in the federal bureaucracy traditionally given to deserving Afro-American party workers went to whites instead; and diplomatic posts, such as the ministry to Haiti, similarly were awarded to white men where blacks had formerly been given these few plums. When such men as Trotter, who had helped mobilize the 1912 black vote for Wilson, sought to counsel him on patronage appointments, they were spurned; and the President cut himself off from his liaisons with the black community. When Wilson did propose the appointment of a few prominent Afro-Americans to high Federal offices, six months after he became President, southern racist leaders in Congress—among them, James K. Vardaman, Hoke Smith, and Ben Tillman—mobilized an extremist opposition; and then Wilson backed down.[3]

Black Americans' failure to obtain political patronage on accustomed lines was a disappointment to them, and doubtless it cost Wilson nearly all his support among the black leadership and the spokesmen for the N.A.A.C.P. Even so, the President could conceivably have held his gains among rank-and-file black voters had he not compounded this record by condoning a calculated, humiliating extension of segregation in the federal offices and bureaus, both in Washington and in the field. The Post Office Department, headed by a Texan, Albert S. Burleson, in-

---

[2] Washington quoted in *The New York Times* (hereafter cited *NYT*), March 2, 1913, sec. ii, 2; editorial, *Crisis,* V (December 1912), 75; Link, "Campaign of 1912," 87. Trotter, a Harvard graduate, had founded the *Guardian* in 1901, largely to combat the accomodationist ideas of the Booker T. Washington-Tuskegee leadership group. See Francis L. Broderick and August Meier, *Negro Protest Thought in the Twentieth Century* (New York, 1965), 25ff.

[3] *NYT,* May 4, 1913, sec. ii, 13; Wolgemuth, "Woodrow Wilson's Appointment Policy," 458ff.; Wolgemuth, "Woodrow Wilson and Federal Segregation," *Journal of Negro History,* XLIV (April 1959), 159-173; Constance McLaughlin Green, *The Secret City: A History of Race Relations in the Nation's Capital* (Princeton, 1967), 171-177; "Democracy and Fair Play," *The Independent,* LXXV (Aug. 21, 1913), 426.

augurated Jim Crow window service. The Treasury and Navy Departments—headed, respectively, by cabinet secretaries William G. McAdoo and Josephus Daniels, both southerners—adopted a stated policy of segregating white from black employees in their Washington headquarters; they also mandated separate restrooms and transferred numerous personnel in order to "correct" situations in which a black superior might be supervising white people, especially white women.[4] McAdoo, other cabinet members, and indeed the President himself issued explanatory statements justifying the new segregation practices on grounds that they would eliminate damaging racial friction—for which, in fact, there was no sound evidence—and would promote the good of black as well as white workers![5] By late 1913, these moves by Cabinet members and subordinate officers in the departments had run their course. There were a few isolated efforts later to adopt new discriminatory practices; and though nothing was done to redress the segregationist innovations of 1913, at least most of these later measures were reversed.[6]

The result was thorough disillusionment with the Wilson Administration on the part of Afro-Americans. In the 1916 *Republican Campaign Text-Book,* Henry Lincoln Johnson drove the point home: "The persistent aim of the Democratic Party [since 1913] has been to eliminate and humiliate the Negro"; and, citing chapter and verse, Johnson documented the decline in employment of blacks, department by department, and the fact that generally only menial jobs were available to them.[7] Black leaders privately declared that there was a southern-led "damnable conspiracy" to shut out their people from American political life.[8]

The 1916 election returns confirmed the loss of Wilson's support

[4] Wolgemuth, "Wilson and Federal Segregation," *passim;* also, a petition of 10,000 black citizens, in New York *Evening Post,* Nov. 6, 1913; *ibid.,* Dec. 16, 1913, Nov. 13, 1914; *The Nation,* XCIX (Nov. 19, 1914), 595; Link, *Wilson: The New Freedom* (Princeton, 1956), 243ff.

[5] Wilson quoted in Link, *op. cit.,* 251; see also *Literary Digest,* Nov. 28, 1914, p. 1,052, quoting the New York *World,* generally a pro-Administration paper, assaulting claims of racial friction; and the attack on Wilson's "resort to evasive rhetoric" by the Boston *Transcript,* quoted *Evening Post,* Nov. 18, 1914, 6.

[6] See *Evening Post,* Dec. 1, 1914, 12; Washington *Bee,* Aug. 19, 1916, Sept. 9, 1916; "Segregation in the Departments," *Harper's Weekly* LIX (Dec. 26, 1914), 620-21; Link, *Woodrow Wilson and the Progressive Era* (New York, 1954), 66.

[7] Johnson, "The Negro Under Wilson," *Republican Campaign Text-Book, 1916* (Washington, 1916), 376ff. See also *Crisis,* XIII (Nov. 1916), 4.

[8] Robert Bruce to Charles W. Anderson, June 17, 1916, Bruce Papers, Schomburg Collection, New York Public Library. Some black spokesmen saw little hope for regaining their previous status even if the Republicans were returned. See *Crisis,* XII (Oct. 1916), 268.

among the black voters. Although his Republican opponent, Charles Evans Hughes, did not receive unqualified endorsement from Afro-American leaders, he took most of the black American vote from Wilson. Typical of views expressed during the campaign was a retrospective analysis in the *Crisis* in December 1916. "Mr. Wilson," the editors asserted, "was still the representative of the southern Negro-hating oligarchy and [he] acknowledged its leadership." The demands of the N.A.A.C.P. and other spokesmen—that Wilson and candidates for Congress take a stand on the rising incidence of lynching in the South, on securing "equal opportunity in public office and public service," on reapportionment of seats in Congress, on peonage labor practices in the South, on segregation in interstate transport, and the like—had gone largely unanswered. Replying to the N.A.A.C.P., Wilson instructed his secretary only to write that the President "stands by his original assurances [of 1912]"; he could say "with a clear conscience that he has tried to live up to them, though in some cases his endeavors have been defeated."[9]

This laconic letter to the N.A.A.C.P.—not even written over Wilson's own signature—signified the President's indifference to the black vote and to the black leadership. Had he not led the nation into war three months later, Afro-Americans probably would have faced four more years of unconcern and evasion in their dealings with the White House and with Federal officialdom. But as this essay will seek to demonstrate, the nation's entry into the war dramatically changed the Wilson Administration's attitude toward Black America.

During the war years, Wilson and his war Cabinet took initiatives to re-establish liaison with the black leadership; they abandoned, in large part, the posture of arrogant indifference to Afro-Americans that had prevailed during 1913-16; and they met in some degree—to say "halfway" would be to exaggerate—the demands of black spokesmen, reversing a few of the most objectionable policies of the first administration. The new posture of the Administration was strictly a wartime measure: what emerged, in effect, was a policy for mobilization of black manpower in aid of the war effort—nothing more.

As soon as America entered the war in April, rumors began circulating that the Germans were undertaking propaganda efforts among black

---

[9] *Crisis,* XIII (Dec. 1916), 59; N.A.A.C.P. circular letter, *ibid.* (Nov. 1916), 17ff.; Wilson, in *ibid.* (Dec. 1916), 84.

Americans, especially in the South. Several alleged German agents were arrested only a few weeks after Congress approved the war resolution; and the Justice Department charged publicly that German propagandists in the Deep South were encouraging Afro-Americans to desert the cotton fields and coal mines, and to migrate to Mexico.[10] This propaganda had absolutely no effect on black Americans. But it was hardly implausible to fear that any efforts the Germans made might succeed. For among the white majority of the population, there were many leaders—old-line progressives, spokesmen for the advanced social-justice movement, and militant left-wing labor spokesmen—who publicly denounced Wilson's interventionist war policy, who threatened to oppose conscription and other war measures, and who persisted in their opposition despite new repressive legislation to put down dissent.[11] The pacifists included among their number several members of the N.A.A.C.P. Board of Directors.[12] If a phalanx of respectable whites, including half a dozen United States Senators, could threaten national unity in wartime, how much more reason there was for black Americans to refuse cooperation in prosecuting a war. For they had long suffered systematic discrimination by the majority population, and now by the Wilson Administration itself as well.

Nevertheless, the traditional accomodationist leaders, associated with the Tuskegee and Hampton Institutes, were quick to declare the unswerving loyalty of their race as the nation moved toward war.[13] The response of the more militant elements remained in doubt until May 1917, when the N.A.A.C.P. held a national conference of its branches and of delegates from other Afro-American organizations. The resolutions adopted—though tracing "the real cause of this world war to the despising of the darker races by the dominant groups" of colonial powers—urged "colored fellow citizens to join heartily in this fight for eventual world liberty, . . . to enlist in the army, to join in the pressing work of providing food supplies, to labor in all ways by hand and

---

[10] *NYT*, April 7, 1917, 7; April 9, 1917, 2; April 13, 1917, 6; Aug. 27, 1917.
[11] Harry N. Scheiber, *The Wilson Administration and Civil Liberties, 1917-1921* (Ithaca, N. Y., 1960); H. C. Peterson and Gilbert C. Fite, *Opponents of War, 1917-1918* (Madison, 1957); and Donald Johnson, *The Challenge to American Freedoms* (Lexington, Kentucky, 1963), all treat wartime dissent and the Administration's repression of war opponents. See also John Higham, *Strangers in the Land* (New Brunswick, N. J., 1955).
[12] Charles Flint Kellogg, *N.A.A.C.P.: A History of the National Association for the Advancement of Colored People, Volume One: 1909-1920* (Baltimore, 1967), 248-249.
[13] *NYT*, April 6, 1917, 11; Emmett J. Scott, *Scott's Official History of the American Negro in the World War* (Chicago, 1919), 42.

thought in increasing the efficiency of our country." Even while thus extending its support to the government, the conference admitted "deep sympathy with the reasonable and deep-seated feeling of revolt among Negroes at the persistent insult and discrimination to which they are subject." Furthermore, the delegates declared: "Absolute loyalty in arms and in civil duties need not for a moment lead us to abate our just complaints and just demands." Among these demands were enumerated the right to serve as enlisted men and officers, to vote, to enjoy educational opportunity, and to have protection against lynching and Jim Crow practices. Pointedly linking the struggle at home with worldwide democracy, the conference insisted that "neither the world nor America can be happy and democratic so long as 12 million Americans are lynched, disfranchised, and insulted."[14]

The themes struck at this May 1917 conference were to characterize the position taken by most Afro-American leaders during the ensuing war period. They advocated loyalty, but also insisted on fair treatment of their race at home. Equally important, they were optimistic that the situation of their race was bound to improve as a result of the "war for democracy" in Europe. The conviction that the war would improve conditions at home did much to sustain Afro-Americans' support of the war effort and may well have served to negate the effects of German propaganda. Most of the leadership agreed with the sentiment voiced in the N.A.A.C.P. annual report for 1916:

> If thousands of American black men do fight in this world war, . . . then who can hold from them the freedom that should be theirs in the end? Or if, on the other hand, they do not fight in actual battle, they will take up the economic burden [on the home front]. . . . In either case their significance will be tremendous.[15]

For the more militant black leaders, there was yet another reason to urge participation in the war effort; for if they took up arms, black men would "learn the fighting game and cease to be so 'aisily lynched.' "[16] While the leaders were formulating their position on the war-partici-

[14] *Crisis,* XIV (June 1917), 59.
[15] For similar expressions, see E. J. Scott to Rosenwald, April 7, 1917, in Scott, *Official History,* 43; *Crisis,* XIV (Aug. 1917), 165; address of H. B. Frissell, principal of Hampton Institute, in *NYT,* April 13, 1917, 6; and Earl E. Thorpe, *The Mind of The Negro* (Baton Rouge, La., 1961), 206.
[16] *Crisis,* XIV (June 1917), 61-62. That this was a possibility was not lost on Negrophobic southerners, some of whom opposed drafting blacks for military service. See *Crisis,* XIV (May 1917), 23; *ibid.,* XIV (June 1917), 61; *ibid.,* XV (Dec. 1917), 79.

pation issue, hundreds of thousands of Afro-Americans demonstrated their loyalty by mass patriotic rallies and by volunteering for service or answering draft calls. Thus the blacks, in this as in every American war since the Revolution, were in the vanguard when the nation called its citizens to the colors.

In the early months of American intervention, Wilson and other high Federal officials took this loyalty for granted, it seemed; at any rate, they made few gestures to cultivate or acknowledge such support from the black community. In mid-April, for instance, Wilson declined to join "the Colored American Citizens" of Washington in a mass patriotic rally when invited by Pastor J. Milton Waldron of the city's Shiloh Baptist Church. Waldron told Wilson that men of his race were "loyal citizens"; yet he felt it necessary to warn the President that "not many of them are enthusiastic in support of yourself." An appearance by Wilson, Waldron declared, would help in persuading black Americans to begin in earnest to undertake "the duty of carrying on the war." But on this occasion as on many others in future months, Wilson did not appear interested in addressing Afro-Americans face to face. Confiding to his secretary that Waldron's letter "puzzled" him, Wilson finally responded to the pastor that his letter was "the first notice I had that many of the members of the colored race were not enthusiastic in the support of the Government in this crisis"—yet he was confident there was no need for a statement of "sweeping character."[17]

Whether the President's "puzzlement" was genuine or in fact disingenuous in April 1917, events soon forced the White House and the Cabinet to confront and re-evaluate government policies of deep concern to black Americans. First, there was a controversy over segregation of Army troops being raised under conscription laws, and a related debate over the desirability of training and commissioning black officers. Then, there arose a series of issues respecting the use of Afro-Americans by the Red Cross and other agencies. On July 2, 1917, a disastrous and bloody race riot at East St. Louis led to demands—which the President failed to heed—that the federal government intervene to overcome the manifest failure of local authorities to protect black residents. Afro-American newspapers were quick to point out the in-

---

[17] Waldron to Wilson, April 12, 1917; Wilson to Tumulty, n. d. (attached); and Wilson to Waldron, April 19, 1917, File VI-152, Woodrow Wilson Papers, Manuscripts Division, Library of Congress.

consistency of a "war to save democracy" with what was transpiring on the streets of a major American city; and indignation, rallies, and marches by black people attracted wide attention to the leadership's demands for Federal action.[18] A small minority of militants now took a hard line: the Rev. Adam Clayton Powell, Sr., for example, asserted that his people should withhold support from the war effort until they had been assured that civil rights would be extended to them, and the "property and lives of the members of our race" protected.[19]

The Wilson cabinet also came under heavy pressure from black leaders who demanded representation in the policymaking and administrative councils of the government. As the war went on, Federal agencies found it necessary to organize special programs to mobilize the support of black Americans—who comprised more than 10 percent of the nation's population.[20] Meanwhile, the Afro-American leaders kept up unremitting pressure for federal laws or Executive Orders to require private business and labor unions to extend equal rights; and they demanded government action to counteract racial violence—especially the lynching of black men in the South. Though the Wilson Administration responded only gradually at first, by the autumn months of 1917 it began to react on a broad front to demands from the black community.

The first manpower-policy issue to be raised concerned mobilization for the armed services. Secretary of War Newton D. Baker faced a bewildering array of problems respecting Afro-Americans. Should they serve in the Army, and if so in what capacity? Should the traditional Army policy of segregation be upheld? In what sections of the country should black Americans be trained? And what could be done to minimize racial friction and to handle any controversies arising from racial questions?

When war was declared in April 1917, there were four Negro units

---

[18] Elliot M. Rudwick, *Race Riot at East St. Louis, July 2, 1917* (Cleveland, 1966), 65 *et passim;* Roscoe E. Lewis, "The Role of Pressure Groups in Maintaining Morale among Negroes," *Journal of Negro Education,* XII (Summer 1943), 464.

[19] Powell, quoted in *Crisis,* XIV (July 1917), 138. See also statement of 3,200 members of Powell's Harlem congregation, in *NYT,* July 9, 1917, 7; and W.E.B. Du Bois, *Dusk of Dawn* (New York, 1940), 246.

[20] One government intelligence report of 1918 noted: "The cooperation of this large element of our population in all civilian and military activities is of vital importance; the alienation, or worse, of eleven million people would be a serious menace to the successful prosecution of the war." (Memorandum, J. E. Spingarn to Col. Churchill, July 22, 1918, File A.G. 291.21, Office of Adjutant General Records, R.G. 94, National Archives.)

in the regular army and eight in the National Guard.[21] Black volunteers brought these existing units to full strength within a week; then the War Department suspended further enlistments by black men until Congress and the Department could decide upon further action regarding organization of black troops. Afro-American spokesmen became "anxious to learn what if any part the Negro will be permitted to take in this War. . . . It is beginning to look as if the Negro will, as a burglar, have to break into this War," as one leader wrote.[22] They received a tentative answer when the Selective Service Law was enacted on May 18. Secretary Baker had already gone on record as being opposed to any bill which would "prevent the enlistment or reenlistment of people of the colored race in the military service."[23] In Congress, however, sentiment was sharply divided. In framing selective service legislation, some northern Congressmen wished to include provisions outlawing discrimination against blacks in the draft, though perpetuating segregated Army units; but racist southerners took another line, with Vardaman of Mississippi opposing universal conscription on grounds that "millions of Negroes who will come under the measure will be armed, [and] I know of no greater menace to the South than this."[24] The conscription bill as passed made no mention of race, though it did require each state to contribute men in proportion to total population, regardless of exemptions—in effect requiring any southern states where local draft boards might exclude black recruits to conscript a compensating number of whites. But the system of segregating Army units was perpetuated.[25]

---

[21] These were the 9th and 10th Cavalries and the 24th and 25th Infantries of the Reglaur Army; and the 8th Illinois and 15th New York Regiments, the Separate Battalions of the District of Columbia and of Ohio, and separate companies of the National Guards of Connecticut, Maryland, Massachusetts, and Tennessee.

[22] George A. Myers to E. H. Baker, May 4, 1917, George A. Myers Papers, Ohio Historical Society (Columbus); *Crisis*, XIV (June 1917), 61, 85; Scott, *op. cit.*, 34. The *Tulsa Star*, June 22, 1917, complained that, having been denied the right to volunteer, Negroes were being conscripted without being able to choose which branch of service they wanted. (Clipping, Wilson Papers, File VI-4107).

[23] Baker to Sen. Thomas Taggart, Aug. 30, 1916, in Washington *Bee*, Sept. 9, 1916. Cf. Daniel R. Beaver, *Newton D. Baker and the American War Effort, 1917-19* (Lincoln, 1966), 224-231.

[24] Quoted in *Crisis*, XIV (May 1917), 23; also *ibid.*, XIV (June 1917), 61, an editorial declaring that "these Bourbons and Copperheads know that if Negroes fight well they will get credit for it."

[25] Kellogg, *op. cit.*, 252. According to Tasker H. Bliss, assistant to the chief of staff, a provision that "white and colored enlisted or enrolled men shall not be organized in or assigned to the same company, battalion, or regiment" was "in line with the existing policy of Congress." (Memorandum for Adj. Gen. of Army, April 14, 1917, Report #13186, General Staff Records, R. G. 165, National Archives.) On September 1, 1917, The *New York Times* reprinted an order to local draft boards from the Adjutant General requiring them to note "white" or "colored" opposite the names

Determined to serve as officers, and not merely in the ranks, several highly educated Afro-Americans applied for admission to the officers' training camp opened at Plattsburgh before the U. S. entry into the war.[26] When they were denied admission, many N.A.A.C.P. and other spokesmen for the black community demanded a segregated training camp for black officers. Although this was controversial—to many, it seemed a capitulation to the segregation principle—Du Bois and others justified the proposal on grounds it was the only realistic hope for getting Afro-American officers commissioned.[27] In Army circles, there was considerable opposition to even this proposal: for instance, the chief of the Army War College Division, viewing the use of black officers as "more of a political than a military question," still put forward his professional opinions that black officers could not be placed in charge of white troops (a view that "requires no argument"), and further that "our colored citizens make better soldiers if commanded by white officers. . . ."[28] Secretary Baker resisted such pressures, however; and after conferring with black spokesmen and N.A.A.C.P. leaders, he approved in May the establishment at Des Moines, Iowa, of a segregated facility for officers' training. The issue was thus "settled wisely," Baker said, "from the point of view of the army, and certainly . . . of the colored men."[29] In October, the first group of 639 black officers was commissioned, and all were assigned to segregated units.

The War Department still needed to decide on the mode of organization and the training of black draftees. During the summer months of 1917, several alternatives were considered: using all the draftees in special service and engineering units; "utilization of a large number of the quota in providing cooks"; and creation of an additional (10th) infantry regiment "of colored men and colored company officers" in each of the sixteen divisional areas of the National Army, with the remainder of black men drafted to be held for use in line-of-communi-

of men certified for service "in order to provide for the segregation of races in the regiments . . . and to arrange for compliance with State laws requiring the races to travel in separate coaches."

[26] *Crisis*, XII (Oct. 1916), 299-300; Robert S. Beighter, "The Record of the Negro in the Armed Forces of the United States and the Evolution of Armed Forces Policy in regard to Negro Personnel" (M.B.A. thesis, Ohio State University, 1950).

[27] On the officers' camp controversy, see Kellogg, *op. cit.*, 250-256; *Crisis* XIII (April 1917), 270-272; *ibid.*, XIV (June 1917), 60-61; John Hope Franklin, *From Slavery to Freedom* (2nd edition, New York, 1956), 448-449; Scott, *op. cit.*, 82-90.

[28] Brig. Gen. J. E. Kuhn, Memorandum for Chief of Staff, May 6, 1917, Report #13290, General Staff Records.

[29] Baker to Woodrow Wilson, May 17, 1917, Wilson Papers, File VI-152.

cation troops.[30] It was this last alternative, for creation of new regiments, that was recommended by the War College Division and approved by Secretary Baker.

But Baker soon came under pressure from southern state governors, who wanted him to adopt a policy against stationing any black units in the South, or permitting any integration of southern training camps. The agitation came to a head in mid-August, when a racial incident involving black regular army troops in Houston, Texas, resulted in several deaths. Court-martial convictions and death sentences were meted out to thirty black soldiers, and another forty were given life imprisonment.[31] The Houston riot intensified pressures from the southern governors, and Baker ordered that no further black troops be called up until a policy on their location for training could be determined.[32]

The N.A.A.C.P. and the Afro-American newspapers expressed grave concern over the suspension of call-ups and other Administration policies. In this situation, Baker convened a special conference of "men interested in the Negro question, most of them educators," on August 31, 1917.[33] The result of the conference was War Department approval, in early September, of plans to create a segregated combat division, and to permit black conscripts to volunteer for auxiliary services.[34] As to the location for training of black troops, General Tasker Bliss announced that "instead of concentrating all of the colored men in the few cantonments of the Southern States, the policy . . . will be to distribute them more or less evenly throughout all of the sixteen national army cantonments."[35] The new combat division—the famous Ninety-Second —was officially activated in October 1917; but its various units were never assembled until they reached France for combat service. Mean-

---

[30] Brig. Gen. Kuhn, Memorandum for Chief of Staff, July 31, 1917, Report #13568, General Staff Records.

[31] Kellogg, *op. cit.*, 261; Baker to Wilson, Aug. 22, 1918, and enclosures, Wilson Papers, File VI-152; *NYT*, Aug. 24, Aug. 25, 1917. Wilson subsequently commuted the death sentences of ten of the convicted men. Thirteen, however, were summarily (and probably illegally) hanged in December 1917. See E. A. Schuler, "The Houston Race Riot, 1917," *Journal of Negro History*, XXIX (July 1944), 300-338; Kellogg, *op. cit.*, 261-262.

[32] This was done at the recommendation of General Bliss, who said that further "racial trouble" would result if recruitment of Afro-American registrants was not suspended. (Bliss to Baker, Aug. 24, 1917, Report #13568, General Staff Records.)

[33] *NYT*, Sept. 1, 1917.

[34] Tasker Bliss, Memorandum for Adj. Gen., Sept. 8, 1917, Report #13568, General Staff Records.

[35] Quoted in *NYT*, Oct. 10, 1917.

while, black contingents of the National Guard were trained with the rest of their units in the same camps, despite the southern governors' objections.

Troop segregation, location of training facilities, and provision of an officer corps were the most prominent questions—but not the only ones —that required War Department action during the early months of war. During the first weeks of recruiting in April, many black Americans had objected to an Army regulation requiring information of race on recruitment applications. Furthermore, National Guard units were called up with instructions that in effect required assignment of black servicemen to service units (such as stevedores in the quartermaster corps, communications units, etc.)—thus preventing their being assigned to the combat divisions that were being formed.[36] In addition, some local draft boards were found to be discriminating against black men; and from the Army came many complaints that black troops were given inferior equipment and made to suffer personal indignities to which white recruits were not subjected. The Navy was not admitting Afro-Americans except as messmen; and blacks were barred altogether from the Marine Corps, from medical units in all services, and from the Army's air arm. "Up to the present," a *Crisis* editorial declared, offers of service had been received "with sullen and ungracious silence."[37]

Secretary Baker's decision to form the 92nd Division for combat and to continue integration of southern training camps was followed later in 1917 by other liberalizations of War Department policy that were responsive to some of these grievances. The Medical Corps began to accept physicians and supportive medical personnel from among black volunteers, specialized army training camps (including several in the South) were gradually integrated, and graduates of the segregated Des Moines officers' training camp were assigned to command all-black units.[38]

---

[36] Sara Brown to Wilson, May 30, 1917, Wilson Papers, File VI-152; George A. Myers to E. H. Baker, May 4, 1917, Myers to Newton Baker, July 22, 1917 and reply, Aug. 1, 1917, Myers Papers; Memorandum from the Adjutant General, Aug. 7, 1917, Report #13368, General Staff Records; Memorandum from Gen. Kuhn, July 31, 1917, *ibid.* In addition to voicing the grievances cited in the text, above, the Negro press responded angrily to the retirement for "medical reasons," which were deemed highly questionable, of the Army's highest ranking black American officer, Col. Charles Young; see Beaver, *op. cit.*, 225.

[37] *Crisis*, XIV (June 1917), 61; also *Tulsa Star*, June 22, 1917, clipping in Wilson Papers, File VI-4107, Robert Moton to Wilson, July 7, 1917, *ibid.;* Kellogg, *op. cit.*, 257.

[38] Commissions for the Des Moines-trained officers had been delayed pending the decision

The War Department's record on troop segregation and discrimination reflected Baker's desire to meet demands from the black community so far as appeared possible—but it also reflected the Secretary's view that "this is not the time to raise the race question" with a view toward any permanent solution either in the army, or in the nation.[39] The concessions that Baker made during 1917-18 were substantial—the acceptance of blacks into specialized units, integration of some training facilities, dismissal of draft-board personnnel who were blatantly discriminatory, the decision to form black combat units, etc. The *Crisis* responded to Baker's personal efforts with a laudatory editorial in December 1917, asserting he had not done "everything we could wish, but he has accomplished so much more than President Wilson or any other member of this administration that he deserves all praise." The editorial admitted that "we are segregated, but that was according to a foolish law for which the Secretary was not responsible."[40]

And yet there were many practices that continued unabated: the general pattern of segregation in formation of units, the public assertions (given wide coverage in the press) by white officers that Afro-American combat troops lacked courage and were overrated as fighting men; discriminatory practices in granting leaves and providing recreational facilities; and, not least, continued resistance to any integration in the services other than the Army.[41] In sum, then, the War Department under Baker, despite opposition from within the Army's officer corps and from Congress, moved far toward adopting policies being demanded from the N.A.A.C.P. and other spokesmen. Its policy concessions were

---

as to organization and assignment of black draftees. (Adj. Gen. to Secretary of War, Sept. 4, 1917, copy, Report #13290, General Staff Records.) See also T. W. Hammond, Memorandum for the Chief of Staff, with accompanying documents, Nov. 2, 1917, *ibid.*; N.A.A.C.P. *Annual Report, 1917,* 9ff; *NYT,* Oct. 10, 1917, 4; Charles H. Garvin, "The Negro in the Special Services of the U. S. Army," *Journal of Negro Education,* XII (Summer 1943), 335ff.; Beighter, "Record of the Negro in the Armed Forces," 12ff.

[39] "After we have succeeded in the great objective of this war would be a more appropriate time to raise questions of changing existing army customs than now." Baker to Wilson, April 17, 1917, Wilson Papers, File VI-4013. In November 1917 Baker wrote to Scott on the same lines, arguing that the War Department could not be expected to solve all America's racial problems. The full letter appears in the U. S. Committee on Public Information's *Official Bulletin,* Dec. 4, 1917.

[40] *Crisis,* XV (Dec. 1917), 61-62; see also L. D. Reddick, "The Negro Policy of the U. S. Army, 1775-1945," *Journal of Negro History,* XXXIV (1949), 20ff.; Garvin, "Special Services," 335ff.; George E. Haynes, *The Trend of the Races* (New York, 1922), 113ff. Scott's *Official History* is the fullest source on the black in military service during the war. Edward M. Coffman, *The War to End Wars* (New York, 1968), 58-72 *et passim* is also important.

[41] J. H. Franklin, *op. cit.,* 447-468.

no doubt important to the government's success in mobilizing Afro-Americans for military service, and in partially blunting the potentially demoralizing effects of the various discriminatory practices which were continued.

As part of his efforts to expedite mobilization for the war effort and to ease racial friction, Baker appointed in October 1917 a Special Assistant who would: "advise in matters affecting primarily the interests of colored draftees and colored soldiers, as well as to render counsel and assistance in those matters, including the interests of soldiers, families, and dependents, and, in a sense, the morale of Colored Americans generally during the war."[42] Emmett Scott—an Afro-American who had long been closely associated with Booker T. Washington, was an officer of Tuskegee Institute, and was a moderate accommodationist in his racial views—was named to the new post. Scott's office was then the only one in the Federal government, other than a Division of Racial Groups in the Bureau of Education, specifically concerned with racial aspects of departmental affairs.[43]

According to Scott's own account, he enjoyed Secretary Baker's full cooperation when he assumed the role of advocate within the War Department for the black troops. He visited training camps to ascertain conditions and boost morale, investigated complaints from individuals and groups, and initiated action by Baker against several draft boards in the South that discriminated against black registrants. Scott also conducted a protracted and frustrating campaign to force the Surgeon General's Office to employ black physicians and nurses.[44]

It was probably no surprise to those who knew his moderate views that Scott became a faithful and often uncritical servant of the war effort. Thus, when he convened a conference of Afro-American editors in June 1918, at the request of George Creel (who headed the U. S. propaganda machine), he said:

> This is not the time to discuss race problems. Our first duty is to fight, and to continue to fight until this war is won. Then we can adjust the problems that remain in the life of the colored men. This is the doctrine we are preaching to the Negroes of the country.[45]

---

[42] Scott, *op. cit.*, 50; also, Kellogg, *op. cit.*, 258. Such an appointment had been suggested by Robert Moton in August. (Scott, p. 41.)
[43] *Negro Status and Race Relations in the United States, 1911-1946*, Report of the Phelps-Stokes Fund (New York, 1948), 46.
[44] Scott, *op. cit.*, *passim*.
[45] Quoted in *NYT*, July 7, 1918.

But Scott spoke directly to the President in much stronger terms. Reporting on the editors' conference, he informed Wilson that influential men of "divergent views on many matters of racial interest and national policy" had affirmed their loyalty to the government and their intention to support mobilization until victory was won. He also spelled out in full, however, a resolution adopted for private circulation by the conferees, to the effect that "justifiable grievances of the colored people are producing not disloyalty, but an amount of unrest and bitterness which even the best efforts of their leaders may not be able always to guide unless they can have the active and sympathetic cooperation of the National and State governments." German propaganda, they declared, was powerless, "but the apparent indifference of our Government may be dangerous."[46]

In conveying this resolution, Scott urged the President to issue a public statement "addressed to colored Americans generally," giving his support to the black leadership's activities in the war effort. But Wilson responded with silence. Then, as throughout the war, Wilson was unwilling to make any formal statements that would seem to ally him with black leaders—perhaps because to do so would identify him with their demands for racial equality as *quid pro quo* for their wartime efforts.

Even though Wilson refused to speak on the basic issue that troubled black Americans, Scott was given a fairly free hand in organizing Afro-American war efforts through both governmental and voluntary agencies. Scott worked closely with the Committee on Public Information (C.P.I.), headed by Creel, to maintain liaison between the propaganda officers of the government and the Afro-American press. He also developed ties with the numerous voluntary black agencies formed to extend hospitality to Afro-American soldiers in the training camps; to aid their families and dependents; to develop special (segregated) programs through the YMCA, the Red Cross, and other agencies; and to coordinate voluntary with governmental efforts in all war-related fields of activity. By Scott's own admission, many of these efforts fell short of obtaining the full cooperation that he expected, and of extending to black troops the same comforts and recreational outlets as white soldiers enjoyed. But at the very least, the presence of a highly placed Afro-American in Secretary Baker's office must have aided greatly in

---

[46] Scott to Wilson, June 26, 1918, Wilson Papers, File VI-152.

gaining access to training camps for black voluntary organizations."
   One program organized at Scott's initiative resulted in Federal fund-
ing of vocational programs for more than 3,000 soldiers on training
assignment at thirteen Negro colleges. In addition, Scott organized the
Students' Army Training Corps (S.A.T.C.), which gave special grants
to schools and colleges for vocational instruction. The S.A.T.C. also
undertook academic instruction designed to qualify applicants for the
Army's officer-training camps. These programs, however, typified the
accommodationist "Tuskegee" approach: they were restricted to schools
and colleges which already followed a policy of enrolling black students, and the emphasis was largely on vocational training in the
"practical arts."[48]
   Although the War Department was the first to appoint a high official
with special wartime duties relating to black Americans, several of the
government agencies engaged in the equally important task of manpower mobilization on the home front soon followed suit. In May 1918,
the Secretary of Labor, mindful of the fact that Afro-Americans comprised one-seventh of the nation's work force, and aware of the social
frictions being generated by mass migration of black workers to the
North during the war, created an office of Director of Negro Economics.[49] Appointed to this post was Dr. George E. Haynes, a professor of
sociology and economics at Fisk University. As director, Haynes organized "cooperative committees of white and colored citizens in the
States and localities where problems of Negro labor arise." He also developed a public-relations campaign "to create good feeling between
the races"; and he built up a staff of Afro-American appointees who
coordinated Labor Department activities with State and local organizations—especially those concerned with tasks of "mobilizing and sta-
bilizing Negro labor for winning the war."[50] Racially integrated ad-
visory committees in several states brought several hundred black

[47] Scott, *op. cit.*, 428-437, 442-447 *et passim*. Since such service organizations as the Red
      Cross and the YMCA had the official authorization of the government to perform
      these tasks at military installations, blacks were particularly irate at instances of
      discrimination. See Carroll L. Miller, "The Negro and Volunteer War Agencies,"
      Journal of Negro Education, XII (Summer 1943), 438-451.
[48] Scott, *op. cit.*, 329ff.
[49] Estimates of the numbers involved in the black migration northward range up to one
      million, but the Labor Department placed the figure at 400,000 to 500,000. The
      migration had been closely related to the race riots that occurred during 1917 in East
      St. Louis, and in Philadelphia and Chester, Pa., and in Newark, New Jersey. See
      U. S. Labor Department, *Negro at Work*, 10-12; Emmett J. Scott, *Negro Migration
      during the War* (New York, 1920); and Henderson H. Donald, "The Negro Migra-
      tion of 1916-1918," *Journal of Negro History*, VI (Oct. 1921), 383-498.
[50] U. S. Labor Dept., *Negro at Work*, 12-13.

Americans into research and action on problems of Afro-American labor. A few of the state committees undertook liaison with the U. S. Employment Service to open job opportunities to blacks; and in Ohio the committee exerted pressure on manufacturing firms to improve substandard housing maintained for black workers, and it claimed to have improved considerably the attitude of employers generally toward black job applicants and employees. Haynes' own office collaborated with the U. S. Civil Service Commission to expedite screening and hiring of Afro-Americans; and Haynes also obtained appointment of several black people to represent Afro-Americans' interests in several Labor Department bureaus. Like Scott in the War Department, however, Haynes attempted reforms strictly from within the Wilson Administration, and his task was wholly war-oriented—that is, designed to aid mobilization. Haynes' public attitude was epitomized in a July Fourth address in 1918, read to more than a million black people at patriotic rallies: "Do not forget that any person, black or white, who does not work hard, who lags in any way, who fails to buy a Liberty bond or a War Savings stamp, if he can, is against his country and is, therefore, our bitter enemy."[51]

Measured by white workers' acceptance of black co-laborers, or by the labor unions' attitudes, the gains made by the black worker during the war were slim indeed. Thus, while Haynes' efforts no doubt contributed to morale, the substantial gains for his race were few. One scholar, appraising the Labor Department's efforts to aid in mobilization of the black worker, goes further and says the main accomplishment was to excite false hopes.[52]

The Food Administration, like the Labor Department, established special offices concentrating on mobilization of the black community. A Negro Press Section set up within the Administration's press department publicized the need for food production and conservation, and provided informational materials for use by organizers of war rallies held for black farm workers. Food Administrator Herbert Hoover expanded his agency's activity by organizing as well special field office programs, first in Alabama and then in the South generally, to work with black farmers and workers. From September 1918 to January 1919, Ernest T. Atwell served as national director of a Negro Section of

---

[51] Quoted in *ibid.*, 137-138; see also *ibid.*, 19ff, 105, *et passim.*
[52] Leon A. Ransom, "Combatting Discrimination in . . . War Industries and Government Agencies," *Journal of Negro Education*, XII (Summer 1943), 407.

the Food Administration; his office coordinated activities down the administrative line to the local level, through Negro State Directors and county deputies. Even more than in the Labor Department, however, the purposes of these activities were exhortative—to urge black people to work harder, to produce more, and to help win the war. There was no emphasis on reform.[53]

The publicity efforts of the Food Administration and other agencies were undertaken in close collaboration with George Creel's Committee on Public Information. The C.P.I., which engaged hundreds of journalists, advertising men, and academic people—and which organized special programs to appeal to nearly every interest group in American society—missed few opportunities to seek Afro-Americans' support of the war effort. Like other agencies, the C.P.I., too, eventually appointed a black American to undertake special tasks. The June 1918 conference of black journalists, for example, was formally organized under Scott's jurisdiction in the War Department, though Creel and the C.P.I. were the initiators behind the scenes. As Creel wrote to Wilson before the conference, its purpose was "to get a working agreement and an organization" that would "take care of" the morale problems being created by "rumor and ugly whisperings" about Army and government treatment of Afro-Americans.[54] Creel learned during the conference itself that the editors were deeply concerned over information filtering back from France—information that black units were suffering discrimination, were being used almost exclusively as shock troops, and were being slandered by their white officers. Soon afterward, Creel appointed Ralph W. Tyler, a Columbus, Ohio, journalist and Republican party worker, to report on the morale and welfare of black soldiers in Europe. Ironically, Tyler had been forced out of a Federal office (as Auditor of the Navy) when Wilson succeeded Taft in 1913. Now, Tyler became a C.P.I. journalist stationed overseas, and most of his reports—at least those published—followed the government's official line, asserting that in the Army in France "men's racial identity is not considered" and denying charges of maltreatment.[55]

---

[53] *Crisis*, XV (April 1918), 293; *ibid.*, XVI (May 1918), 9; "Notes for County Food Administrators," MS., Wilson Papers, File VI-152; Scott, *Official History*, 355ff., 362-364. Atwell had been business manager of Tuskegee Institute for 15 years.

[54] George Creel to Wilson, June 17, 1918, Wilson Papers, File VI-152.

[55] Scott, *Official History*, 293, 324; Scott to Joseph Tumulty, Oct. 23, 1918, Wilson Papers, File VI-152. During the Taft Administration, Tyler had set up a Colored Press Bureau in Washington, an organization supported by the Republican Party. (Herbert

The policy of appointing Afro-Americans to relatively high-level government posts did not always have the desired effect of unifying the black population behind the war effort. This was so largely because of divisions within the black leadership itself. When the Army Intelligence Bureau offered an officer's commission to W. E. B. Du Bois, for example, it provoked great controversy. As editor of *Crisis,* the N.A.A.C.P. journal, Du Bois had been steadily critical of segregationist policies, but he had still supported wartime cooperation by black people. Now he declared himself willing to accept the Army commission if the N.A.A.C.P. board retained him as *Crisis* editor. But this evoked a storm of criticism from the Afro-American press, which questioned how the editorial integrity of *Crisis* could survive such an arrangement. Finally, the Army withdrew its offer.[56]

Even sharper controversy surrounded the government's appointment of Dr. Robert R. Moton, president of Tuskegee and acknowledged successor to Booker T. Washington as leader of the accommodationists, to investigate conditions among black troops in France following the November 1918 Armistice. The more militant leaders had little confidence in Moton; and he confirmed their worst expectations when he made a widely publicized address to black troops counselling them to return home "as you have carried yourselves over here—in a straightforward, manly, and modest way." This advice could be translated, as Ralph W. Tyler noted, as meaning "come back with your tail between your legs."[57] In light of the notorious Army treatment of black troops at the time (they had been excluded from the Paris victory parade, they were confined closely to encampments "to prevent men coming in contact with white women," and their units were kept busy with constant drilling until being returned home), this adventure of Moton's brought down upon both him and the government the wrath of critics who perceived a transparent accommodationist tactic.[58]

Aptheker, ed., *A Documentary History of the Negro People in the United States,* vol. II [New York, 1964], 848.)

[56] Elliott M. Rudwick, "W. E. B. DuBois in the Role of *Crisis* Editor," *Journal of Negro History,* XLIII (July 1958), 227; Kellogg, *op. cit.,* 273-274.

[57] Moton quoted in Franklin, *op. cit.,* 461; Ralph W. Tyler to George Myers, Jan. 26, 1919, Myers Papers. In 1917, Moton had triggered an outraged reaction when he advised Southern black workers to remain where they were, and not migrate to the North seeking better jobs. (*Crisis,* XIII [Jan. 1917], 139.)

[58] Black troops and their treatment in France are discussed at length in W.E.B. Du Bois, "The Negro Soldier in Service Abroad during the First World War," *Journal of Negro Education,* XII (Summer, 1943), 324-334; the Army order confining troops to

In sum, the appointment of a few black leaders to government positions was pursued largely as a policy of co-optation—absorption into the system of an aggrieved group's spokesmen to eliminate or appease "potential sources of opposition."[59] This tactic may have blunted the edge of criticism: at least it was a departure from the blatantly exclusionist and lily-white policies of 1913-1916. But certainly the government's success in gaining black support in both civilian and military mobilization was, in the end, much more the result of an independent decision made by the black community to cooperate wholeheartedly in the war effort. In large part, that decision was a result of deeply-felt patriotism. But patriotism was coupled with hope—expressed best, perhaps, in the famous June 1918 "Close Ranks" editorial in *Crisis*—that a record of important contributions to the war effort would help win the battle against discrimination at home after the war.[60]

Neither President Wilson nor the majority of his Cabinet—the main exception was Newton D. Baker—proved willing to encourage such hopes with explicit statements of appreciation or support. In effect, Wilson asked the black American for cooperation despite pre-existing and continuing racial grievances; yet he never committed himself or his Administration to relieving the unjust conditions in which black Americans lived.

---

camp is quoted in *ibid.*, 328; see also Benjamin E. Mays, "Veterans—It Need Not Happen Again," *Phylon*, VI (1945), 205-206. Kellogg, *op. cit.*, 274-275, reports Du Bois's attack on Moton for his statements in France, and also for Moton's alleged refusal to accept an invitation to participate in the Paris Peace Conference because he "hurried home to attend a Tuskegee conference" instead. In fact, Moton did indicate his willingness to address the peace conference on the problem of the black race, after being invited by Colonel House; but he said that he would not do so unless President Wilson was prepared to support his views. Wilson promptly declined Moton's offer! (Newton D. Baker to Wilson, Feb. 28, 1919, and reply, March 1, 1919; Stanley King to Moton, March 21, 1919, Newton D. Baker Papers, Library of Congress.)

[59] As co-optation is defined in Philip Selznick, *TVA and the Grass Roots* (reprint edition, New York, 1966), 217.

[60] An editorial in the August 1917 issue of *Crisis* (XIV, 165), asserted: "Never again are we going to cope with the same conditions and the same social forces that we have faced in the last half-century. . . . It is [the Negro's] business actually to put himself into the turmoil and work effectively for a new democracy that shall know no color. The first method of doing this is, of course, to take part in the war. . . ." In December 1917, another *Crisis* editorial (Vol. XV, 77) declared: "The tide against the Negro . . . has been turned, and . . . we may expect to see the walls of prejudice gradually crumble." Dr. Kenneth B. Clark later wrote: "It appears that the pattern of morale was to a large extent determined by a high concentration of positive hope and expectancy in the consequences of an allied victory. The Negro felt that such a victory would improve his condition in America." (Clark, "Morale of the Negro on the Home Front," *Journal of Negro Education*, XII [Summer, 1943], 423.) See also Guion G. Johnson, "The Impact of War Upon the Negroes," *ibid.*, X (July 1941), 606-607; and R. E. Clement, "Problems of Demobilization and Rehabilitation of the Negro Soldier," *ibid.*, XII (Summer 1943), 536-537.

There were unusual opportunities to do something for the black American when the abrupt centralization of emergency Federal power during 1917-18 led to nationalization of the railroads and to a vast extension of governmental control over industry and labor. The Wilson Administration had an opportunity to move dramatically to aid Afro-Americans in the basic matter of personal safety, too, when the white population directed an increasing mob violence against black people and when, during the war period, individual lynchings reached new proportions. But these opportunities passed without substantial action by the government.

A few gains were made by black workers when the railways came under Federal control. Under Secretary McAdoo and Walker Hines, the Railroad Administration imposed a new policy of equal wages for white and black labor on the same jobs—a policy which benefitted the Afro-American so long as there was a labor shortage and the railroads had to hire black men. But the same policy proved a two-edged sword immediately after the Armistice; for then the railroads, acting with the approval of Federal authorities, began to exclude black workers from the train crews in the absence of the earlier incentive to engage Afro-Americans because their labor came cheaper. Of more enduring positive significance was the Railroad Administration's decision to bargain with the organized black employees of the Pullman Company, which had long resisted unionization.[61] Yet the Railroad Administration also acknowledged that the "abstract principle of equality" was "irreconcilable" with the "realities [of] racial prejudices"; and so this Federal agency accepted the separate-but-equal policy in its passenger operations. Although facilities for Afro-Americans were upgraded in stations and on trains, the Railroad Administration deferred to Jim Crow laws in the southern states that mandated segregation of passengers. Nor were black men in military uniform or government officials travelling on Federal war business exempted from Jim Crow rules! All this was perpetuated despite the legal opinion rendered by a Railroad Administration counsel that the Federal agency had the implicit constitutional power to overrule the states' segregationist laws and informal codes.[62]

---

[61] Sterling D. Spero and Abram L. Harris, *The Black Worker* (reprint edition, New York, 1968), 295-305; Walker D. Hines, *War History of American Railroads* (New Haven, 1928), 169; Brailsford R. Brazeal, *The Brotherhood of Sleeping Car Porters* New York, 1946), 6-20; William G. McAdoo to E. T. Atwell, Nov. 21, 1918, U. S. Railroad Administration Records, File P19-3, National Archives.

[62] The legal opinion of Judge Payne is in MS Extract of Minutes, Conference of Nov.

In addition, the Federal railroad authorities continued an earlier policy of the private companies—adopted to stem the flow of black migration northward—of refusing to sell prepaid tickets in northern ticket offices for use on one-way trips from the south. The ban on such sales was continued until June 1919, when the N.A.A.C.P. obtained Senator Warren Harding's aid in overturning it.[63]

What seemed even less defensible, however, was the Federal government's failure to eliminate discriminatory practices in the hiring and management of its own employees. Afro-Americans continued to be assigned mainly to menial jobs; they were segregated in most Federal offices; and the "last hired, first-fired" rule prevailed, as they found when they did obtain white-collar jobs, for black secretarial and clerical workers were often discharged without cause if white applicants came forward. Though a handful of prominent black men had been appointed to high posts, there was no thorough-going effort to reform internal management practices nor any overturning of the established pattern of race relations in the civil service.[64]

The continuing humiliations and reverses suffered by black workers in the war period did not create much difficulty for the government's mobilization efforts. No doubt this may be attributed partly to the prospect of repressive action if black militants had adopted a tactic of anti-war opposition. Had such a move occurred, had Afro-American leaders counselled resistance to the draft or to involvement of their people in war industries, probably such spokesmen would have suffered the same suppressionist counter-measures as the government did take, in fact, against the I.W.W., the Socialists, and other organized op-

---

21, 1918, Railroad Administration Records; see also W. D. Hines to McAdoo, May 26, 1918, and McAdoo to Atwell, Nov. 21, 1918, *ibid*. Pressure on the Wilson Administration from black spokesmen to abolish discriminatory practices in railroad operations began from the moment the government seized the railroads; see A. Grimke and others to Wilson, telegram, Dec. 27, 1917, Wilson Papers, File VI-152; and *Crisis*, XV (Feb. 1918), 164.

[63] H. E. Davis, memorandum of complaints of N.A.A.C.P., endorsed by Senator Harding, June 5, June 16, 1919; Edw. C. Niles to Harding, June 12, 1919; Max Thelen, Memorandum and Instructions, July 25, 1919, all in Railroad Administration Records.

[64] There was no increase in the percentage of Afro-Americans among total civil service workers, despite a rise in Federal civil service employment of black people from 20,000 in 1912 to 45,000 in 1918. On the civil service, see Ransom, "Combatting Discrimination," 408-409; *Crisis*, XIV (July 1917), 114; *ibid.*, XV (March 1918), 249; Mary Church Terrell, *A Colored Woman in a White World* (Washington, 1940), 252-255; National Equal Rights League to Wilson, May 3, 1917, and National Race Congress to Wilson, Oct. 1, 1918, Wilson Papers, File VI-152(A); Thomas N. Roberts, "The Negro in Government War Agencies," *Journal of Negro Education*, XII (Summer 1943), 372.

ponents of the war.[65]

But cooperation by Afro-Americans was not based solely on fear. For despite inequality of treatment, hope still persisted. "If the colored citizens of this country seize this opportunity to emphasize their American citizenship for effective war activities," a *Crisis* editorial asserted in May 1918, "they will score tremendously. When men fight together and save together, this foolishness of race prejudice disappears." The same month, even the militant Chicago *Defender* editorialized that "out of this great struggle may come industrial and civil freedom. . . . The colored soldier . . . will hardly be begrudged a fair chance when the victorious armies return." Similarly, James Weldon Johnson predicted in the *New York Age* that "the indirect results of the war will be a fuller realization of democracy for all the submerged races and classes of the world." A Hampton Institute official declared that a black American who proved his loyalty during the war crisis could not any longer "be put off with the crumbs that fall from a rich man's table."[66] And Du Bois' famous *Crisis* article urging his people to "Close Ranks" with the whites appeared as late as July 1918, when angry disillusionment over the treatment of black combat troops in France had already begun to compound disaffection over treatment of their brethren at home.

The first sign that such high hopes were misguided appeared early in the war, with the East St. Louis riot of July 1917. The riot itself was part of an intensifying pattern of violence directed against Afro-Americans, given new impetus by reactions in the North to the mass migration of black workers. (In 1916, there had also been nearly sixty lynchings recorded, mainly in the South.) Events at East St. Louis brought home to Afro-Americans that the northern industrial cities were no haven against violent assaults or lawless killing: East St. Louis foreshadowed the terrifying Washington and Chicago riots of 1919.[67] But the Federal government's response to East St. Louis was no less prophetic of future

[65] See works cited in note 11, *supra*, for data on the repression of dissident white groups. In the Spring of 1918, the Justice Department cautioned Du Bois that criticism of the government by *Crisis* was harming the war effort, and could bring suspension of mailing privileges under the Sedition Act. (Rudwick, "Du Bois as *Crisis* Editor," 226.) The black journal *Messenger*, a Socialist organ, was denied mailing privileges and its editors sentenced to jail terms. (Franklin, *op. cit.*, 467.)

[66] *Crisis*, XVI (May 1918), 7; Johnson and a Hampton Institute official, quoted in Charles H. Wesley, "The Negro Citizen in Our Wars for Freedom," *Negro History Bulletin*, VII (Jan. 1944), 84, 93; the *Defender*, in Lester M. Jones, "The Editorial Policy of the Negro Newspapers of 1917-1918," *Journal of Negro History*, XXIX (Jan. 1944), 24-25.

[67] Rudwick, *East S. Louis*, *passim*; Allan D. Grimshaw, "Lawlessness and Violence in America . . .," *Journal of Negro History*, XLIV (Jan. 1959), 52-72.

events: despite angry pressures for action, President Wilson himself again stood aloof, treating the problem of violence, as one black leader charged, "as a regrettable phase of social pathology, to be treated with cautious and calculated neglect."[68]

With the intensification of violence—an estimated 140 to 222 black Americans died at the hands of mobs during the war—disaffection and militancy developed new impetus in the black community.[69] Although the Afro-American periodicals continued to preach cooperation, white progressives and black spokesmen alike besieged the White House with letters and telegrams urging that lynching be made a Federal crime and that Wilson speak out against such atrocities. But in February 1918, the Justice Department advised the President that there was no constitutional basis for Federal anti-lynching laws; nor, it ruled, were lynching incidents "connected with the war in any such way as to justify the action of the Federal Government under the war power."[70]

Wilson turned his back on pleas that he invoke the moral power of the Presidency against lynching by making a public address. He responded to pleas that he speak out either by ignoring them or by making vague promises of "seeking an opportunity" to say something.[71] By early summer of 1918, as German propagandists stepped up a campaign to create discontent among black Americans, Wilson had begun to come under pressures from within his Cabinet to take a stand on lynchings and violence. Newton Baker warned Wilson that there was "more unrest among [Negroes] than has existed before for years"; and Attorney General Thomas W. Gregory, a Texan, himself denounced lynching in a speech of June 1918, and privately urged Wilson to speak out.[72] A high-ranking Army intelligence officer who had been a founder of the N.A.A.C.P. recommended in July the immediate enactment of a Federal anti-lynching law based on the constitutional war powers, "to

---

[68] Open letter from Dean Kelly Miller, Howard University, to President Wilson, Aug. 4, 1917, Wilson Papers, File VI-152. In contrast to Wilson's stand, Congress undertook a full investigation of the riots.

[69] Memorandum, J. Spingarn to Col. Churchill, July 22, 1918, Military Intell. Branch Report, #10996-36, cited in Fn. 20, *supra*.

[70] J. R. Shillady to Jos. P. Tumulty, Feb. 18, 1918, Wilson Papers, File VI-543. This same file contains dozens of telegrams urging Wilson to speak out, or to sponsor an anti-lynching bill in Congress.

[71] James Weldon Johnson, *Along This Way* (New York, 1933), 324; Wilson to Robt. Moton, June 18, 1918, in Ray S. Baker, *Woodrow Wilson: Life and Letters* (New York, 1927-1939), VIII, 218.

[72] Baker to Wilson, July 1, 1918, Wilson Papers, File VI-152; Gregory, quoted in *Crisis*, XVI (June 1918), 71; Gregory to T. H. Franklin, Aug. 17, 1918, Thomas W. Gregory Papers, Library of Congress.

cope with the danger which the growth of unrest and dissatisfaction among colored people involves with respect to the successful prosecution of the war."[73] When Wilson finally did concede, and made a public statement in July deploring mob violence, he made no specific mention of the racial dimension—and in any event, this was to be the last time he would make such an appeal, despite the wave of new lynchings and urban riots in the ensuing months.[74]

The demobilization which followed the November 1918 Armistice brought only further travails for black Americans. Wilson gave them no representation on a special council (which did little in any event) formed to consider post-war demobilization of industry; and, absorbed with the Paris Peace Conference, he was a silent bystander when Afro-Americans endured blatant discrimination from private employers and, worse, during the riots and lynchings of 1918-19. The black soldier returned to find the Ku Klux Klan revitalized, denial of suffrage and residential segregation remaining as before, and a gathering of racial and political tensions that led to the "Red Summer" of 1919. In one year, seventy-seven blacks were lynched, including several soldiers in uniform; and twenty-six American cities, including Washington and Chicago, suffered race riots.[75] Once more, President Wilson responded to appeals that he take a public stand against these events with vague statements and assurances that he was "thinking the matter over."[76]

Few Afro-American leaders had been as realistic as one militant who said: "I have had no illusions on the subject of democracy for the Black and colored races after the war, for I have not seen anything to indicate that those who have the power to establish the principle, have any wish or intention to extend its blessings and benefits." But those men who had continued to hope for democracy recognized soon enough that their faith was illusory; and many found themselves moving toward this same spokesman's position when he said that "equality

[73] Memorandum, J. Spingarn to Col. Churchill, cited note 69, *supra;* also, Spingarn's testimony before the Committee on the Judiciary, House of Rep., 65th Cong., 2nd Sess., *Hearings* on H. R. 11279, 3-4. One Army intelligence officer attributed Wilson's statement on lynching directly to fear of the situation being caused by German propaganda among Afro-Americans. (Testimony of Capt. George Lester, reported in *NYT*, Dec. 15, 1918.)

[74] Scheiber, *Wilson Administration,* 50-51; *NYT,* July 27, 1918; see also Johnson, *Along This Way,* 323-324; and N.A.A.C.P. to Wilson, July 25, 1918, Wilson Papers, File VI-543.

[75] Du Bois, *Dusk of Dawn,* 263-264. For a full analysis of the riots, see Arthur I. Waskow, *From Race Riot to Sit-In, 1919 and the 1960s* (New York, 1966).

[76] Wilson to J. E. McCulloch, Aug. 18, 1919, Wilson to Moton, Aug. 12, 1919, Wilson Papers, File VI-543; other telegrams to Wilson are in File VI-152, *ibid.*

is not obtained by gift but by struggle."[77] For if the war had not basically
changed American society's racism, it had changed the Afro-American.
Having heard so long the slogans of a holy war for democracy, having
witnessed at first hand a society, in France, free from racial discrimination, and despairing now of concessions from a Federal government
that no longer required their services, returning black soldiers were
ready to follow Du Bois as he proclaimed: *"We return. We return from
fighting. We return fighting."*[78] As for the black laborer on the home
front, "the effect of the war . . . was to create in him new aspirations
for higher standards of living" and a desire "for some of the real, substantial things of American democracy," asserted Dr. George Haynes of
the Labor Department in December 1918: "Negroes . . . seek this as
part of the democracy for which they have shared their possessions,
their labor and their blood. . . . They are coming to believe in themselves as men and women to whom the blessings of the world are to
come, and by whom the enjoyment of these blessings are to be shared."[79]
The Afro-American press, which underwent a swift expansion following the war, was unanimous in denouncing injustices and nearly unanimous in advocating self-defense in the face of racial violence.[80] Assess-
ing the new militancy that prevailed in the press, the Justice Department found a "dangerous spirit of defiance and vengeance at work
among the Negro leaders, and, to an ever-increasing extent, among their
followers"—language typical of the government's increasingly rigid
response to black demands as the flames of prejudice were fanned during the Red Scare of 1919.[81]

But whether conservative or militant, nearly every black American
must have shared the feelings of Emmett J. Scott, who had sought to
work from within the government to promote racial justice. "As one
who recalls the assurances of 1917 and 1918," Scott said in retrospect,
"I confess personally a deep sense of disappointment, of poignant pain
that a great country in time of need should promise so much and afterward perform so little."[82]

---

[77] Address, n.d. but 1919, Bruce Collection.
[78] *Crisis,* XVIII (May 1919), 13-14.
[79] Haynes, "Effect of War Conditions on Negro Labor," *Proceedings of the Academy of
Political Science,* VIII (1918-20), 308-310. On emergence of the "new Negro," see
Spero and Harris, *op. cit.,* 385ff.
[80] Robert T. Kerlin, *The Voice of the Negro, 1919* (New York, 1920), 11, 23.
[81] "Investigation Activities of the Department of Justice," 66th Cong., 1st Sess., *Sen.
Doc.,* XII (May 19-Nov. 19, 1919), 162, 187.
[82] Scott, Address, Oct. 3, 1933, quoted in Pittsburgh *Courier,* Oct. 7, 1933, clipping in
Scott File, Schomburg Collection.

6

Closed Shop and White Shop: The Negro Response to Collective Bargaining, 1933-1935

RAYMOND WOLTERS

According to President Franklin D. Roosevelt, the purpose of the National Industrial Recovery Act was to put people back to work at wages that would provide more than a bare living. The crucial point in inducing recovery was thought to be the expansion of purchasing power, and the preamble of the legislation declared that the economy would be invigorated by "increas[ing] the consumption of industrial and agricultural products by increasing purchasing power."

The legislation authorized a wide range of governmental activity, and one of the most important aspects of the new program was its effort to encourage the development of trade unions. Several important New Deal advisers believed that without the countervailing power of well-organized unions the excess supply of labor would put workers at a serious disadvantage when bargaining with employers, with the result that the wage earners' real income would not be large enough to sustain the mass purchasing power that would stimulate recovery. It was felt that by encouraging collective bargaining the government would enable workers to wrest higher wages from management and that the resulting increase in consumer spending would benefit the entire economy. Accordingly, Section 7a of the National Industrial Recovery Act provided

> 1) that employees shall have the right to organize and bargain collectively through representatives of their own choosing, and shall be free from the interference, restraint or coercion of employers of labor, or their agents, in the designation of such representatives . . . .
> 2) that no employee and no one seeking employment shall be required as a condition of employment to join any company union or to refrain from

RAYMOND WOLTERS *is an Assistant Professor of History at the University of Delaware.*

joining, organizing, or assisting a labor organization of his own choosing. . . .[1]

Yet it soon became apparent that there was much disagreement as to the meaning of collective bargaining "through representatives of their own choosing." Labor leaders such as John L. Lewis insisted that President Roosevelt wanted workers to join independent unions, but many businessmen noted that the legislation had not specified the manner in which representatives were to be chosen, and they sought to comply with the terms of Section 7a by establishing company unions. Almost from the beginning of the NRA experiment, it was apparent that Section 7a did not ensure labor's right to organize independent unions. Determined employers were able to avoid meaningful negotiation with outside unions.[2]

Historians and economists often have assumed that all wage earners would have benefited if the NRA had supported collective bargaining more enthusiastically and had provided adequate legislative protection of the workers' right to organize in independent unions. Yet insofar as Negro workers are concerned, this assumption is questionable. The great majority of Negro wage earners were members of the working class, but during the early years of the New Deal Negroes were rarely found in the ranks of organized labor. Altogether in 1930 there were at least nineteen independent unions which excluded Negroes from membership, either by constitutional provision or by initiation ritual. An additional ten unions admitted Negroes to membership only in segregated auxiliary locals. Of course these were only the more blatant examples of union discrimination. Many unions prohibited Negro membership by tacit consent, while others permitted only token membership. Still others—perhaps a majority—discriminated against colored workers in more subtle ways. While admitting that it was impossible to determine exactly the number of Negro trade union members, the

[1] "Presidential Statement on NIRA," *The Public Papers and Addresses of Franklin D. Roosevelt,* (New York, 1938-1950) II, 251. *United States Statutes at Large,* XLVIII, 195. See the following for some representative examples of New Deal thinking with regard to collective bargaining: Hugh Johnson, *The Blue Eagle* (New York, 1935), 334-350; testimony of Donald Richberg, United States House of Representatives, *Hearings Before the House Committee on Ways and Means,* 73rd Congress, 1st Session, 68-69; testimony of Robert F. Wagner, *ibid.,* 105. Irving Bernstein has written perceptively on the formulation of *The New Deal Collective Bargaining Policy* (Berkeley and Los Angeles, 1950). *United States Statutes at Large,* XLVIII, 195.
[2] Arthur M. Schlesinger, Jr., *The Coming of the New Deal* (Boston, 1959) chapter 9. Irving Bernstein, *op. cit.,* chapters 3 and 4.

N.A.A.C.P. felt it was "safe to say that there were in 1930 no more than 50,000 colored members of national unions," and almost half of these were members of the Brotherhood of Sleeping Car Porters. These colored union members represented about 3 percent of the 1,500,000 Negroes engaged in transportation, extraction of minerals and manufacturing in 1930 (compared with a figure of about 10 percent for all non-agricultural American workers).[3]

From its inception the A.F.L. showed little enthusiasm for the task of organizing unskilled, industrial workers. Indeed, some writers have interpreted the emergence of the A.F.L. and the decline of the Knights of Labor in the late 1880s and early 1890s as the turning point which "marked the triumph of craft individualism over industrial brotherhood." Although the A.F.L. occasionally issued statements concerning the need to organize the mass-production industries, it had not made a major attempt in this direction since the abortive steel strike of 1919. During the 1920s membership in the Federation's largest industrial unions declined precipitously, and this reinforced the general impression that the Federation represented only those skilled workers who composed the "aristocracy of labor." During the early years of the Depression several federal labor unions were chartered for the express purpose of organizing mass-production industries, but these federal unions were largely unsuccessful, and they did not receive enthusiastic support from A.F.L. headquarters; Horace Cayton and George Mitchell expressed the skepticism of most Negroes when they noted that "the national office did nothing until its position became so paradoxical that some gesture was necessary to prevent a new union movement. . . ."[4]

---

[3] Herbert Northrup, *Organized Labor and the Negro* (New York, 1944) 2-4. Sterling D. Spero and Abram L. Harris, *The Black Worker* (New York, 1931) 58, 85-86. Irving Bernstein, *op. cit.*, 84. Herbert Hill, "Labor Unions and the Negro," *Commentary*, XXVIII (December, 1959) 482. N.A.A.C.P. Office Memorandum, "The Negro and Trade Unions," n.d. N.A.A.C.P. Files. National Urban League, *Negro Membership in American Labor Unions*, 1930 pamphlet in Urban League Files. Interdepartmental group concerned with the special problems of Negroes, "Report on Negro Labor," NA RG 48.

[4] Sterling Spero and Abram Harris, *op. cit.*, 53. Norman Ware, *The Labor Movement in the United States, 1860-1895* (New York), *passim*. Irving Bernstein has written that union membership, which rose to slightly more than 5,000,000 in 1920, fell to less than 3,500,000 by 1930. By this later date union members constituted only 10.2 percent of the 30 million nonagricultural employeees counted in the census, compared with 19.4 percent in 1920. "A significant feature of labor's decline in the 1920's is that it struck especially hard at organizations that were either wholly or predominantly industrial in structure. . . . At the same time many craft unions either held their own or made gains." Membership in the largest industrial unions, the United Mine Workers, the International Ladies Garment Workers, and the Amalgamated Clothing Workers of America, declined from a total of about 670,000 in 1920 to 150,000 in

Since a disproportionately large number of Negroes were either semi-skilled or unskilled workers, it was inevitable that they would play a minor role in craft unions. Of the 825,000 Negroes employed in manufacturing industries in 1920, Spero and Harris calculated that only 16.6 percent were skilled workers; 67.9 percent were laborers, and 15.5 percent were semi-skilled. The percentages for white workers were 32.4 skilled, 19.1 semi-skilled, and 48.5 laborers. Thus, if skill was to be made the prerequisite for trade union membership, less than one-third of the Negro workers, and only slightly more than half of the whites, were eligible for organization. Statistics such as this convinced the National Urban League that there was "little hope for the black worker so long as [the A.F.L.] remains structurally a craft organization."[5]

The effects of race prejudice and the craft system of organization were compounded further by the large degree of independence which the A.F.L. gave its constituent members. The A.F.L.'s official declarations that all workers should be organized without regard to race, creed, or color were ineffectual, because authority in matters of membership and participation was left in the hands of the local union. Thus, while the A.F.L. itself barred racial discrimination in union membership, the policy was of little significance because admission standards were set by the independent unions.[6]

Yet Negro spokesmen believed that there was much that Federation officials could have done in the way of informal persuasion to break down the pattern of racial discrimination. Unfortunately, it seemed to Negro leaders that the Federation's constitutional difficulties were complicated by a fundamental unwillingness to actively persuade member unions to remove Negro exclusion clauses from their constitutions. Ira De A. Reid of the Urban League declared that "Through the American Federation of Labor has uttered pronouncement upon pronouncement

---

1930. Bernstein, *The Lean Years* (Boston, 1960), 85-86, 335. See also Schlesinger, *op. cit.*, 138. Horace Cayton and George Mitchell, *Black Workers, and the New Unions* (Chapel Hill, 1939) 125.

[5] "The AFL and the Negro," *Opportunity*, VII (November, 1929) 338. Sterling Spero and Abram Harris, *op. cit.*, 85-86.

[6] Herbert Northup has observed that "In a very real sense the government of labor unions can be compared to the American federal system. Unions have their national, state, and local organizations as does the government of our country. In the administration of programs of relief, housing, industrial training, etc., Negroes receive the most equitable treatment, as a rule, when the federal government administers the program directly. . . . The same results are observable in matters of union policy. Negroes almost invariably fare better when national officers assume charge than they do when such questions as admissions or promotions are left for the local leaders to handle." Northrup, *op. cit.*, 236-237.

favoring the admission of Negro workers, that body has failed to convince the masses of Negro workers that it is rendering other than lip
service to such expressed principles." W. E. B. Du Bois of the
N.A.A.C.P. was even more emphatic: "The A. F. of L. has from the
beginning of its organization stood up and lied brazenly about its
attitude toward Negro labor," he proclaimed. "They have affirmed and
still affirm that they wish to organize Negro labor when this is a flat
and proven falsehood." T. Arnold Hill, the Industrial Secretary of the
Urban League, complained that the A.F.L. had never "campaigned
among its members for its idea of fair play reiterated in frequent
resolutions."[7]

William Green, the President of the A.F.L., admitted that the Federation's bi-racial ideals had not always been realized, but he reminded
Negroes of the enormous problems faced by those who would change
popular attitudes. He suggested that the A.F.L. as a whole was not to
be condemned because some of its affiliates discriminated against black
workers, any more than a church should be condemned because all
church members were not leading perfect lives. This explanation failed
to satisfy most Negroes; indeed, many agreed with Elmer Carter, the
editor of the Urban League's journal, *Opportunity,* who maintained
that Green's reference to the church was singularly unfortunate. "For
the church," Carter observed, "does not pursue a laissez faire policy;
it does not wait until its candidates are ready . . . as is the policy of the
A.F.L. The church makes its candidates ready. It seeks them out, peti-
tions, urges, pleads, cajoles, threatens; it goes into the far places where
dwelleth the heathen and by every means of persuasion seeks to lure
them under its enfolding mantle."[8]

The A.F.L.'s lack of enthusiasm for organizing mass-production
workers and the fundamental inconsistency between the racial policies
of the member unions and the affirmations of the parent body caused
many Negroes to reject the assumption that all workers would benefit
by increasing the power of organized labor. Roy Wilkins, the Assistant
Secretary of the N.A.A.C.P., expressed views that were widely shared

---

[7] Ira De A. Reid, "Lilly White Labor," *Opportunity,* VIII (June, 1930) 170. W. E. B.
Du Bois, "The A. F. of L.," *Crisis,* XL (December, 1933) 292. T. Arnold Hill,
"Letter to William Green," *Opportunity,* VIII (February, 1930) 56.
[8] William Green to Elmer A. Carter, November 7, 1929. *Opportunity,* VII (December,
1929) 381-382. "The President of the AFL Replies," *Opportunity,* VII (December,
1929) 367.

in the Negro community when he observed that "while Section 7a was a powerful weapon for the workers if they would use it and fight for the correct interpretation of it, we came shortly to realize . . . that while the American Federation of Labor was seizing upon Section 7a to carry on the most stupendous drive for membership in its history, it was doing little or nothing to include Negroes in the organizing." Jesse O. Thomas, the Urban League's Southern Field Secretary, made the same point when he noted that "While Section 7a has greatly increased the security of labor in general, insofar as the different labor organizations thus benefited deny and exclude Negroes from their membership by constitutions or rituals, the position of Negro labor has been made less favorable." Thomas believed that in passing this legislation Congress had intended to benefit all workers; but because of the "unsportsman-like and anti-social attitude of the majority of the membership and heads of many of the unions and crafts, the position of Negroes has been made even more disadvantageous." W. E. B. Du Bois expressed a prevalent attitude most succinctly when he wrote that "The American Federation of Labor is not a labor movement. It is a monopoly of skilled laborers, who join the capitalists in exploiting the masses of labor, whenever and wherever they can. . . ." "The most sinister power that the NRA has reinforced is the American Federation of Labor."[9]

Negro leaders were apprehensive about the prospect of A.F.L. unions taking advantage of the encouragement and protection offered by Section 7a to organize workers and establish themselves as the sole representative of labor. In a special memorandum prepared for President Roosevelt, the Urban League warned of the dangers inherent in the new recovery legislation. The League pointed out that Section 7a did not explicitly accord protection "to minority groups of workers whom the union wishes, for racial or religious reasons, to exclude from employment." Consequently, there was the danger that after establishing itself as the sole collective bargaining agent, organized labor would demand that management discharge black employees. Such incidents had occurred in the past, and the League feared that the practice would become more serious in the immediate future when it was likely that union membership would become a necessary prerequisite for an increas-

---

[9] Roy Wilkins to Horace Cayton, October 30, 1934. Cayton and Mitchell, *op. cit.,* 413-414. Jesse O. Thomas, "Negro Workers and Organized Labor," *Opportunity,* XII (September, 1934) 278. W. E. B. Du Bois to Martha Adamson, March 27, 1936. Du Bois Papers. Du Bois, "The A. F. of L.," *Crisis,* XL (December, 1933) 292.

ing number of jobs.[10]

During the 1930s several examples of trade unions' using their power to force the dismissal of colored workers came to the attention of Negro leaders, an experience which understandably served to confirm their original pessimistic suspicions. In Long Island City, New York, the Brotherhood of Electrical Workers, Local No. 3, organized several electrical supply shops, refused membership to the Negro workers already employed there, and used its newly won power to force the managements to discharge several dozen Negro employees. In Manhattan, some locals of the Building Service Employees' Union demanded that employers discharge Negro workers and fill the vacancies with white unionists. As a result, several hotels, restaurants, and office buildings were forced to discharge Negro elevator operators and restaurant workers and hire whites. In Milwaukee the Urban League reported that the A.F.L. affiliate had called a strike at the open shop Wehr Steel Foundry but had not informed the Negro workers in the plant. According to the League, "The blanket demand made by the union was that the A.F.L. be recognized. They did not strike for higher wages, shorter hours or better working conditions. . . . After the plant was closed entirely, the specific demand of the A.F.L. union was dismissal of Negroes from the plant." In St. Louis the depth of this anti-Negro sentiment was strikingly illustrated when all the A.F.L. men working on the Homer Phillips Hospital (a $2,000,000 colored hospital erected in the middle of a Negro neighborhood) walked off the job and halted construction for two months in protest against the General Tile Company's decision to employ a black man as a tile setter. Examples such as these naturally made other employers reluctant to hire black labor; they knew, as one independent contractor observed, that if they did so they would run the risk of having their white employees "suddenly become ill, or have to take care of personal business, or for any number of other fictitious reasons quit work." It was for this reason that the Building Committee of the St. Louis Board of Education would not allow black workers to do repair work on any of the city's seventeen colored schools. Other large contractors followed suit, and St. Louis' Negro mechanics were effectively barred from work on everything except small jobs.[11]

[10] Urban League Memorandum. "The Negro Working Population and National Recovery," January 4, 1937. Urban League Files.

[11] Urban League Memorandum, "The Negro Working Population and National Recovery," January 4, 1937. Urban League Files. Workers' Council Bulletin 17, "Labor Re-

Roy Wilkins stated the viewpoint of many Negro leaders when he declared that all too often the A.F.L.'s strategy was to take advantage of Section 7a "to organize a union for all the workers, and to either agree with the employers to push Negroes out of the industry or, having effected an agreement with the employer, to proceed to make the union lily-white." The editor of the *Baltimore Afro-American* concluded that "unless the A.F.L. is able to make its locals throughout the country open their doors to colored members in all crafts, it may be necessary for colored labor to organize and join in a country-wide fight on the union." And when Horace Cayton and George Mitchell interviewed Negro workers they discovered that resentment of the A.F.L. was widely shared. One Homestead, Pennsylvania, steel worker told them that outside unions wanted Negroes to go out on strike with white workers, but that after the battle was won the black worker would be made the victim and cast aside. Another steel worker in Cleveland told Cayton that the Negroes in his plant had "decided after studying that if labor organizations were to get a footing the colored would lose out. There are [a] few jobs that the colored hold which they [white union workers] would like to get; that is one reason why we have to fight against the labor organizations." According to the N.A.A.C.P., most Negroes believed "that labor unions usually oppose the economic interests of Negroes. This follows from the fact that every union seeks to establish a closed-shop or as near the closed-shop as possible. Since American unions have largely excluded Negroes, the closed-shop has meant an arrangement under which there are no job opportunities offered black workers."[12]

Throughout the country and in a variety of ways, Negroes protested against the practice of union discrimination. Walter White, the Executive Secretary of the N.A.A.C.P., urged the A.F.L. "not only to make unequivocal pronouncement of opposition to any discrimination based

---

lations and the Position of Negro Minorities," September 23, 1937. Copy in N.A.A.C.P. Files. Charles Lionel Franklin, *The Negro Labor Unionist of New York* (New York, 1936) 241. *Chicago Defender,* August 25, 1934. St. Louis Branch of the Urban League, "Report on Local Labor Conditions, 1934," typescript in N.A.A.C.P. Files. John T. Clark to Donald Richberg, *Chicago Defender,* March 31, 1934. Interdepartmental group concerned with the special problems of Negroes, "Report on Negro Labor," NA RG 48. Jesse O. Thomas, "Negro Workers and Organized Labor," *Opportunity, XII* (September, 1934) 277-278. Lester B. Granger, "Negro Workers and Recovery," *Opportunity,* XII (May, 1934) 153.
[12] Roy Wilkins to Horace Cayton, October 30, 1934. Cayton and Mitchell, *op. cit.,* 413-414, 175 *Baltimore Afro-American,* April 19, 1934. N.A.A.C.P. office memorandum, "The Negro and Trade Unions," n.d. N.A.A.C.P. Files.

on color but to take tangible steps to put the pronouncement into practice." The delegates to the N.A.A.C.P.'s 1934 annnual conference reminded the Federation of the essential solidarity of interests of all labor and suggested that "there can and will be no industrial peace for white labor as long as black labor can be excluded from union membership." When the annual convention of the A.F.L. met in San Francisco in 1934, local Negroes ringed the convention hall with pickets bearing signs proclaiming that "White Labor Cannot Be Free While Black Labor is Enslaved," and that "White Unions Make Black Scabs." On the floor of the convention, A. Philip Randolph, the Negro President of the Brotherhood of Sleeping Car Porters, proposed that the A.F.L. expel "any union maintaining the color bar." The resolutions committee rejected Randolph's motion on the ground that "The American Federation of Labor . . . cannot interfere with the autonomy of National and International Unions." However, the committee did accept an amendment authorizing the appointment of a five member committee "to investigate the conditions of the colored workers of this country and report to the next convention."[13]

The A.F.L.'s Committee of Five to Investigate Conditions of the Colored Workers met in Washington on July 12, 1935, and heard the testimony of a number of witnesses familiar with the problems of Negro workers. (The members of this all-white Committee of Five were: John Brophy of the United Mine Workers, Chairman; John E. Rooney of the Operative Plasters and Cement Finishers; John Garvey of the Hod Carriers and Common Laborers; Jerry L. Hanks of the Journeyman Bargers; and T. C. Carroll of the Maintenance of Way Employees.) Specific examples of union discrimination were described by Reginald Johnson of the Urban League, Charles Houston of the N.A.A.C.P., and A. Philip Randolph. In addition, several black workers appeared to tell of the difficulties they encountered when they tried to join union locals. In the course of his testimony, Houston informed the Committee that a number of N.A.A.C.P. branches were "assembling data on discrimination against Negro workers in their cities" and urged that additional hearings be held in other sections of the country. Believing that suffi-

---

[13] Walter White telegram to William Green, *The New York Times,* October 4, 1933, 4:3. Resolutions of the 25th Annual Conference of the N.A.A.C.P., 1934. N.A.A.C.P. Press Release, August 2, 1935. N.A.A.C.P. Files. *Pittsburgh Courier,* October 13, 1934. *Report of the Proceedings of the Fifty-fourth Annual Convention of the American Federation of Labor* (Washington, 1934) 330-332. Northrup, *op. cit.,* 11.

cient information had been uncovered at the first and only hearing in Washington, however, President Green informed the N.A.A.C.P. that the Federation had decided that additional regional hearings were not necessary. Ever suspicious, Walter White reminded Green that this refusal "to go further into this vitally important question will be construed as justification of the skepticism widely expressed of the sincerity of the American Federation of Labor's action."[14]

After concluding its hearings, the Committee of Five recommended a threefold plan: 1) that all international unions which discriminated against colored workers should take up the "Negro question at their next convention for the purpose of harmonizing constitution rules and practices to conform with the oft-repeated declarations of the A.F.L. conventions on equality of treatment of all races within the trade union movement"; 2) that the A.F.L. should issue no more charters to unions practicing discrimination; and 3) that the A.F.L. should begin an educational campaign "to get the white worker to see more completely the weaknesses of division and the necessity of unity between white and black workers to the end that all workers may be organized."[15]

The Committee had been specifically instructed to report to the next convention, and if its recommendations had been accepted and implemented significant internal reform of the A.F.L. might have been achieved. The Federation's Executive Council had grave reservations concerning the wisdom of the report, however, and President William Green arranged for it to be submitted to the Council rather than to the open convention. At the same time the Council also received a second report on the Negro question from one of its own members, George Harrison, the President of the exclusionist Railway Clerks. Harrison's report, advocating no action except "education," was considerably less forceful than the Committee's recommendations. But because of its innocuousness, it was more to the liking of President Green and the Council, who refused to release the Committee's report and instead arranged for Harrison's inoffensive document to be presented to the convention. Even so, Harrison delayed his presentation until about 10 p.m. on the eleventh and last day of the 1935 convention. By then

---

[14] N.A.A.C.P. Press Releases, July 12, 1935, July 19, 1935, July 26, 1935 and September 26, 1935. N.A.A.C.P. Files. "Reports of the Executive Secretary of the Joint Committee on National Recovery," June 19, 1935, and September 20, 1935. NA RG 183. Oxley File.

[15] *Report of the Proceedings of the Fifty-fifth Annual Convention of the American Federation of Labor* (Washington, 1935) 809. Northup, *op. cit.*, 11.

the delegates were exhausted and divided by the craft versus industrial union controversy (this was the convention which saw the final split in labor's ranks and the emergence of the C.I.O. as an independent body) and were ready to accept any report that speeded progress toward adjournment.[16]

This sabotage of the Committee's report by the A.F.L.'s Executive Council seemed to destroy the Negro's last hope for reform coming from within the Federation. Writing to John L. Lewis, Walter White observed that "the recent hypocritical attitude of the American Federation of Labor in suppressing the report of the Committee . . . has destroyed the last vestige of the confidence which Negro workers ever had in the A.F.L." The Committee's chairman, John Brophy of the United Mine Workers, was even more outspoken. In a sharply worded letter of resignation, Brophy charged that the "maneuvering on the part of the executive council plainly indicated that [they] wanted the Committee of Five . . . to be merely a face saving device for the American Federation of Labor, rather than an honest attempt to find a solution of the Negro problem in the American labor movement."[17]

Given the record of A.F.L. discrimination and the Negro's distrust of organized labor, it could be argued that colored workers were fortunate that Section 7a did not adequately safeguard labor's right to organize independent unions. Certainly many Negroes were convinced that their position would have been even more desperate if the Recovery Act had established effective machinery for enforcing its collective bargaining provisions. Moreover, while Negroes realized that company unions were not altogether satisfactory—that, especially during the NRA period, many employers had encouraged the organization of company unions as a defense against real collective bargaining—they understandably did not share the aversion which many white workers felt toward these management-controlled employee representation programs.[18]

Yet organized labor and large segments of the American liberal

---

[16] "Report of the Executive Secretary of the Joint Committee on National Recovery," November 23, 1935. NA RG 183. Northup, *op. cit.*, 12.

[17] Walter White to John L. Lewis, November 27, 1935. N.A.A.C.P. Press Release, November 15, 1935. N.A.A.C.P. Files.

[18] See Spero and Harris. *op. cit.*, chapter VII, and Cayton and Mitchell, *op. cit.*, 61-63 and 171-175. The attitudes of important Negro leaders in this regard are stated in the following letters: Trevor Bowen to Roy Wilkins, March 30, 1934; Wilkins to Walter White, March 21, 1934; White to Franklin D. Roosevelt, March 21, 1934. N.A.A.C.P. Files. Also see Lloyd N. Bailer, "Negro Labor in the Automobile Industry" (unpublished Ph.D. dissertation, University of Michigan, 1943) *passim.*

community believed that proliferation of company unions was under-mining the entire recovery program. Recalling the earlier argument that strong trade unions were needed to force management to increase mass purchasing power, the liberal-labor group maintained that NRA had failed to stimulate full recovery largely because ambiguities in the language of the recovery bill and the absence of enforcement powers had "enabled a minority of employers to deviate from the clear intent of the law and to threaten our entire program with destruction." Rally-ing behind the leadership of Senator Robert F. Wagner of New York, this group maintained that new legislation was needed to establish another labor board with the power to enforce its decisions and to clearly prohibit employers from dominating or supporting workers' organizations. Consequently, early in 1934 Senator Wagner and his assistants began to work on a new bill that would "clarify and fortify the provisions of Section 7a." As it finally emerged, the new legislation proposed to establish a strengthened National Labor Relations Board (N.L.R.B.) with the authority to investigate any disputes involving Section 7a, to order elections so that employees might choose their own representatives for collective bargaining *with membership in the union chosen by the majority a mandatory prerequisite for continued employ-ment,* and the power to prohibit certain "unfair" employer practices such as company domination of the workers' organization. The legisla-tion also provided that the N.L.R.B. was to be an independent admin-istrative agency with the power to enforce its decisions.[19]

---

[19] J. Joseph Huthmacher, *Senator Robert F. Wagner and the Rise of Urban Liberalism* (New York, 1968) chapters 5 through 10. National Labor Relations Board, "Article by Senator Robert F. Wagner on Labor Unions," *Legislative History of the National Labor Relations Act, 1935* (Washington: United States Government Printing Office, 1949) 22-26. Bernstein, *The New Deal Collective Bargaining Policy,* chapters 5 through 10.

The bill Senator Wagner introduced in February 1935 differed in some respects from the original 1934 version; most significantly, it emphasized the NLRB's position as a Supreme Court of labor relations by stressing the enforcement of labor's rights rather than the adjustment of differences and by providing that all members of the Board would represent the public (thus rejecting the earlier proposal to create a tripartite body with representation from management, labor, and the public). These changes were of considerable importance, but they did not affect black workers specifically and were not commented on by black leaders; indeed, Negro comment on the Wagner bill focussed almost wholly on the 1934 measure. At first I suspected that some of the N.A.A.C.P. and Urban League files for 1935 had been misplaced, but Negro newspapers also ignored the revised 1935 bill, and I have concluded that black people decided they had stated their case and done what they could in 1934 and that nothing further could be done in 1935. There is another interesting aspect to this, one that relates to the factional struggle within the N.A.A.C.P., but limitations of space prevent a full discussion here. Briefly, it is that the pro-labor forces within the Association—those who thought that the economic problems of black and white workers were inextricably intertwined and could be solved only by bi-racial working-

Negro leaders were not entirely out of sympathy with Senator Wagner's approach to collective bargaining. They approved of the requirement that certain conditions, among them free elections and majority choice, had to be fulfilled before a union could be certified as a legitimate bargaining agent. But Negro leaders also insisted that it was essential that the Wagner bill be amended so as to outlaw racial discrimination by unions. Without such an amendment, they reasoned, there was the very real danger that discriminatory unions would use their power to restrict the Negro's economic opportunities. With such an amendment Negroes would have, as Washington attorney William Hastie noted, "a strong weapon . . . for compelling unions to accept into membership all qualified employees."[20]

The demand for an anti-discrimination clause in the Wagner bill was widespread in the Negro community. T. Arnold Hill warned that "If the Wagner Bill passes in its present form, the power and influence of the labor movement will be greatly enhanced with the consequent danger of greater restrictions being practiced against Negro workers by organized labor." Dean Kelly Miller of Howard University insisted that "Every effort should be made to amend the Wagner Bill so as to safeguard the rights of the Negro. . . . Unless this is done it is easy to foretell the doom of the Negro in American industry." Roy Wilkins observed that the Wagner Bill "rigidly enforces and legalizes the closed shop," and he noted that "the act plainly empowers organized labor to exclude from employment in any industry those who do not belong to a union." He thought it was "needless to point out the fact that thousands of Negro workers are barred from membership in American labor unions and, therefore, that if the closed shop is legalized by this act Negro workers will be absolutely shut out of employment." Harry E. Davis, a member of the N.A.A.C.P.s' Board of Directors, summed up the sentiments of many Negroes when he observed that "it is not a 'closed' shop which is in the offing, but a 'white' shop."[21]

Negroes also pointed out that the Wagner legislation would require

---

class cooperation—had become so strong by 1935 that the national officers decided to forego further criticism of trade unions. I have discussed this matter in some detail in a forthcoming book, *Negroes and the Great Depression: The Problem of Economic Recovery.*

[20] William Hastie to Walter White, March 27, 1934. N.A.A.C.P. Files.

[21] T. Arnold Hill to Walter White, April 3, 1934. N.A.A.C.P. Files. Hill, "Labor Marches On," *Opportunity,* XII (April, 1934) 120-121. Kelly Miller, "Amend the Wagner Bill," *Norfolk Journal and Guide,* March 31, 1934. Roy Wilkins memorandum to N.A.A.C.P. Office Staff, March 23, 1934. Harry E. Davis to Walter White, March 20, 1934. N.A.A.C.P. Files.

employers to rehire all striking employees after a settlement had been reached. According to the N.A.A.C.P. and the Urban League, this would jeopardize the position of Negro strikebreakers who had been given employment while union men were off the job. While they "deplore[d] the necessity for strikebreaking," the Negro protest organizations maintained that "it is the one weapon left to the Negro worker whereby he may break the stranglehold that certain organized labor groups have utilized in preventing his complete absorption in the American labor market." The N.A.A.C.P. viewed the prospect of indirectly penalizing strikebreakers with particular alarm; it was convinced that "practically every important entry that the Negro has made into industries previously closed to him has been through his activity as a strikebreaker."[22]

While Congress was considering the Wagner bill, the N.A.A.C.P. and the Urban League urged the inclusion of an amendment which would have denied the benefits of the legislation to any union which discriminated on the basis of race. Elmer Carter was sent to Washington, where he acted as the League's chief lobbyist, and T. Arnold Hill and Lester B. Granger prepared for the Senate Committee on Labor and Education a "Statement of Opinion" which summarized the League's objections to the unamended Wagner legislation. William Hastie prepared a similar document for the N.A.A.C.P., and Walter White kept in close touch with Senator Wagner and his secretary, Leon Keyserling. From Keyserling, White learned that "The Act as originally drafted by Senator Wagner provided that the closed shop should be legal only when there were no restrictions upon members in the labor union to which the majority of workers belonged." But, according to Keyserling, "The American Federation of Labor fought bitterly to eliminate this clause and much against his will Senator Wagner had to consent to the elimination in order to prevent scuttling of the entire bill."[23]

[22] N.A.A.C.P. office memorandum, "The Negro and Trade Unions," n.d. Workers' Council Bulletin 17, "Labor Relations Legislation and the Position of the Negro Minorities," September 23, 1937. N.A.A.C.P. Files. National Urban League, "A Statement of Opinion on Senate Bill S 2926," Urban League Files. Interdepartmental group concerned with the special problems of Negroes, "Report on Negro Labor," NA RG 48.

[23] National Urban League, "A Statement of Opinion on Senate Bill S 2926," Urban League Files. The proposed N.A.A.C.P. amendment read as follows: "Provided, however, that the term labor organization shall not include any organization, labor union, association, corporation, or society of any kind, which by its organic law or by any rule or regulation, or any practice excludes any employee or employees from membership in the organization or from equal participation, with other employees by reason of race, creed or color." It should be noted that Senator Wagner supported

Negro spokesmen also presented their objections to the Wagner bill in correspondence to and informal conferences with labor leaders and government officials. Walter White, for example, wrote to William Green, specifically requesting Green's support for the proposed N.A.A.C.P.-Urban League amendment. Green, however, answered in an equivocal fashion that, in White's view, "boiled down, means precisely nothing." The N.A.A.C.P. leader forwarded a copy of Green's reply to Senator Wagner "so that you may see how he dodges answering our specific question as to whether or not he and the American Federation of Labor will support a provision to eliminate discrimination by labor unions." White also wrote to President Roosevelt, reminding him that unions "with ill grace can ask benefits for white labor while these unions discriminate against black labor," and he demanded that "full safeguards . . . be given to prevent this." "We rely on you," he declared, "to prevent [the] sacrifice of [the] Negro to Jim Crow unionism." Within the Roosevelt administration, Clark Foreman, Secretary of Interior Harold Ickes' adviser on the special problems of Negroes, called attention to "the fact that the American Federation of Labor was being recognized more and more by government agencies as the spokesman of labor—although quite commonly Negroes are excluded from local unions belonging to the A.F.L." Foreman maintained that "if we could assume, as had been claimed, that Negro workers were better off under the company unions than under the A.F.L., the Administration should be advised before sponsoring any measures which would indirectly worsen the condition of the Negro." He suggested that "whether or not the A.F.L. or other labor organizations were involved, the government should not do anything against any element of the population or negotiate preferential agreements with any organization which discriminated against certain elements of the population."[24]

The opposition to the proposed N.A.A.C.P.-Urban League amendment was led by the American Federation of Labor (though it is significant that the leaders of the emerging industrial unions of the C.I.O.

the N.A.A.C.P.'s attempt to add this anti-discrimination clause to the Wagner bill. Robert F. Wagner telegram to Walter White, April 16, 1934. White to William Hastie, March 28, 1934 and April 17, 1934. N.A.A.C.P. Files.

[24] Walter White to William Green, April 17, 1934. Green to White, May 2, 1934. White to Robert Wagner, May 15, 1934. Also see William Hastie telegram to White, March 29, 1934 and White to Hastie, May 16, 1934. White telegram to Franklin D. Roosevelt, March 21, 1934. N.A.A.C.P. Files. Minutes of the second meeting of the interdepartmental group concerned with the special problems of Negroes, March 2, 1934. NA RG 48.

were not recorded in opposition). The A.F.L. maintained that re-
calcitrant employers would use this amendment as an excuse to involve
even non-discriminatory unions in costly litigation and thus delay the recognition of the unions' right to bargain collectively with the employer.
Employing the rhetoric of working-class solidarity, the A.F.L. warned
Negroes that they should not support legislation which would impede
the progress of trade unionism, "for in the progress of honest trade
unionism lies the future security of all workers, of both minority and
majority groups." Some Negro leaders admitted that the A.F.L.'s position in this regard was not entirely without merit. Nevertheless, most
concluded, as the Urban League did, that while "it is a dangerous thing
for Negroes to request governmental interference in the internal affairs
of unions, the least that Negroes can demand is that [the] government
shall not protect a union in its campaign to keep them out of present
and future jobs."[25]

Despite the essential validity of their arguments, Negroes suffered a
defeat in 1935 when Congress passed and President Roosevelt signed
the National Labor Relations (Wagner) Act without the N.A.A.C.P.-
Urban League amendment. The reason for this seems clear: the American Federation of Labor had more political power and influence than
the two Negro protest organizations. Government officials candidly explained that "because there was no organization of Negroes, and therefore no one who could command the support of any considerable number of Negro workers, there was little likelihood of their gaining" special consideration. Negroes learned once again that insofar as labor was
concerned the dominating forces in the government were, as Clark
Foreman explained during the NRA's first year, "the industrialists and
the A.F.L., both of whom are hostile to Negro labor, the former because
they want to keep Negroes as a reserve of cheap labor, and the latter
because they want to eliminate Negro competitive labor." Negro leaders
had appealed for an amendment on grounds of equity and justice, but
their request was not granted because it conflicted with the claims of
better organized and more powerful white interests.[26]

---

[25] The AFL arguments were summarized by the Urban League, Workers' Council Bulletin
    17, "Labor Relations Legislation and the Position of the Negro Minorities," Sep-
    tember 23, 1937. N.A.A.C.P. Files. The quotation attributed to the League is from
    this document.
[26] Minutes of the second meeting of the interdepartmental group concerned with the
    special problems of Negroes, March 2, 1934. Clark Foreman to Harold Ickes, De-
    cember 13, 1933. NA RG 48.

7

Race, Class, and Progress: Black Leadership and Industrial Unionism, 1936-1945

JAMES S. OLSON

Paradoxically, the traditional relationship between black men and organized labor has been strained and uneasy. Although they shared many goals, conflict and hostility marked their association before 1936. The fundamental structure of the A.F.L., by virtually guaranteeing craft and local autonomy, prevented uniform levels of racial justice in unions throughout the nation. Moreover, craft unionism's exclusiveness, both racial and occupational, created still greater friction. Local omnipotence, racial prejudice, fears of job competition—all combined to segregate and often exclude Negroes from membership in organized labor's most powerful institution.

The massive migration of Negroes to northern cities during World War I enhanced this disaffection. For the first time black and white workers came into daily contact, and their mutual antagonism, growing out of white prejudice and anger over Negro strikebreaking activities, increased. Recognizing this hostility as a fundamental flaw in the labor movement, employers capitalized on it and, by cultivating relations with the Negro community, solidified black anti-union sentiment. Finally, with most black workers employed in mass production industries, the A.F.L.'s opposition to industrial unionism further alienated the Negro community. This gulf between the two movements prevailed throughout the post-war years.

During the Great Depression, millions of black workers lost their jobs. New Deal labor legislation, upholding the right of collective bargaining, alleviated many of labor's problems, but because A.F.L. racial barriers remained intact, Negro workers, by virtue of their exclusion

JAMES S. OLSON *is a graduate student at the State University of New York, Stony Brook.*

from unions, largely found themselves without federal protection. With the economic situation desperate, more and more black leaders realized the urgent need for organizing Negro workers.[1] Nevertheless, confusion dominated the Negro organizations' approach to labor-management disputes. They questioned the sincerity of management's overtures to the black community because they understood industry's self-serving interest in dividing the labor movement. But labor, on the other hand, could not be trusted because of its discriminatory practices. Consequently, black leadership was caught in a power vacuum. Furthermore, it knew that by not making some commitment it might lose its institutional relevance with the Negro worker. The rise of the C.I.O. solved this dilemma.

With most Negro workers employed in mass-production industries, national black leadership immediately endorsed the principle of industrial unionism. This principle was, for example, supported in 1936 by the National Negro Congress,[2] which sought "to secure definite cooperation with the Committee on Industrial Organization in the organization of Negro workers in mass production into industrial unions."[3] The *Pittsburgh Courier,* a leading Negro newspaper, expressed similar sentiments.[4] The C.I.O., in sum, was for black institutional leaders, the long-sought-after viable alternative to industrial paternalism and union exclusion, and they responded by supporting it in the jurisdictional dispute that developed with A.F.L. organizers.

Black leadership, to be sure, remained skeptical, despite its initial sympathy, owing to its past experience with organized labor. Beyond calling for racial equality, the C.I.O. had yet to prove itself by actually organizing Negro workers. Caution prevailed. Writing for the National Urban League, Lester Granger warned Negro workers against "jubilantly rushing toward what they assume to be a new day for labor and a new organization to take the place of the A.F. of L."[5] Although they

---

[1] James Welden Johnson, *Negro Americans, What Now?* (New York, 1934), 67.
[2] An analysis of the response of Negro Communists to the C.I.O. has not been attempted because Communists never exterted a critical influence on the Negro masses during this period. (See Wilson Record, *The Negro and the Communist Party* (Chapel Hill, 1951), Ch. 8.). Because the National Negro Congress was captured by the Communists in 1940 (Gunmar Myrdal, *An American Dilemma* (New York, 1944), 818), and most of the non-Communist members deserted it, the Congress ceased to be a leading black organization, and has not been considered in this study's post-1940 analysis of black leadership.
[3] National Negro Congress, *Proceedings,* 1936, 21.
[4] *The Pittsburgh Courier,* July 11, 1936.
[5] Lester B. Granger, "Industrial Unionism and the Negro," *Opportunity,* XIV (January, 1936), 29.

appreciated the C.I.O.'s promises, black leadership nevertheless awaited their fulfillment. Like the Urban League, the N.A.A.C.P. assumed a wait-and-see posture, and demanded proof of C.I.O. sincerity.[6]

In 1936-37 the organizing drives in the steel and automobile industries provided the first crucial test of C.I.O. intentions. Its leadership, by seeking to impartially organize black workers across the country, produced a favorable reaction among black officials. Under the direction of A. Philip Randolph, the National Negro Congress contributed several of its organizers to the Steel Workers Organizing Committee (S.W.O.C.).[7] The National Urban League praised the attitudes of the "liberal C.I.O. unions."[8] Robert L. Vann, editor of the *Pittsburgh Courier*, participated in the S.W.O.C.'s drives in Pittsburgh, wholeheartedly supporting the campaign.[9] Finally, the N.A.A.C.P. told black workers that they had "nothing to lose and everything to gain by affiliation with the C.I.O. . . ."[10] For the first time a national labor organization was attempting to organize workers without regard to race, and black leadership, seeing the start of interracial worker unity, was able to make a tentative commitment in labor-management struggles.

Throughout the pre-war years the C.I.O. fulfilled its promise of impartiality. Witness, for instance, its southern organizers. When the Georgia Ku Klux Klan declared war upon the Textile Workers Organizing Committee in 1939 for its interracial program, the N.A.A.C.P. remarked: "It has often been said that you can tell a man by the kind of enemies he makes. If this is true of organizations also, then the C.I.O. is certainly an unparalleled blessing in our land."[11] Equally impressive to the black community were the leadership assignments given to Negroes in C.I.O. unions. The *Chicago Defender*, for example, praised the appointment of Henry Johnson, a Negro, as assistant national director of the Packinghouse Workers Organization Committee.[12] Finally, the C.I.O. proved its ability to hold racial prejudice in check at the local level. In late 1940, for example, 500 white workers at the Curtiss-Wright aircraft plant in Columbus, Ohio, struck when a Negro

---

[6] "Industrial Unions and the Negro Worker," *Crisis*, XLIII (September, 1936), 273.
[7] National Negro Congress, *Proceedings*, 1937, n.p.
[8] Lester G. Granger and T. Arnold Hill, *Occupational Opportunities for Negroes* (New York, 1937), 14.
[9] *The Pittsburgh Courier*, July 31, 1937.
[10] Blood for the Cause," *Crisis*, XLIV (July, 1937), 209. The *Chicago Defender* likewise endorsed the C.I.O. during these years. See *The Chicago Defender*, June 5, 1937.
[11] "From the Press of the Nation," *Crisis*, XLVI (January, 1939), 19.
[12] *The Chicago Defender*, September 16, 1939.

was promoted to the tool and die department. R. J. Thomas, president of the U.A.W.-C.I.O., immediately removed the local union official who had endorsed the strike, and ordered the men back to work, an equivocal directive that won N.A.A.C.P. praise.[13] Similar actions were not lost upon black leadership and, by the outbreak of World War II, its relationship with the C.I.O. was amicable and secure.

The National Negro Congress (N.N.C.) provided the C.I.O. with the most militant support. From its outset in 1936 the Congress had been a left-wing, worker-oriented organization.[14] The powerful Communist element strengthened this orientation, as did the organization's financial dependence upon Party-dominated C.I.O. unions.[15] Little wonder, then, that it militantly endorsed an industrial workers' movement.

But the response of black institutions was not uniform. In contrast to the N.N.C., the Urban League was much more reserved. Before organized labor welcomed the black man, the League had for years tried to convince industry of the necessity of hiring Negroes and, as a result, was management conscious. It had praised the C.I.O.'s repudiation of the color line, but could not be too laudatory for fear of endangering the relationship it had cultivated with management. The conservatism of those business and professional people who dominated the League further restrained its enthusiasm.[16]

The attitude of the N.A.A.C.P. differed from that of the Congress and of the League. Unlike the Congress, the N.A.A.C.P. did not commit organizers to the C.I.O. campaigns; unlike the League, it was not reserved. N.A.A.C.P. opinion of the C.I.O. reflected the nature of its own concerns. Seeking to publicize civil rights issues and to pursue legal cases of general significance to the black community, it propagandized for the C.I.O. in its various house organs—the N.A.A.C.P. *Bulletin* and the N.A.A.C.P. *Press Service*. The N.A.A.C.P. was more enthusiastic than the League—indeed it proved to be one of the C.I.O.'s most vigorous advocates—because it had never been management oriented, and because its financial backing came largely from rank-and-file membership dues rather than from upper-class white philanthropy.[17]

The national Negro press[18] played a similar role. Acting as a sounding

---

[13] *N.A.A.C.P. Press Service*, November 21, 1941.
[14] National Negro Congress, *Proceedings*, 1937, n.p.
[15] Record, *op. cit.*, 159.
[16] E. Franklin Frazier, *Black Bourgeoisie* (Glencoe, Illinois, 1957), 100.
[17] Gunnar Myrdal, *op. cit.*, 822.
[18] In his study, Myrdal concluded that the most influential representatives of the Negro

board for Negro opinion, it began, after early cautiousness, to report favorably C.I.O. activities. Because the press represented the attitudes of two of the Negro's most important agencies (N.A.A.C.P. and the Urban League) and because the two major press representatives—the *Chicago Defender* and the *Pittsburgh Courier*—published national editions that were free from the pressures of local politics, their attitude toward the C.I.O. was positive. Both papers were guided by editors with well-established reputations for militancy on the issue of racism in American labor, and both quickly endorsed the C.I.O. when it invited Negroes to join.[19]

Despite differences in the degree of their support of the C.I.O., black periodicals shared a common theme, in that they all gradually began to express sympathy with the doctrine of labor solidarity. For years before the C.I.O., young black intellectuals and white radicals had argued that the solution to Negro economic distress lay in the unity of black and white workers.[20] Moderate Negro leadership generally shunnned the concept until the rise of the C.I.O. made it seem more relevant. Late in 1936 a *Crisis* editorial remarked: "The ultimate security of black and white labor will be achieved only in a union of all workers for their attainment of a common objective in the face of a common enemy . . . an enemy that has too long played the one against the other for the exploitation of both."[21] Even the Urban League now spoke favorably of working-class unity.[22] This doctrine was still in a germinal stage, to be sure, and black leadership did not yet see it as the most important antidote to racism. But its use did add the dimension of class consciousness and of class protest to racial protest, and stimulated the movement of black workers in the C.I.O.

The national Negro business and professional organizations, being aloof from the masses, were apathetic about the rise of industrial union-

---

newspaper press were the *Chicago Defender* and the *Pittsburgh Courier* (Myrdal, *op. cit.*, 1423). He also considered the most influential representatives of the periodical press to be the *Crisis*, published by the N.A.A.C.P., and *Opportunity*, published by the National Urban League (*ibid.*, 909). In this study, I have accepted Myrdal's conclusions about the most influential elements of the Negro press.

[19] Sterling D. Spero and Abram L. Harris, *The Black Worker* (New York, 1930), 435. For years before 1936, the *Chicago Defender* published its "Platform for America," which was written by its editor, Robert S. Abbott. One of the key planks of that platform was "the opening up of all trades and trade unions to blacks as well as whites." (*The Chicago Defender*, January 26, 1935).

[20] Spero and Harris, *op. cit.*, 387.

[21] "Industrial Unions and the Negro Worker," *Crisis*, XLIII (September, 1936), 273; also see *The Chicago Defender*, August 29, 1936.

[22] "Editorial," *Opportunity*, XV (May, 1937), 133.

ism. They were much less active than the other national organizations, and their interests and goals allowed them to ignore labor issues. When they did protest racial prejudice, it was against the aspects of prejudice which they had personally experienced, such as segregation in theaters, hotels, and restaurants.[23] They generally overlooked the problems of the lower classes, and consequently ignored the relationship of black workers to labor unions. Most important, unlike the more influential elements of black leadership, they did not find validity in the labor-solidarity doctrine, but rather saw the Negroes' salvation in terms of a separate, black business structure, completely independent of white capitalism.[24] In this sense they were more racially-oriented than class-oriented, and conceived of black progress in terms of racial solidarity rather than interracial labor unity.[25] Throughout the decade, therefore, these national Negro business and professional organizations played no part in Negro-C.I.O. relations. Their community status and social-political values discouraged conceptualization of the issue of Negro-labor relations.

Despite the apathy of business and professional groups, the most influential elements of black institutional leadership had accepted the C.I.O., and by 1942 they were ready to move from acceptance to complete alignment. Unfortunately, the outlook of black leadership at the local level was not nearly so positive.

Indeed the divergence between local and national leadership was striking. After touring the nation as a labor correspondent for the *Pittsburgh Courier* in 1936-37, George Schuyler wrote: "The most disheartening observation in connection with this labor revolution has been the indifference, hostility, and open opposition of so many edu-

---

[23] Professor Myrdal names the National Negro Business League, the National Negro Bankers' Association, the National Negro Insurance Association, the National Medical Association and the National Bar Association as the most important organizations in this element of black leadership (Myrdal, *op. cit.,* 816). Of these organizations, only the National Bar Association endorsed the C.I.O. (Horace R. Cayton and George S. Mitchell, *Black Workers and the New Unions* (Chapel Hill, 1939), 383-389). See also Myrdal, *op. cit.,* 795.

[24] Ralph Bunche, "Conceptions and Ideologies of the Negro Problem," 122-124. This is an unpublished manuscript prepared for the Myrdal study in 1940, and is now deposited in the Schomburg Collection of the New York Public Library.

[25] An example of the entire combination of factors affecting Negro professional and business leaders can be seen in the 1938 conference of the National Negro Insurance Association. When dealing with the question of how to improve labor conditions and employment opportunities for black workers, the Association completely ignored the potential of industrial unionism and felt that surveying business organizations for job vacancies and making the information available to Negro workers would be the best approach. Likewise, in dealing with the best means of strengthening the whole race, they concentrated only on the hope of establishing an independent, black capitalism (National Negro Insurance Association, *Proceedings,* 1938, 82).

cated Negroes holding positions of trust and leadership in the community."[26] Many local leaders maintained their traditional suspicion of labor unions, while others upheld their loyalty to local industries which had hired Negroes. A black businessman in Akron, for example, praised the Firestone Corporation because "during the height of the depression whites were clamoring for the discharge of Negroes but Firestone did not discharge a single one."[27] Unlike the national leaders, prominent local figures could not detach themselves from parochial needs and circumstances, and consider the situation in larger terms. Being business and professional men holding secure positions in the community, they looked with dismay upon the economic dislocation which accompanied militant labor activity. They were simply unable to see black progress in terms of black- and white-labor solidarity. Finally, the local Negro community depended financially upon steady industrial production and steady wages to Negro employees.[28] Strikes of course halted wages, and local shopkeepers and professionals suffered because the sales of their goods and services were adversely affected. In sum, economic anxieties and political conservatism combined to generate considerable hostility toward the C.I.O. among the local leaders.

To further hurt the C.I.O., industrial management often cultivated relations with black community leaders. By means of financial contributions to local Negro organizations, management gained their allegiance and increased their dependence upon local industry. The black church became the focal point of this support, and the most sophisticated practitioner of the policy was the Ford Motor Company. Ford made financial contributions to selected Negro churches, and then in effect used the ministers as employment agents. Prospective workers were hired, upon presenting a written ministerial recommendation from their minister to company officials. Negro ministers welcomed Ford's assistance because it increased church attendance, helped keep the church financially solvent, and strengthened their community leadership position.[29] Once having secured company approval, a minister was anxious to keep it, and thus willing to follow Ford's anti-C.I.O. position.

---

[26] George S. Schuyler, "Reflections on Negro Leadership," *Crisis*, XLIV (November, 1937), 327.
[27] *The Pittsburgh Courier*, August 28, 1937.
[28] *Ibid.*, July 24, 1937.
[29] Lloyd H. Bailer, "Negro Labor in the Automobile Industry," unpublished Ph.D. dissertation, University of Michigan, 1943, 113.

Walter White, executive secretary of the N.A.A.C.P., recalled the occasion in 1937 when a belligerent delegation of Detroit Negro ministers
threatened to boycott the N.A.A.C.P. convention unless U.A.W.-C.I.O.
speakers were removed from the program.[30] Horace White created a sen-
sation by asking, in the February 1938 *Christian Century*, "Who Owns
the Negro Church?"; and by concluding that when the black worker
sought aid from his local minister, he found that "his church, which
he thought was the one institution belonging to the Negro, is actually
the property of the big white industrialist."[31] Given these local conditions, C.I.O. attempts to organize the black worker met stiff resistance.

Such intransigence embarrassed black leadership on the national level.
For example, while the N.A.A.C.P. endorsed the C.I.O., the president
of the Indianapolis N.A.A.C.P. chapter, in referring to the local
S.W.O.C. campaign in 1936, declared, "I have come to the conclusion
that Negroes had better stay out of the unions."[32] Usually business and
progressional men, these branch officers—joined by ministers and an
often corrupt local press—endorsed typical anti-C.I.O. beliefs and posed
a serious dilemma for the pro-C.I.O. elements of national leadership.[33]

The 1941 Ford strike aptly revealed the crisis in attitudes. Both national and local black leadership played conspicious roles and, as such,
this walkout provides a case study of the problem of the response of
black leadership to the C.I.O.

In making their most concerted attempt to organize the Ford workers,
U.A.W. officials knew that their greatest challenge would be provided
by local black leaders—if they maintained their loyalty to the company
and urged Ford's 17,000 black workers to resist C.I.O. overtures. Union
anxieties were fully justified. Walter White wrote that the atmosphere
of one local N.A.A.C.P. meeting was as "anti-union as would have
been that of a meeting of the board of directors of the Ford Motor
Company."[34] Ford also pressured black clergymen into condemning the
strike, the U.A.W.-C.I.O., and industrial unionism generally.[35] The
hostility manifested by these local leaders, combined with the indecision
of many black workers about the value of unionization, had serious

[30] Walter White, *A Man Called White*, (New York, 1948), 212.
[31] Horace White, "Who Owns the Negro Church," *Christian Century*, LV (February 9,
    1938), 176-177.
[32] *The Pittsburgh Courier*, September 11, 1936.
[33] Myrdal, *op. cit.*, 909; also see *The Pittsburgh Courier*, September 11, 1936.
[34] W. White, *op. cit.*, 215.
[35] *The Detroit Tribune*, April 26, 1941; see also Lloyd Bailer, "Negro Labor in the
    Automobile Industry," 234.

consequences: 1,500 black workers refused to stop working at the River Rouge plant in Dearborn.

This 1941 strike presented a crisis in loyalty, for national black leadership, since it had praised Henry Ford for his long-time policy of employing Negroes. The *Pittsburgh Courier*, as late as 1940, had characterized him as "one of America's most broadminded men. Race, creed, and color are secondary."[36] The clash between the U.A.W. and Ford necessitated a momentous decision for black leadership, because loyalty to Ford was clearly incompatible with support of industrial unionism. Yet this leadership, after considering the alternatives, unhesitatingly decided that the workers' interests demanded C.I.O. organization.[37]

Black leadership now faced the dual necessity of overcoming local antagonism and of convincing the confused workers to align themselves with the union. Walter White exemplifies the black leadership's situation. After much pleading, he convinced local N.A.A.C.P. chapters to endorse the U.A.W. and to provide sound trucks that would urge the strikebreakers to leave the River Rouge plant.[38] White then marched in a U.A.W. picket line and praised the union's race policies.[39] Under the combined urgings of local and national black leadership, the workers did indeed walk out. Shortly afterwards, Ford recognized the U.A.W.-C.I.O. and agreed to a union shop, grievance machinery, and wage increases—concessions that constituted a remarkable victory for the U.A.W. and black leadership alike. With Ford's capitulation, the ties between them strengthened and, by the eve of World War II, both groups were on the verge of complete alignment.

The tempo of Negro praise for the C.I.O. altered, under the threat of war in 1941, as other issues—such as discrimination in defense industries and in the armed services—replaced industrial unionism in immediate importance. But black support for the C.I.O., though subsiding, remained enthusiastic. And when the C.I.O. complied with black leadership demands for an extension of C.I.O. racial activities, Negroes moved from zealous support to informal alliance with the union.

In part reacting positively to these demands, the C.I.O., during the war, expanded its activities into the area of civil rights and industrial discrimination. Just three weeks after the Ford strike the National

---

[36] *The Pittsburgh Courier,* July 6, 1940; *The Chicago Defender,* March 7, 1936.
[37] *N.A.A.C.P. Annual Report,* 1941, 31; *The Pittsburgh Courier,* April 19, 1941 and May 31, 1941; *The Chicago Defender,* April 19, 1941.
[38] W. White, *op. cit.,* 215.
[39] "N.A.A.C.P. Acts in Ford Strike," *N.A.A.C.P. Bulletin,* I (May, 1941), 1.

Urban League charged the C.I.O. with being reluctant to deal with employment discrimination.[40] Later in the year the N.A.A.C.P. accused it of being deaf "to pleas for assistance in breaking down the barriers to the ballot box in the South."[41] Early in 1942, Philip Murray, President of the C.I.O., appointed a committee to investigate the problem of equality of opportunity for Negro workers in American industry, and this body quickly evolved into the permanent Committee to Abolish Racial Discrimination. Under its direction, the transition and expansion of C.I.O. racial policies began.

In mid-1941, faced with the threat of A. Philip Randolph's March on Washington movement, Franklin D. Roosevelt established the Fair Employment Practices Committee (F.E.P.C.) to deal with industrial discrimination. But, because the F.E.P.C. was unpopular in some circles, Congress often reduced its funds and threatened its very existence. The C.I.O. and its Committee to Abolish Racial Discrimination throughout the war joined black leadership in opposing these cutbacks and in demanding the maintenance of the F.E.P.C.[42] The union's firm stand impressed black leadership and made it more aware of the value of complete alignment.

Another rationale for black identification with industrial unionism was the C.I.O.'s new interest in civil rights. The U.A.W.-C.I.O. intervened in Detroit's Sojourner Truth controversy in 1942, when local whites called for segregation of the new federal housing project; and union demands for integration of all the facilities drew praise from black leadership.[43] In 1944 the N.A.A.C.P. lauded the C.I.O.'s support of integration of the armed forces and of an end to lynching and the poll tax.[44] Finally, the C.I.O.'s Political Action Committee denounced all forms of discrimination, and its cooperation with black leadership to achieve that goal convinced prominent Negroes that industrial unionism was the black man's most powerful ally in America.[45]

Declining antagonism of local black leaders to the C.I.O. further strengthened the bond between blacks and the union. The real source of local anti-C.I.O. opposition had been the tendency of local black leaders

---

[40] "Editorial," *Opportunity*, XIX (May, 1941), 130.
[41] "South in the Saddle, Riding Labor," *Crisis*, XLVII (December, 1941), 556.
[42] *The Chicago Defender*, March 6, 1943.
[43] *N.A.A.C.P. Bulletin*, II (July, 1942), 3.
[44] *Ibid.*, III (December, 1943), 4; *The Pittsburgh Courier*, November 13, 1943.
[45] "Allies of the Negro," *Opportunity*, XXI (July, 1944), 117; *The Chicago Defender*, August 5, 1944.

to gravitate to the political and social power center. When the C.I.O. was powerless they refused to support it for fear of angering management. But once management capitulated, and the C.I.O. became part of this power structure, local leaders ended their anti-union activities. Moreover, management, after recognizing the C.I.O., ended its conspicuous relations with the black community and no longer demanded or commanded loyalty. Finally, the F.E.P.C., despite its inherent weaknesses, caused many employers to end discrimination. The assurance that black workers would not be fired because of race or of pro-union sympathies removed the local fear of massive economic dislocation resulting from jobless black workers. The Ford strike of 1941 was the last marked evidence of local antagonism, and this issue, during the war years, ceased to mar the black leadership's relationship with the C.I.O.

No longer confronted by parochial hostility, black leadership completed its informal alliance with the C.I.O. Perhaps the National Urban League best illustrates this commitment. By 1942 the League had no reservations. With the union firmly embedded in the power structure, there was now little need to fear management's wrath. Cooperation with the C.I.O. existed in many areas,[46] and the union's interest in civil rights convinced the League that the C.I.O. was the Negro's "most important historical experience in 75 years of struggle. . . ."[47] The League had unequivocally allied with the C.I.O. by 1945, and this alliance was duplicated by other influential elements of black leadership.

Acceptance of the labor solidarity doctrine accompanied alignment with the C.I.O. During the war years black leadership realized that the concept of labor solidarity would benefit not only black workers but the black man generally. Ralph Bunche best expressed what black leadership came to advocate when he wrote:

> The overwhelming majority of Negroes are working class, and most of these are unskilled. Thus, practically the entire Negro race would be included in the scope of this ideology. The black and white masses, once

---

[46] In 1943 the League collaborated with the C.I.O. in publishing the pamphlet, "Working and Fighting Together." (National Urban League, *Annual Report*, 1943, 9-10). The 1943 Urban League conference program reads like a C.I.O. convention. Among the speakers were James Carey, Secretary-Treasurer of the C.I.O.; Walter Hardin, international representative of the U.A.W.-C.I.O.; George Weaver, Director of the C.I.O. Committee to Abolish Racial Discrimination; Ferdinand Smith, Secretary of the National Maritime Union, C.I.O.; and Willard Townsend, president of the United Transport and Service Employees of America, C.I.O. (National Urban League, *Annual Conference Program*, 1943, 3-4).

[47] Monroe Sweettance, "The CIO and the Negro American," *Opportunity*, XX (October, 1942), 292.

[48] Bunche, *op. cit.*, 131-132.

united, could employ the terrifying power of their numbers to wring concessions from the employers and from the government itself.[48]

After years of witnessing the C.I.O.'s ability to elevate the status of the black worker, black leadership appreciated the potentialities of industrial unionism and accepted the concept of labor solidarity. In 1943 the N.A.A.C.P. explained:

> every attack on labor is an attack on the Negro, for the Negro is largely a worker. . . . Organized labor is now our national ally. The C.I.O. has proved that it stands for our people within the unions and outside the unions. . . . If labor loses a battle, the Negro loses also.[49]

Similar sentiments were expressed by the other elements of black leadership.[50] By 1945 it had run the gamut of opinion about the C.I.O.; its response had evolved from the skepticism of 1936 to near total identification of 1945, and at the war's end, it looked upon the C.I.O. and the idea of labor solidarity as the black man's greatest hope for social and economic progress in the post-war world.

---

[49] "The 1943 Line-up vs. the Negro," *The N.A.A.C.P. Bulletin*, III (February, 1943), 1.
[50] George Clifton Edwards, "Negro Progress and White Justice," *Crisis*, LII (September, 1945), 251; National Urban League, *Annual Report*, 1945, 9-10; *The Chicago Defender*, April 17, 1943. Surprisingly, even business and professional organziations demonstrated a recognition of the need at least partially to cooperate with the C.I.O. *(Responsibility: Official Publication of the National Negro Business and Professional Women's Clubs*, II (April, 1944), 11).

Index